The Cross in Our Context

"Subtle, passionate, and knowing . . . a coherent case for
discipleship of an intentional and daring kind. This book
gives ready access to the thinking and faith of one of our
finest thinkers, a welcome addition to a remarkable corpus
of evangelical faith."

—Walter Brueggemann
  Columbia Theological Seminary

Other Works by Douglas John Hall

The Reality of the Gospel and the Unreality of the Churches (1975)

Lighten Our Darkness: Toward an Indigenous Theology of the Cross (1976)

Has the Church a Future? (1980)

Steward: A Biblical Symbol Come of Age (1982)

Christian Mission: The Stewardship of Life in the Kingdom of Death (1985)

God and Human Suffering: An Exercise in the Theology of the Cross (1986)

Imaging God: Dominion as Stewardship (1986)

When You Pray: Thinking Your Way into God's World (1987)

Stewardship of Life in the Kingdom of Death (1988)

Thinking the Faith: Christian Theology in a North American Context (1989)

Professing the Faith: Christian Theology in a North American Context (1993)

Confessing the Faith: Christian Theology in a North American Context (1996)

Remembered Voices: Reclaiming the Legacy of "Neo-Orthodoxy" (1998)

Why Christian? For Those on the Edge of Faith (1998)

The Cross in Our Context

Jesus and the Suffering World

Douglas John Hall

Fortress Press

Minneapolis

THE CROSS IN OUR CONTEXT
Jesus and the Suffering World

Library of Congress Cataloging-in-Publication Data
The cross in our context : Jesus and the suffering world / Douglas John Hall.
    x, 274 p. : ill. ; 22 cm.
    Includes bibliographical references (p. 231–255) and index.
    ISBN 0-8006-3581-7 (alk. paper)
    1. Jesus Christ—Crucifixion. 2. Holy Cross. 3. Suffering of God. 4. Theology, Doctrinal—North America. 5. Suffering—Religious aspects--Christianity. 6. Christianity and culture.
BT453 .H27 2003
52873152   2003273368

Manufactured in the U.S.A.
08   07   06   05   04   2   3   4   5   6   7   8   9   10

To Trinity Lutheran Seminary
in appreciation for
The Joseph Sittler Award

And in memory of
David J. Monge and
Mark A. Olson,
Pastors

Contents

List of Illustrations

Preface

This book had its genesis about five years ago, when Marshall Johnson, then Director of Fortress Press, proposed that I create a one-volume digest of my large three-volume work on "Christian Theology in a North American Context."[1] The present volume cannot be considered a digest or synopsis of the larger work; it is an original essay with its own internal logic and purpose—as I shall explain in the introduction. Yet I have also intended it to incorporate the major motifs and emphases of my trilogy, and the material is arranged in such a way that readers who wish to pursue further any of the subjects treated at greater length in the trilogy may do so without difficulty. To that end, a table is presented at the end of the book, giving the appropriate references in the trilogy for the successive chapters of this work.

Because the trilogy is extensively referenced, I have not attempted in this present work to document everything as fully as might have been done. In the interests of brevity, I have kept longer quotations from other sources to a minimum.

The ten chapters of the book were first given as lectures, and I have intentionally retained the style of direct address in the published version. The lectures were initially developed at Trinity Lutheran Seminary in Columbus, Ohio, in 2002, during my term as Distinguished Visiting Professor, and I am deeply indebted to the faculty and staff of that institution for its support and collegiality throughout that period. I am particularly grateful to the students of my lecture and seminar course there, who will no doubt recognize in these pages some of their own questions and concerns. I am grateful as well to the students of my graduate seminar at McGill University, who during the semester just this week completed, heard and responded to the lectures in their final form.

Finally I should like to take this opportunity of expressing sincere gratitude to my longtime publishers, Fortress Press, and especially to Michael West, editor in chief, whose insightful, encouraging, and cheerful support have made the necessarily solitary vocation of writing both more companionable and more rewarding personally.

Introduction

> "*Theologia crucis* is not a single chapter in theology, but the key signature for all Christian theology."
>
> —Jürgen Moltmann

"RELIGION KILLS!"

These words were scrawled on the graffiti-inviting outer wall of the Presbyterian College of Montreal in the days immediately following the shattering events of September 11, 2001. They are words to which every religious person and institution in these perilous times ought to pay close and thoughtful attention. For most of the violence, death-dealing, and terrorizing afoot in our world is inspired—if not initiated—by some religion or other, and the question that is being put to all world religions today is whether they are, *at base,* life-affirming or agencies of death.

At base: that is to say, is the violence in which a religion is involved (for what religion is *not* so involved?) coincidental, perhaps even accidental, or can it be traced to core beliefs or unthinking presuppositions of the faith in question? That religion can be used by all sorts of inherently violent causes is self-evident. What must be asked today, however, is whether a religion directly or indirectly *courts* such usage—whether its foundational teaching and tone render it open to use or misuse by those who have other axes to grind, or whether (to be still more concrete) it manifests any clear checks and balances *against* co-optation by such mentalities.

The advent of terrorism on a global scale has evoked these questions of Islam in particular. In a brief article titled "Islam's Bloody Borders," the well-known American journalist Charles Krauthammer asks whether Islam is "an inherently violent religion"—a question which, as he says, "has received much attention of late." His own answer is that "the question is absurd." It is "like asking whether Christianity is a religion of peace." On that topic he responds, "Well, there is Francis of Assisi. And there is the Thirty Years' War. Which do you choose?" In other words, religion is as religion does. What may be said of Islam at the present time, he affirms (with Samuel Huntington), is that "'Islam has bloody borders'"; and he names a number of these. Yet Islam has known "periods of tolerance," and "most Muslims are obviously peaceful people living within the rules of civilized behavior." "Which," asks Krauthammer, "stands for the real Islam?" The question is "not just unanswerable," he writes, "it is irrelevant. The real issue is not the essence of an abstraction—who can say what is the real Christianity or the real Judaism?—but the actions of modern Muslims."[1]

A Christian theologian recollecting the words of the one who said "by their fruits ye shall know them" will not dismiss Krauthammer's empirical approach. Neither will he or she find it satisfactory, for it assumes, in effect, that the content of belief as such is peripheral if not irrelevant—"the essence of an abstraction"—that what matters is not the theological and ethical substance of a religion but the actions of its avowed adherents. No serious Christian could fault the journalist's determination to pay particular attention to what religious people actually *do*. But unless and until one is ready to consign theology (and perhaps human theory as a whole) to abstraction, if not to the nether regions of rationalization and hypocrisy, one is surely bound to affirm that the actions of believers are usually the acting out of foundational beliefs, whether in conscious or unconscious ways. To state the matter the other way around: the foundational beliefs of a religious faith will find expression, one way or another, in the deeds and deportment of its membership. That airy abstraction, rationalization, and hypocrisy exist—abound, even!—among the religious; that gross discrepancies can be found in every faith between thought and act, what is desired and what is done: these can readily be admitted. But such an admission does not obviate the fact that there are definite consequences of belief, as of disbelief. Nor does it rule out the necessity, in every religious faith, of distinguishing between authentic and inauthentic expressions of that faith. Without such vigilance, no religious faith could survive. It would quickly dissolve into contradictory and chaotic factions—a danger of which North American Christians, with our literally thousands of churches and sects, are particularly conscious.

It may appear defensive and self-serving when a theologian asserts, in effect, that theology matters. But if by *theology* one means the continuous process of disciplined and prayerful *thought* through which a community of faith seeks to understand what it believes and thus to be guided in its living out of that belief (and that is what I mean), then to deny that theology matters, and matters very concretely, is tantamount to opening up the ever-ready floodgates of irrationality and mindless, boundless spiritualism. Worse still, it is to make a gift of that spiritual energy to powers and principalities that have vested interests in deploying it. It is of course pretentious in the extreme when the doctrinal guardians of a religion claim to define for good and all the "real" Christianity/Judaism/Islam/etc., but a religious community must always be busy with sifting its essence from historical accidents and extraneous associations—"rightly dividing the word of truth" (2 Tim. 2:15, KJV). This is more conspicuously the case today than ever before, for the future well-being of the entire planet is at stake.

The geopolitical situation has confronted Islam in particular with the challenge to dissociate itself from its extremes and its "bloody borders," and one is grateful for the fact that there are Muslim scholars and faithful people who are responding precisely to that challenge. But Christians—and especially Western Christians—who imagine that the epithet "Religion Kills!" has no application to themselves and their religion are greatly deceived. Not only does the whole history of the Christian religion bear ample evidence of the accuracy of such a charge, and not only does the present-day world situation confirm the suspicion of many that Christianity has by no means repented of its propensity to aggressive behavior; but, at a more subtle yet also more deadly level, the association of the Christian religion with white Western/Northern economic, military, and cultural imperialism constitutes possibly the single most insidious cause of global peril. It can in fact be argued (and is) that the current bellicosity of the militant forms of Islam represents a reaction of the Muslim world to its humiliation by the powerful technocratic West, especially as the latter is embodied in the one remaining planetary superpower—which just happens to be the most avowedly Christian of all the nations of the world.

Insofar as that charge is true (and in my opinion its truth cannot be wholly gainsaid), it follows that Christianity, even more insistently than Islam, is being challenged today to examine itself with a view to ascertaining what elements within it are contributing to the volatile character of the age and what could be done to change that situation.

Precisely here we are thrown back upon basic belief—theology! For it matters little that Christians, and especially North American Christians, are "very nice people" whose "actions" (Krauthammer) are on the whole generous and peaceful. Neither does it suffice to claim that Christianity promulgates a morality of love, justice, peace, compassion, goodwill, etc., etc. So long as Christian faith is unable to distinguish itself at the level of foundational belief from the Western imperial peoples with which it has been and is inextricably linked, its actions and ethical claims will be ambiguous, even when they are inspired by apparently Christian motives. As it is, thankfully, a significant (if not yet significant *enough*!) portion of Christian people in North America, Europe, and other traditionally Christian lands *have* participated in acts of disengagement from the present official policies of their host societies—for example in the current protests of mainstream Christians in the United States and elsewhere against the evident desire of the governing authorities of America and its allies to undertake, with or without United Nations' approval, a "preventive" war against Iraq. Such acts of dissent from the dominant culture must be lauded by all who discern the signs of the times and realize, therefore, that violence, even when it is called anti-terrorism, can only beget more violence—including more terrorism. But while such actions on the part of Christian persons and denominations are admirable, they are neither self-sustaining nor sufficiently far-reaching.

For both durability and profundity, change must be undertaken at the level of the faith that informs and sustains the act—that is to say, at the level of theology. It is well, christianly speaking, when a religious community manifests a sufficient degree of the knowledge of the love of God to see the world from the perspective of its nation's real or alleged enemies; when it is sufficiently liberated from the immodest behavior of its own racial, ethnic, cultural, and cultic loyalties to consider the rights of "the other." But a modest church that is still under the spell of an immodest theology has not yet begun to deal with the fact that "Religion Kills."

For what "kills" in religion is not only, or primarily, the exclusionary deed, the aggressive and proselytizing stance, the crusading attitude and act, but the underlying doctrine that functions both as inspiration and justification for all such actions. A religious community that believes itself to be in possession of "the Truth" is a community equipped with the most lethal weapon of any warfare: the sense of its own superiority and mandate to mastery.

In short, it is the theological triumphalism of Christendom that must be altered if the Christian faith is to exist in the world of today and tomorrow as a force for life and not death. Enlightenment humanism has ensured that most Christians of the Northern Hemisphere, even those who decry humanism as a great evil, have been influenced by a spirit of decency that is appalled by overt acts of violence and obvious wickedness. But the liberalization of our behavior, so far as it is true, has only rarely extended itself into modesty at the level of basic belief. We continue—even we who are liberal or moderate churchfolk—to look upon our belief system as something inherently superior to all alternatives, and with few exceptions we tend to think that our superior cultus is reflected in our superior culture.

It would of course be an exercise in absurdity for a Christian theologian to propose that his or her fellow Christians should cease thinking their faith significant enough to warrant its being the vehicle of their "ultimate concern" (Paul Tillich). But significance, even ultimate significance, does not forthwith translate into the kind of credal exclusivity that sets people at war, potentially, with every other claim to significance. It is possible—and now it is absolutely necessary!—to hold firmly to a faith that not only does *not* kill but opens a community to life-enhancing communion with others of our kind, and of otherkind as well. *At base,* that is precisely what the "theology of the cross" means to me.

Does it seem strange that a theology centered in the violent death of a man should be *at base* a theology defiant of death and oriented toward life "more abundantly"? I shall ask this question again many times, explicitly or implicitly, in the chapters that follow, and my whole intention therein is to respond to it both affirmatively and as persuasively as possible: Yes, it *is* strange; yet this strangeness conceals a profound logic of its own. That logic is grounded in the foundational claim of this theology, which is that the cross of the Christ hides—and reveals—the decision of God, *vere Deus,* to absorb in his own person the compulsions of the alienated human spirit to kill, and so to create "a new spirit within us," a spirit that has passed through death to the life that is possible on death's far side.

In all of my previous works, both written and spoken, it has been my hope to enunciate for myself and others the depths that I have felt in this "never much loved" (Jürgen Moltmann)[2] theological tradition that Martin Luther insightfully called the "theology of the cross" *(theologia crucis).* Indeed, I should not have found Christianity very gripping, beyond childhood and adolescence, had I not been led by Luther, Dietrich Bonhoeffer, the early Karl Barth, and others to the contemplation of this "thin tradition." Historical Christianity—Christendom—has steadfastly avoided the *theologia crucis* because such a theology could only call into question the whole imperialistic bent of Christendom. But with the demise of Christendom in the modern and postmodern periods, it has become possible for serious Christians to reconsider the meaning and role of this submerged "critical theology."[3] In fact most of the creative movements in Christian theology from the so-called neo-orthodox movement onward—including liberation theology and much Christian feminism—have had, if not explicit, then implicit links with this approach to the Christian faith. But now the *possibility* of such a reconsideration has become a grave *necessity,* for there is no place in a world on the brink of self-destruction for a religion that is driven by the quest for power and glory, or even for survival. Such a religion can only be "part of the problem, not its solution."

While my previous work has all been informed by the theology of the cross, my purpose in this present offering is to be quite intentional in articulating the ways in which, in my understanding, the spirit and method of this theological tradition works itself out in relation to the major areas of Christian doctrine. I am in complete agreement with Jürgen Moltmann in his assertion, quoted above, that the theology of the cross must be seen to apply to *the whole faith* as its informing perspective—its "key signature." Although the nomenclature apparently suggests to the uninformed or unreflective that this is a theology narrowly concentrated on the crucifixion of Christ and the doctrine of atonement, a careful examination of the works of any Christian who has adopted this posture, from St. Paul to Luther to Søren Kierkegaard to Dorothee Soelle, will immediately demonstrate that it connotes a spirit and method of theological meditation that touches upon every aspect of faith and life. *As does the cross of Jesus Christ!*

Accordingly, I have planned this brief volume to address, in turn, the traditional concerns of Christian systematic theological reflection, in each case asking how that particular aspect of doctrine is affected by viewing it from the perspective of the *theologia crucis.* Thus, after an initial chapter in which I attempt to define this theology in a preliminary manner, the second and third chapters are concerned with epistemological and methodological questions (the so-called prolegomena). With the fourth chapter we move to matters of content: the doctrines of God (chapter 4), humankind (chapter 5), the Christ (chapter 6), the church (chapter 7). Chapter 8, "The Theology of the Cross and the Crisis of Christendom," represents something of an excursus, but one made necessary by the reality of the church in the world today. It would be irresponsible, I feel, to discuss the doctrine of the church in our time without addressing the reality of the church's effective disestablishment, and the theology of the cross can speak to this reality in a way that the usual triumphalistic ecclesiology (such as one has it, for example, in so-called church-growth movements) simply cannot. Then in chapter 9 I turn to Christian ethics and outreach (missiology)—which are always more than merely ethics and mission, hence my chapter heading, "On Being Christian Today." Finally, chapter 10 asks after the eschatology appropriate to this theological posture.

It will be obvious, then, that I intend this book as a comprehensive statement of Christian faith, in the sense that it touches upon all of the major dimensions of Christian theological tradition. I certainly do *not* offer it, however, as a full-fledged discussion of Christian teaching, whether in its parts (chapters) or as a whole. I have attempted such fullness of thought in my major systematic work, the trilogy mentioned in the preface, and I am hopeful that those readers who are inspired, incensed, or at least made curious by what is contained in this small work will consult my more discursive treatment of the faith in those three volumes. My intention here, to repeat, is not to cover the waterfront but to concentrate specifically on trying to discern what Christian doctrine might look like were it to be subjected to an intentionally critical examination from the vantage point of this critical and constructive theological approach. Or, to alter the metaphor from sight to the more appropriate biblical metaphor of hearing, what would Christianity sound like if it were played in this key?

Some, I suppose, will conclude that the *theologia crucis* must adopt a minor key, for it will seem to them gloomy and lacking in the celebratory jubilation that characterizes so much popular Christianity today. Well, but life often plays itself out in the minor keys, and those who neglect those keys in favor of the always brilliant, always predictable major keys and "all things bright and beautiful," as so much anglosaxon Christianity has done, are found, in the end, to be out of touch with life. But it is, to begin with, a superficial judgment, at best, to think that a theology that focuses a good deal on that which negates life is "half in love with easeful death"![4] The only way of affirming life among a species and in a world that is preoccupied with repressing its knowledge of death while in its actions pursuing death with a wondrous single-mindedness—the only way of saying yes to life in such a context is to discover, somehow, the courage that is needed to confront the culture's repressed and therefore highly effective no. The theology of the cross is for Christians the most reliable expression of the Source of that courage.

So if it is a theology that makes a good deal of use of the minor key (and, let us hope, avoids the sentimental diminished or dominant fifths and sevenths), it is also a theology that modulates frequently between minor and major keys, and with great artistry and inventiveness—at least when it is in the hands of a real musician, like Luther or Bonhoeffer. (I can only do my best as a lesser composer of this music!) It is in this respect, one could say—and without in the least stretching the analogy—comparable to the music of Johann Sebastian Bach, which also modulates frequently and unpredictably between minor and major harmonies, and for the very good reason that Bach was himself an acknowledged disciple of this same Lutheran (but also trans-Lutheran) theological tradition. That is to say, he knew enough about death to look for life in the midst of it and not by pretending that death in all its guises did not exist.

At this point in time, standing just inside the portal of a new century, a new millennium, the future of the Christian faith in the world seems quite uncertain. Will Christian churches still exist a century hence? five centuries? a millennium? Will they be recognizably Christian still? Many of our contemporaries, including some very thoughtful Christians, are skeptical. Christianity entered the *twentieth* century convinced of a victorious future: this would be "the

Christian Century"! We know now that it was not that; indeed, we know that the previous century, perhaps the most violent hundred years in human history, contained many manifestations of what, from the perspective of biblical faith, must be labeled anti-Christian if not positively demonic. We also know that the previous century saw the distinct decline and humiliation of Christendom, at least in its historical Western form. This glaring discrepancy between twentieth-century ecclesiastical hopes and realities has made, in some sense, skeptics of us all. We face the future with grave, if for the most part undemonstrative, uncertainty.

But one thing may be said with certainty: Whatever survives into the near and distant future as Christian faith will have to achieve greater depths of wisdom and courage than most of what has transpired—more or less automatically as "culture religion" (Peter Berger and others)—throughout the fifteen-hundred-odd years of Christendom. And this wisdom and this courage will have to do in particular with the disciple community's capacity to comprehend the mystery of the strange relatedness of opposites—faith and doubt, hope and despair, love and hate, life and death—to comprehend this mystery in such a way as to affirm, in thought, word, and deed, the positive (faith, hope, love—life!) yet without the superficiality and sentimentality that is bound to result from a myopic and repressive neglect of the negative (doubt, despair, hate—death!). And that, I shall once again argue here, is precisely what the "thin tradition" Luther called *theologia crucis* can do for us and that its still-popular antithesis, *theologia gloriae,* never has done and never will do.

Part One

Theology of the Cross

Crucifixion
by Matthias Grünewald

chapter 1

What *Is* the Theology of the Cross?

The past four or five decades have witnessed a new and in many ways provocative wave of interest in the theology of the cross. Not only in Germanic and Scandinavian Protestantism, where the term *theologia crucis* was never totally foreign, but even in some anglosaxon Christian circles, this "thin tradition," as I called it in an earlier work,[1] has recently achieved a certain currency. That this is so is quite surprising, because heretofore, as many northern European scholars could (with Ernst Käsemann[2]) legitimately complain, in the English-speaking churches the concept of a theology of the cross denoted little more than the attempt to explain the significance of Christ's crucifixion. Today, at least among informed students of Christian theology, but even to some extent within the larger discourse of the churches, anglo-Christians often sense in this term a more profound significance. Unfortunately, the suspicion of such a significance is rarely more than that, however; on the whole there is still a marked uncertainty about the deeper meaning of the term. The purpose of this chapter is to address that uncertainty.

I shall do so first by going straight to the source of the term itself: Martin Luther, whose peculiar spirituality is the locus of this nomenclature. Luther invented the language *theologia crucis;* he did not invent the thought behind the language, which is chiefly biblical. But by giving a linguistic designation to this thought Luther clarified its significance for Christians. If therefore we can discover something of what moved the Wittenberg Reformer to use this particular terminology, we shall begin to grasp the spirit of this whole approach.[3]

Before we proceed to that task, one further introductory remark—perhaps even a caveat—is called for. While our anglosaxon uncertainty about the meaning of the "thin tradition" is attributable in part to a general unfamiliarity with the Lutheran branch of the Protestant Reformation, the problem is much more complex than could be explained by a mere lack of historical information.[4] We had better recognize from the outset that Christendom has had grave *difficulty* with this theological tradition—that its being "thin" has, in fact, little to do with a dearth of historical or doctrinal knowledge. It is true, certainly, that Luther, while honored by English-speaking Christians as the first great Reformer, has been the least known of the sixteenth-century Reformers in anglo-Protestant settings. And it is also true that the reforming spirits most influential in English-speaking cultures (John Wyclif, John Calvin, John Knox, John Wesley, and others), both individually and collectively fostered certain theological emphases significantly different from, if not inimical to, Luther's theology of the cross. Nevertheless, what has kept the churches from exploring this tradition lies in another direction entirely—a fact that is demonstrated, if by nothing else, by the reluctance also of many Lutheran Protestants themselves to give this tradition much more than a theoretical or reverential nod.[5] Jürgen Moltmann puts his finger on the real reason for the neglect of the "thin tradition" when he remarks, "There is a good deal of support in the tradition for the theology of the cross, *but it was never much loved.*"[6]

Why was this theological approach "never much loved"? My full response to that question must await the unfolding of the tradition in the chapters that follow. Perhaps it will suffice for the present to say that for a triumphant religion such as Western Christianity has been (and still, for the most part, wishes to be), serious contemplation of such a tradition would involve a transvaluation of values so radical that the prospect of actually *embodying* them is discouraged from the outset. At least for the two northernmost countries of North America, it would be necessary, I think, to say that conventional Christianity needs to experience a greater failure than has yet befallen it before it is ready to discard the accumulated assumptions, beliefs, and practices of sixteen centuries of establishment and explore seriously such a radical alternative as is signaled by this tradition. That being said, however, it would be necessary to add that wherever the actual failure of established Christianity *has* been "marked, learned, and inwardly digested" (and even in North America there are clear instances of this), the Christians involved frequently find themselves turning to something like the theology of the cross, whether wittingly or unwittingly, in their quest for an alternative tradition, gospel, and lifestyle.

And precisely in this is to be found the deepest reason for the new currency of this old biblical and Reformation theme: namely, that it does represent another way, a different approach, an alternative interpretation of the message and mission of the Christian movement. As long as the trappings of Christian Establishment persist, the church is able to draw upon the doctrinal and political assumptions of sixteen centuries of Christendom. But as Western Christendom fades (and it has been fading for two centuries), serious Christians know that they must either hearken to a different theological and missiological drumbeat or quietly concede to the forces of disintegration and decay.[7]

It is not my intention in what follows to attempt anything approaching a full-blown interpretation of Luther's understanding of the subject. For that the reader may turn to various Luther scholars, such as Gerhard Forde, Gerhart Ebeling, Peter Manns, O. H. Pesch, Walther von Loewenich, Bernhard Lohse, and others. The British theologian Alister McGrath might also be consulted.[8] One of the most eloquent American expressions of this theological tradition is that of the late Alan E. Lewis, provocatively titled *Between Cross and Resurrection: A Theology of Holy Saturday.*[9] My purpose here is to look for the spirit and mood beneath the language and to suggest a theological stance that is, I hope, Luther's, but also larger than Luther—as Luther himself would have wished. I will imply that the spirituality that induced Luther to deploy this language is of a piece with the whole early character of the Reformation, the thing that provoked its detractors to name its adherents "*Protest*-ants," even if it bears the marks of a particular (Germanic) culture. For the theology of the cross has its genesis, as we may say, in a great refusal.

The Great Refusal

A few months after he had achieved notoriety through the unexpectedly wide circulation of his Ninety-Five Theses—to be specific, in April of 1518—Luther was required by the head of his Augustinian order to present an account of himself at the Chapter meeting in Heidelberg. It was in this presentation that he first explicitly introduced the rudiments of his theology of the cross.[10] The key sentences or theses are numbers 19, 20, and 21. I shall cite them in their context, starting with the sixteenth thesis:

> [16] The person who believes that he can obtain grace by doing what is in him adds sin to sin so that he becomes doubly guilty.
> [17] Nor does speaking in this manner give cause for despair, but for arousing the desire to humble oneself and seek the grace of Christ.
> [18] It is certain that man must utterly despair of his own ability before he is prepared to receive the grace of Christ.
> [19] That person does not deserve to be called a theologian who looks upon the invisible things of God as though they were clearly perceptible in those things which have actually happened (Rom. 1:20).
> [20] He deserves to be called a theologian, however, who comprehends the visible and manifest things of God seen through suffering and the cross.
> [21] A theology of glory *[theologia gloriae]* calls evil good and good evil. A theology of the cross *[theologia crucis]* calls the thing what it actually is.[11]

Theology of glory, theology of the cross: what was Luther getting at in this after all rather arcane—and certainly novel—language? It is advisable, I believe, to look for his meaning first in what he negates. He was, after all, indebted to Nicholas of Cusa[12] and other theologians—including the founder of his monastic order, Augustine himself—who made copious use of the *via negativa* (that is, seeking to glimpse the truth of a thing by discovering and describing what it is *not*).

He names that against which he is directing his critique *theologia gloriae*. The closest we may come in contemporary English to what Luther intended here, I should judge, is the term *triumphalism*.

Triumphalism refers to the tendency in all strongly held worldviews, whether religious or secular, to present themselves as full and complete accounts of reality, leaving little if any room for debate or difference of opinion and expecting of their adherents unflinching belief and loyalty. Such a tendency is triumphalistic in the sense that it triumphs—at least in its own self-estimate—over all ignorance, uncertainty, doubt, and incompleteness, as well, of course, as over every other point of view. Triumphalism so understood is certainly a *fundamentally human* phenomenon, for we all of us are prone to elevating our ideas, simple or complex as they may be, to a status far above their deserving. This temptation infects every genre of human thinking, not only religious thought. There is, however, always something of the religious in it, even when it concerns purely secular matters, for there is no system of interpretation, however comprehensive or profound, that *can* account for the whole of reality, or demonstrate its veracity universally. "Knowledge is always surrounded by ignorance."[13] A prominent element of *belief*, therefore, or at least of the suspension of *disbelief*, is always presupposed, even when the system in question repudiates belief and purports to base itself solely on scientific procedures—and perhaps especially then! Marxism-Leninism in its official Soviet expression was a case in point.

That political phenomenon of our era also demonstrates another important aspect of the triumphalist posture: namely, the need to buttress any such system with the mechanics of authority, to shore up alleged truth with power, potentially with absolute power. The

connection between ideological triumphalism and despotism, imperialism, or hierarchic systems is not accidental; for life continuously
gives the lie to all pretensions to finality, and history (especially
recent history) regularly demonstrates both how far triumphalistic
systems will go to fend off life's insistent questions, *and* how impossible it is, in the long run, to do just that.

While an implicit religiousness thus inheres in all expressions of
triumphalism, explicit religion is particularly prey to the triumphalist temptation. For it belongs to religion (and in this lies its distinction from faith) to ascribe to its foundational or fundamental tenets
and mores their grounding in the Absolute—in God. Prophetic religion or faith, as we have it exemplified in the tradition of Jerusalem,
engages in an ongoing critique of the purely human tendency to
deify fondly held views of the individual or the group: the human
word, however wise or sacred, is never to be equated with the Word
of God. But without this critical dimension, religion (including
Christianity as religion) suffers badly from the deep psychic need of
finite humankind to find security and permanency in expressions of
belief from which all ambiguity, all relativity, and all doubt are
expunged.

The only antidote to religious triumphalism is the readiness of
communities of faith to permit doubt and self-criticism to play a
vital role in the life of faith. Unfortunately, it is unusual when a religious faith leaves room for profound questioning of itself on the part
of its adherents. Even more rarely does religion actually invite and
encourage such questioning. And if we want to understand why historic religions everywhere have been under duress throughout the
modern period, it is surely in large measure because so many human
beings refuse almost intuitively to give a priori assent to any explanation of existence that asks for it on the basis of authority alone—on
the basis, for instance, of long establishment. Triumphalism both
political and religious has been dealt a severe blow throughout the
period, and especially in the previous (twentieth) century. Could one
perhaps say that what we call *post*modernity is precisely the flowering
of human skepticism concerning all triumphalistic systems, above all

modernity itself—a skepticism that was brewing throughout the modern period, and was conspicuously vindicated by the failure of so many of those systems in the latter part of the previous century? While there will always no doubt be people who want to be told by someone else what they ought to believe and do, a spirit of skepticism still pervades our world, and belief of any kind must either come to terms with this skepticism or else content itself with becoming the refuge of a human segment that is afraid of its own humanity and will say amen to whosoever delivers it from itself.

Martin Luther was of course not, in this sense, a postmodern person, but he was already (as was Shakespeare a little later on) highly conscious of the complexity and mystery of the world; he was therefore skeptical of systems that explained the world too handily, that of the Christian Aristotelians in particular,[14] and especially when those systems had to back up their explanations with force—with papal bulls and inquisitions and burnings-at-the-stake. At least in retrospect it may be said that if, on the positive side, Luther's quest was a quest for the grace of faith, on the negative side his whole struggle was against the transmutation of faith into true belief—or, to use the older terms, the transmutation of faith as trust *(fiducia)* into faith as assent to doctrinal propositions *(assensus)*.[15] Contrary to many nineteenth-century interpretations of him, Luther was not an individualist in the modern North American sense, or even in Kierkegaard's sense; yet clearly he wanted a faith that allowed him, with all his warts, to be honest both about the limitations of human comprehension and the hiddenness of the divine. He was in fact an exceptionally—and to his friends often a frustratingly—honest human being, who, in his earlier years especially (but not exclusively), found all answers to his deepest questions inadequate, not least of all his own answers—though when occasion evoked it he could be maddeningly pigheaded, too. For him, an answering theology, even the great answering theology of a Thomas Aquinas, too consistently gave in to the hubris of assuming closure. Luther found peace, relatively speaking, only when he was able to discern like Job an answering God—a God, paradoxically, whose answers were in fact questions,

questions larger and more searing than his own, but a God whose questioning *Presence* was a real response to the Augustinian restless heart *(cor inquietum)* of this monk, the only response he would get, the only response he needed.

It is this rigorous honesty, this truth-orientation, that shines through the twenty-first thesis of the Heidelberg Disputation in particular: "A theologian of glory calls evil good and good evil. A theologian of the cross calls the thing what it actually is."[16] Perhaps Luther quite consciously used the twentieth verse of Isaiah 5 in phrasing this sentence: "Woe to those who call evil good and good evil, who put darkness for light and light for darkness, who put bitter for sweet and sweet for bitter." At the very least, the twenty-first thesis means that the theology of glory confuses people. But it is a particular kind of confusion. It is a confusion that substitutes an obvious, nonparadoxical, unconditional, and immediate awareness of divine presence and glory (*unverborgene Herrlichkeit*—literally, "unhidden glory") for the more concealed, tentative, indirect, and paradoxical knowledge of God revealed through the crucified one. The *theologia gloriae* confuses and distorts because it presents divine revelation in a straightforward, undialectical, and authoritarian manner that silences argument, silences doubt—silences, therefore, real humanity. It overwhelms the human with its brilliance, its incontestability, its certitude. Yet just in this it confuses and distorts, because God's object in the divine self-manifestation is precisely not to overwhelm but to befriend.

Luther's concern here is of a piece with his distinction between the hidden and the revealing God (*Deus absconditus* and *Deus revelatus*). God, he believes, *hides* in the very act of self-manifestation. God's revealing is simultaneously an unveiling and a veiling. God conceals Godself under the opposite of what both religion and reason imagine God to be, namely the Almighty, the majestic transcendent, the absolutely other. In one sense, to be sure, we might say in Luther's behalf that God really is other—even "wholly other" *(totaliter aliter),* to use Rudolf Otto's well-known term. But God's otherness, for Luther, is not to be found in God's absolute distance from us but in

God's willed and costly *proximity* to us. In simpler language (which, however, is the profoundest language of all), God is other than we because God *loves*—and loves, as Anders Nygren insisted, without ulterior motive, spontaneously.[17]

Such God-talk may seem doubletalk until one asks about the *anthropological* presupposition of it. That presupposition is present everywhere in Luther's works, but nowhere more explicitly than in his famous Christmas sermon:

> Let us, then, meditate upon the Nativity just as we see it hap-
> pening in our own babies. I would not have you contemplate
> the deity of Christ, the majesty of Christ, but rather his flesh.
> Look upon the Baby Jesus. Divinity may terrify man. Inexpress-
> ible majesty will crush him. That is why Christ took on our
> humanity, save for sin, that he should console and confirm.[18]

It could even be argued, I think, that Luther's theology of the cross is in considerable measure the *consequence* of his anthropology—or, if not exactly its consequence, that theology is certainly inseparable from his evident feeling for human vulnerability. Though he was not trained in the humanist tradition, as were Phillip Melanchthon, Ulrich Zwingli, and John Calvin, he manifests a human and worldly orientation that is at least as profound as the humanists. I would even argue that it is more profound than most humanism, because it is grounded not in a vain boast of human potentiality but in a deep sympathy with human weakness and wretchedness—a sympathy, alas, that is nearly unique in the history of Christian scholarship, including the scholarship of the Reformation. To be sure, Luther did not consistently manifest this sympathy in his actions or his words—though one could say accurately enough that his very *in*consistency bespeaks the human frailty of which he was sensible. He was capable, certainly, of terrible attacks on human pride and arrogance, but he knew as well (what Savonarola and other preachers against sin, including perhaps Calvin, seem not to have realized) that human pride and arrogance usually masquerade a thinly cloaked anxiety— like the soldier of Luther's famous illustration, frightened by the rustling of a dry leaf being blown along the pavement by a night wind.[19]

Because for Luther human existence is a frail and uncertain business, divinity for him is not first of all sovereign omnipotence (as it was for Calvin) but astonishing *compassion*.

But we should pause here to take note of this important word: *compassion*. The English language, being so thoroughly conditioned by Latin, often does not convey the picture that the word as such contains—especially when, today, only a handful of English-speakers have any knowledge of the Latin roots of so many of our words. *Germania,* which resisted Rome and also the language of Rome, can help us here. For German is the more "primitive" language in the sense that it retains more consistently the immediate connectedness between the word and the experience or feeling that gave and gives rise to the word. What we call *sympathy* or *compassion* (words that are almost technical for us; words that require an extra effort of thought if the experience they represent is to be felt anew in our using these words), is in German *Mitleid*—literally, with-suffering. To feel compassion, deeply and sincerely, is to overcome the subject/object division; it is to suffer *with* the other. Not just to have a certain fellow feeling for him or her, and certainly not only to look with pity upon another—a pity that in its actualization accentuates one's *distance* from the other. Rather, it means to be thrust into a solidarity of spirit with the other—to experience, in one's own person, the highest possible degree of identity with the other. One can see at once how important such language is for the entire Christian narrative, especially the christological center with its motifs of incarnation and atoning representation. Etymologically, of course, the word *compassion* contains the same thrust as does the German *Mitleid: com* (with) + *passio* (suffering). But few of us actually hear this in the word, since we have neither the linguistic tools for doing so nor (in the contemporary world where words have become so cheap) the *attentiveness* to language that are required.

The essence of God, then, is for Luther God's "with-suffering"—which is of course why he could speak of God (not only of the

Christ, but of God) in what, against the background of the patripassian controversy,[20] was a scandalous way: the crucified God *(Deus
crucifixus)*.[21] This is a scandalous designation, however, not only
because it defies longstanding doctrine concerning the divine
"impassability," but because it defies the strange but perennial
human reluctance to have God too deeply implicated in the pain of
created life. It is an astonishing thing when God's willing solidarity
with suffering creation is experienced by human beings. It is entirely
surprising, unanticipated, unpredictable, for it is not at all what
either religion or reason could or should or does expect. The "gracious God" whom Luther finally found (and kept losing and kept
finding!) is a complete reversal of the omnipotent one to whom
inductive reason and religious authority testify, and before whom the
human spirit, guilty, cowers. Such a God must be *revealed* because
neither nature nor rationality nor experience leads the soul to conclude that the Absolute is merciful. Moreover, the compassion of
God must not—and when it is experienced *cannot*—be turned into
a predictable attribute, as if, to be God, it would be *necessary* to manifest compassion always (the sort of thing that Heinrich Heine was
satirizing when, on his deathbed, he announced, "God will pardon
me; that's His profession"). The divine compassion is rather a continuous, utterly gracious movement of the Holy Spirit toward the
human, and partly for that reason the human never truly believes
and appropriates this compassion but remains the unconverted
doubter, finding it impossible above all to believe in the possibility of
forgiveness and a new beginning. *Simul justus et peccator* (we remain
simultaneously justified and sinner).

The glory of God is by no means ruled out by Luther's rejection
of the *theology* of glory, yet it is radically redefined. Irenaeus came
close to Luther's meaning when he said that the glory of God has
more to do with the condition of God's creatures than with God
personally: "The glory of God is humankind [being made] fully
alive" *(Gloria Dei vivens homo)*. Glory and power as they are usually
understood in human parlance are completely rejected by this theology; for the object of the divine omnipotence is not to establish

and vindicate *Itself* but to justify the creature, that is, to make the creature whole, authentic, alive. God will become *our* God; therefore, divine power, to achieve its own aim, must accommodate itself to human weakness.

I am anticipating here what must be more fully considered under the discussion of Theology (God) in this theological tradition, but let me state already what seems to me absolutely vital if we are to comprehend this entire approach: *The theology of the cross, which may be stimulated* (as we have seen) *by a certain kind of anthropological pre-understanding, is nevertheless first of all a statement about God, and what it says about God is not that God thinks humankind so wretched that it deserves death and hell, but that God thinks humankind and the whole creation so good, so beautiful, so precious in its intention and its potentiality, that its actualization, its fulfillment, its redemption is worth dying for.* If this were understood, if the atonement had been enucleated under the aegis of this assumption, instead of being taken over lock, stock, and barrel by Anselmic sacrificial theory (as happened to the whole of Western Christendom), we would not have Christian feminists and humanists today who find the cross of Jesus Christ an obnoxious and ethically dangerous symbol. That they do find it so, in many cases, is because the cross and the God who is self-revealed there have *not* been interpreted under the aegis of a genuine theology of the cross but under that of the theology of glory. As Jon Sobrino has stated in his *Christology at the Crossroads,*

> Our theology of the cross becomes radical only when we consider the presence (or absence) of God on the cross of Jesus. It is at this point that we face the alternative posed by Moltmann: Either the cross of Jesus is the end of all Christian theo-logy or else it is the beginning of a truly Christian theology.[22]

The Anti-Ideological Nature of This Theology

I have been trying to unearth the meaning of the theology of the cross *via negativa* by interpreting what it rejects: *theologia gloriae.* I have done so by equating the theology of glory with the modern term *triumphalism*. It will provide another dimension of what is being negated in Luther's juxtaposition of these two concepts if we contrast the terms *theology* and *ideology*. What Luther means by theology of glory could be interpreted in contemporary language as religious ideology; conversely, there is an anti-ideological thrust in the very character of theological reflection as theology of the cross.

By *ideology* I mean a theoretical statement or system of interpretation that functions for its adherents as a full and sufficient credo, a source of personal authority, and an intellectually and psychologically comforting insulation from the frightening and chaotic mishmash of daily existence.[23] For the ideologue, whether religious or political, it is not necessary to expose oneself constantly to the ongoingness of life; one knows in advance what one is going to find in the world. In fact, the psychic comfort of ideology lies just in its protective capacity, its property as mental and intellectual insulation: one clings to one's system of interpretation as a refuge from the ambiguous, unsettled, and largely undecipherable *fluxus* of the actual. The ideological personality (and in our time there are many such personalities) is constantly on guard against the intrusion of reality, of the unallowable question, of the data that does not "fit" the system; therefore the repressive and suppressive dimension is never far beneath the surface of the ideological inclination. José Míguez Bonino writes of "the ideological misuse of Christianity as a tool of oppression," because he knows that the line between theology and ideology is a very fine one, easily and sometimes unknowingly transgressed.[24]

An illuminating warning about the dangers of ideology comes, refreshingly, from an unusual source—the realm of politics and economics. One of the true luminaries in that field, John Kenneth Galbraith, remarked in a speech to the Liberal Party of Canada: "In recent years, there has been a current of thought—or what is so described—which holds that all possible economic activity must be returned to the market. Privatization is [for these neo-conservatives] a public faith. Conservatives need to be warned that *ideology can be a heavy blanket over thought. Our commitment must always be to thought.*"[25]

This observation needs to be applied to Christian theology—a fortiori! Authentic theology involves a lifelong commitment to *thought* and a concomitant vigilance against the tendency of individuals and communities to turn the products of thought into ironclad systems that discourage or preclude further thought. Now, to think is to be vulnerable. It is to know (as Socrates taught) that one does not know—does not, and never will, *possess* truth. At best, one may be *oriented* towards truth—and, for Christians, this means a truth that is never easily lived with or unambiguously desirable. People who claim to be excitedly pursuing truth have not yet encountered truth in all of its naked critique of the status quo, its unmasking of human disguise, and its demands for repentance and new life. The "freedom of the Christian person," Luther's great discovery and desire, is not synonymous with the freedom about which our entire society speaks with such ease and complacence. Christ makes us free, but his kind of freedom is shunned by fallen humanity both because it entails a new kind of bondage and responsibility and because it frightens us to be delivered up to our own resources. It is a freedom that demands of us that we become, truly, the "thinking animals" that Aristotle insisted is our essence.

Whatever else may be said of him, Martin Luther was *a thinker.*[26] And like his nineteenth-century follower, Søren Kierkegaard, he was well aware of the propensity of thought to "wound from behind." It has been too tempting for subsequent Protestantism to limit Luther the thinker, the ponderer and questioner, to his youth—to the period of his anxious searching before that moment of illumination, the so-called tower experience, his appropriation of Paul's "justification by grace through faith." Certainly that experience calmed the anxious spirit of the young Wittenberg professor, but it is wrong to assume that, afterwards, thought—reasoning in its deepest sense—played only an interpreting role in his life. Neither revelation, nor grace, nor faith, nor the divine Spirit, nor the wondrous Word (the Bible) provided Luther with a finished product, an inviolable system of meaning, in short an ideology from which the struggle and turmoil of wounding thought had been banished. It is impossible to

read his works without realizing at every turn of phrase that faith, for
him, and the driven search for understanding that faith (when it is
really faith) demands of one, is indeed, a struggle. His last written
words (*"Wir sind Bettler, dass ist Wahr"*; We are beggars, that's true)
are symbolic of all the words—the volumes of words—that preceded
them. Flashes of astonishing insight there are, certainly. But they are
flashes, like the lightning that illuminates for a moment the sur-
rounding darkness. The quest for understanding is never satisfied.
Like the medieval mystics, he reserved the "beatific vision" for the
eschatological future—though that did not render his mind less
determined to search for wholeness of vision here and now.

It is instructive in that connection to study the manuscripts of his
ongoing translation of the New Testament. Calvin, having written
his *Institutes of the Christian Religion* early in his career, spent the rest
of his life polishing and improving them, this truly impressive systematic theology. Luther, who seems not to have trusted himself to
such a systematic unfolding of the Christian faith, spent the rest of
his life making revisions to his translation of Erasmus's Greek text of
the New Testament. The search for "just the right words" was bound
to fail, because the incarnate Word that alone deserves the appella-
tion *Truth* cannot be reduced to language. Luther honored the Bible
more than any other source of knowledge: "Abandon Scripture, and
God abandons us to the lies of men."[27] Yet he mistrusted the kind of
certitude that biblicists or Bible-pietists claim to derive from that
source, and on at least one occasion he questioned the overconfi-
dence of the biblical writers themselves. When in conversation his
friend Justus Jonas held up St. Paul as a model of true belief, Luther
blurted out, "I don't think [Paul] *believed* as firmly as he talks. I cannot believe as firmly, either, as I can talk and write about it."[28]

If Luther could not derive ideological security from the Scriptures, he was even less capable of finding peace in the carefully articulated doctrines of the late scholastic theologians. The reality of his
own spiritual inauthenticity would not submit to the exorcisms of
the religious system. The system had an answer for everything, but
its answers were too facile for this introspective man. They did not

squelch the questions of his famous "conscience." That conscience was shaped by the peasant's incapacity for guile and the thinker's commitment to truth. "The theology of glory calls evil good and good evil." It smoothes over the rough places of comprehension, glides past contradictions, explains paradoxes. It stops short of the real struggle and anguish of "thought." It answers questions—yes, some questions. But its answers are like so many bricks in a wall whose function is to prevent open confrontation with the questions that no mere religious answers can extinguish.

Luther, who owes so much to the Germanic mysticism that pre-dates the Reformation, was nevertheless (or perhaps one should say therefore) what Reinhold Niebuhr would have called a "Christian realist." That term connotes many things, but among them it means that *doctrine has always to be submitted to the test of life.* Doctrine must serve life, not life doctrine. Like the Sabbath, Christian theology was and is made for humankind, not humankind for theology. So if, in order to hold onto doctrine I have to lie about life (which is the way of *theologia gloriae*), or repress what is actually happening to me and my world, then doctrine is functioning falsely. A statement of the modern French mystic, Simone Weil, is appropriate here:

> One can never wrestle enough with God if one does so out of a pure regard for the truth. Christ likes us to prefer truth to him because, before being Christ, he is truth. If one turns aside from him to go toward the truth, one will not go far before falling into his arms.[29]

To be sure, the object of faith (which is no object but a living subject) always exceeds, surpasses, and challenges experience. Nor can theological claims ever be simply corroborated or verified by experience. Yet the whole purpose of faith is to free us for life—for full and actual daily living—and to illumine the meaning of what occurs to us, *not* to insulate us from all the confusing and negating dimensions of our finitude, but to give us the courage to enter more deeply into the unknown that is around us and within us. As Luther's whole biography attests, he was one of those who are gifted (and burdened) with the awareness that healing can only occur when the deepest causes of the human malaise have been encountered. It is easy enough to devise theories in which everything has been "finished"—all sins forgiven, all evils banished, death itself victoriously overcome. But to believe such theories one has to pay a high price: the price of substituting credulity for faith, doctrine for truth, ideology for thought. One must forfeit the habit of honesty and give one's attention unconditionally to the worldview, the system, the theory. One must become a true believer, never questioning (as Luther does in Thesis 21 of the Heidelberg Disputation) that what doctrine claims about reality corresponds precisely with what is.

The Theology of the Cross as Faith's "Nevertheless"

What I hope I have established through this commentary on Luther's spirituality could be called the negative basis of his theology of the cross. This theology begins with a great refusal. It refuses any system of belief that capitalizes on and exploits the human need (and it *is* a need, a real one—though it is also the quintessence of sin, biblically understood)—the fallen human need to control and repress truth, to hold to comforting and comfortable partial truths or even downright falsehoods that can seem to assuage the soul's thirst for certainty and ultimacy, and so avoid unprotected exposure to the abyss of meaning over which finite existence is suspended.

The question that emerges out of this existential refusal is whether it is possible to move beyond the refusal into some affirmative form of faith and theology. That was Luther's question, especially prior to 1517. He expressed his anguish in the language of a "quest for a gracious God," but it could as well be termed the quest for a faith that allowed him to be himself, completely, without abandoning him to self alone—for that would be no resolution of his dilemma.

We know that Luther did experience such a gift of faith, and that the experience of "justification," renewed by the divine Spirit and strengthened by biblical contemplation and the support of the *koinonia*, saw him through many bleak moments—*Anfechtungen,* periods of utter abandonment, attacks upon the spirit that also renewed themselves regularly and devastatingly. And we know that at the center of this struggle of faith, for him, the crucified Christ always appeared as the defining revelation both of God and of the human condition.

> In what a terrific tension Luther held his faith! On the one hand, he viewed it with radical seriousness as the work and gift of God who acts upon humankind from without. On the other hand, he experienced it as a concrete personal decision and commitment. In contemplating his tension, one understands why religion was a perpetual crisis and an unceasing battle for Luther.
>
> This is the meaning of the *tentationes,* the agonies of faith, into which he was drawn again and again. He felt that the merciful God was withdrawing from him. . . .
>
> He overcame these *Anfechtungen* (assaults), as he called them in his own tongue, by appealing to Christ and by relying upon the First Commandment: I am the Lord, thy God; thou shalt have no other gods before me. When he was free again and restored in the faith, he knew more definitely than ever before that the inborn and acquired human certainties and safeguards are nothing ultimately sure and that man deceives himself when he pretends to possess certainty in himself. Thus, these agonies appeared to him as a means by which the truth of faith, as a truth from beyond man's reach, was confirmed. A Christian, so he concluded, must be continually in the process of becoming.[30]

The theology of the cross, wrote John Dillenberger, "makes it possible to live with a dimension of trust which leaves unanswered the mystery of [one's] own life, but also . . . does not reduce [one's] life to meaninglessness."[31] While the theology of glory vanquishes (that is, claims to vanquish) all that negates by presenting a triumphant positive, the theology of the cross provides a basis of trust and courage enabling faith to enter more deeply into the sphere of the negative, and to *engage it*—engage, not conquer. This theology, which as we shall see is from start to finish a particular *eschatology,* depicts the negation of the negation, not as a fait accompli but as process, promise, and hope—becoming. The process is not "natural"—that is, history is not as such redemptive; grace and not nature directs the overcoming of that which would denigrate and annihilate life, just as grace alone explains the resurrection of Jesus Christ. The process of redemption is hidden from ordinary sight, yet it becomes visible to the eyes of faith as glimpses of fulfillment, intimations of the yes that overcomes every no. And such faith issues in the *hope* that this gracious process moves towards an end— *eschaton*—that is indeed wholly positive, though the character of *God's* positive may be entirely incommensurate with human expectation. And behind this whole posture of faith there stands the *foundational assumption* of this theology that God, as God is manifested in the crucified one, is faithful: that is, that God has an abiding self-commitment to the creation, that God will not abandon the world and its creatures "prematurely" (Bonhoeffer).

The further explication of the theology of the cross in positive terms will of course be the endeavor of our entire study. Here we can only make a start. In proceeding to the positive, however, we should never forget the great refusal that this positive presupposes. In Christian theology at its best, the negative plays a very important role. For since the truth with which Christians have to do is a *living* truth, it is easier to state what this truth is *not* than to express accurately what it *is.* The late medieval mystical tradition that was so influential for Luther depended on the "way of negation" very prominently, especially, as intimated earlier, in the work of Nicholas of Cusa. Recently the American preacher and theologian Barbara Brown Taylor drew on Nicholas to make an important point over against all fundamentalist and other forms of positive Christianity. Commenting on Nicholas's concept of "learned ignorance," she wrote:

> In Nicholas's scheme, the dumbest people in the world are those who think they know. Their certainty about what is true not only pits them against each other; it also prevents them

from learning anything new. This is truly dangerous knowledge. They do not know that they do not know, and their unlearned ignorance keeps them in the dark about most things that matter.[32]

There is a persistent warning in the theology of the cross to avoid the facile, the simplistic—to offer easy religious answers to difficult human questions. The questions are never abandoned, because the world God loves must not be abandoned, and the questions are there in the world long after all the religious, philosophic, scientific, and other answers have been given.

The theology of the cross is sometimes accused of having a fixation on the negative—indeed on all forms of suffering. This charge is justified when it is leveled against distorted forms of this theology that have not understood *why* suffering—both human and divine, human and therefore divine—must be prominent in any presentation of the Christian gospel. It is not because Christianity is predisposed to pain, but only because *there is pain. The world is full of pain, and God loves the world.* This is why the Japanese theologian Kazuo Kitamori, one of the most consistent Eastern representatives of this theological tradition, placed at the center of his theology (that is, his conception of God) the concept of "the pain *of God.*"[33] A religion, Christian or otherwise, that wishes to accentuate the positive without doing business with the negative may (in affluent and powerful societies) enjoy a certain temporary success. But, as Dostoevsky insisted, it will turn to ashes in the face of one dying child. Certainly it is the object of the biblical God to assuage, and finally to overcome, all pain, to wipe away all tears. Death is not glorified in this theology; it is the enemy—the "last enemy" (1 Cor. 15:26). But the message of the cross is that this enemy, and all the other forms of negation symbolized by the name of this enemy, may only be overcome *from within,* not from above. And therefore the faith that emanates from this cross is a faith that enables its disciples to follow the crucified God into the heart of the world's darkness, into the very kingdom of death, and to look for light that shines *in* the darkness—

the life that is given beyond the baptismal brush with death—and only there.

The most succinct and portable way that I have found to characterize the theology of the cross is to recall the three so-called theological virtues named by Paul in 1 Corinthians 13: faith, hope, and love. But, remembering the importance of the *via negativa* for both Paul and Luther, the three positive virtues should be stated together with what they negate: faith (not sight), hope (not consummation), love (not power). Without the three negations, the three positives too easily devolve into platitudes. It is necessary as always, when speaking of this tradition, to keep before one that which is ruled out—the *theologia gloriae*. The theology of glory, in whatever guise it assumes, is invariably tempted to be a theology of sight, not faith; finality, not hope; and power, not love.

The "thin tradition" throughout the ages of Christendom has had to assume a very modest role. It has been marginalized, often wholly displaced, by the great triumph song of imperial religion. But it has never been without its representatives. I will end this introductory chapter with an illuminating statement of one of the best-known of these:

> One of Luther's most profound insights was that God made Himself small for us in Christ. In so doing, He left us our freedom and our humanity. He shows us His heart, so that our hearts could be won.
>
> When we look at the misery of our world, its evil and its sin . . . we long for divine interference, so that the world and its daemonic rulers might be overcome. We long for a king of peace within history, or for a king of glory above history. We long for a Christ of power. Yet if *He* were to come and transform us and our world, we should have to pay the one price which we could not pay: we would have to lose our freedom, our humanity, and our spiritual dignity. Perhaps we should be happier; but we should also be lower beings, our present misery, struggle and despair notwithstanding. We should be more like blessed animals than human beings made in the image of

God. Those who dream of a better life and try to avoid the Cross as a way, and those who hope for a Christ and attempt to exclude the Crucified have no knowledge of the mystery of God and humanity.[34]

Having thus set the tone for this "not much loved" but finally very much *needed* theological tradition, we shall begin now to consider its application to the major doctrinal themes of the Christian faith.

chapter 2

Theology of the Cross
as Contextual Theology

This Earth Is the Lord's

The cross of Jesus Christ is at the same time a historical reality and a symbol. Like all symbols its meaning transcends all possible explanations of its meaning. As the history of atonement theologies attest, the symbol of the crucified savior is able to absorb many differing interpretations, not all of them mutually compatible. Despite the obvious dangers it courts, this openness must be maintained, for without it the symbol is restricted in its universality and loses, in fact, its symbolic status.

One dimension of the significance of the cross remains steadfast, however, and is the presupposition of all possible interpretations of this event: namely, faith's assumption that the cross of the Christ marks, in a decisive and irrevocable way, the unconditional participation of God in the life of the world, the concretization of God's love for the world, the commitment of God to the fulfillment of creation's promise. "God so loved the world that he gave his only son . . ." (John 3:16).

The theology of the cross, at its most rudimentary, is nothing more nor less than a rapt, ongoing contemplation of and commentary upon this foundational claim of Christian faith. Unlike theologies of glory, which invariably tend to supercede creation in favor of a supramundane redemption, the theology of the cross is bound to this world in all of its materiality, ambiguity, and incompleteness. It will not—cannot—opt for a doctrine of redemption, however theoretically or spiritually appealing, that in effect bypasses or contradicts the biblical affirmation of creation. What God loves and is determined to save is not an abstraction and not a "savable" *part* of the whole, but the real world in its inseparableness and interrelatedness. God is as firmly committed to the life of this world as that cross was planted in the ground at Golgotha, that is, (symbolically) at the very center of death's apparent sovereignty.

The symbol thus understood—but simultaneously misunderstood—was appropriated to the uses of imperial peoples and their sovereigns for a thousand years of Christendom. In the year 1534, for example, while Martin Luther was still actively engaged in his reforming work, the French explorer Jacques Cartier sailed up the St. Lawrence River to the site of the Mohawk village of Hochelaga— the very location today of my employer, McGill University, at the heart of the city of Montréal. With some of his sailors, Cartier made his way to the top of the small mountain that dominates that city and gives it its present-day name (Mont Réal), and he caused a rude cross to be driven into the rocky soil at its summit. By this gesture the French explorer declared: "All this land now belongs to the king of France." Had the indigenous peoples (Mohawks) who were present on that occasion grasped the intent of this act and its future ramifications for their race, they would not have indulged the strange behavior of the newcomers! For unlike the God of the Scriptures, whose cross at Golgotha was the consequence and promise of suffering love *(agape)*, Cartier's cross, like that of so many other wandering European conquerors, bespoke an ownership and a sovereignty from which even tolerance, to say nothing of love, was to be expunged. Even in its distortedness, however, the historic custom of claiming sovereignty through the planting of a cross preserves one dimension of the meaning of the original cross of faith: its insistence that, all appearances to the contrary, the creation is God's own handiwork and the sphere of God's benevolent dominion. The cross of Jesus

Christ is God's claim to this world—the claim, however, not of a despot, yearning for greater power and glory, but of a lover yearning to love and be loved, and thus to liberate the beloved from false masters. "The earth is the Lord's and the fullness thereof" (Ps. 24:1).

Expressing the same thought in other language, the cross of Jesus Christ is the end-consequence of the divine determination to be "with us" *(Emmanuel)* unreservedly. It is the inevitable though not necessary final step in that sequence of events that has its genesis in the divine decision to "visit and redeem my people" (Luke 1:68). The when of that decision certainly cannot be pinpointed. That the Lucan writer believed the annunciation of the Virgin to stand in strict continuity with the history of Israel is clear from the references in Gabriel's address to the central figures of Israel's past, David and Jacob. There is no marcionitic bypassing of Judaism here! The divine determination to "redeem my people" has, as we may say, a long history. That it is perhaps even inappropriate to assign that decision to time has been the rationale of all who have insisted that the incarnation was planned before the foundations of the world—though such a concept runs counter to the biblical assumption that human history is predicated on human freedom and not predetermined. In any case, the when of the divine decision is not as vital as is its character as decision. God's unconditional commitment to the world is not the consequence of destiny—is not necessary, as if by the sheer act of creation the Creator were bound to see the creation through to the realization of its full potential. God, in the biblical tradition, is with us voluntarily—through love alone. And this quality of volition, which is the origin and essence of what the biblical tradition means by *grace,* must be borne in mind in all dimensions of theological reflection, particularly when that reflection has to do with the *suffering* that such a commitment entails—and it always entails suffering, whether it applies to Jesus Christ or to his disciples. Given the conditions of historical existence, genuine world commitment entails "affliction" (Simone Weil). The commitment as such, however, is an act of great freedom—and perhaps the only truly great freedom. It is not necessary; nevertheless, if there is love—if one is moved by love of the world, the commitment and its consequence, the suffering, are inevitable. God, declares the entire Bible, has made Godself vulnerable to love for the world. The incarnation, declares the New Testament, is the (inevitable though not necessary) consequence of that love.

Cross, Incarnation, and Context

The theology of the cross is incarnational theology at its most unalloyed and all-embracing. Characteristically, the incarnation of the divine Word is associated in Christian doctrine and liturgy with the *birth* of the Christ. But we—creatures human and extrahuman—are not only born; we live, and we die. Our being, as the nontheist Martin Heidegger so accurately if starkly stated it, is "being-toward-death." A Creator who through loving and liberating participation in the creaturely condition would redeem it "must" (once the decision has been taken) follow the creature through to that nonbeing "toward" which all creaturely being moves—that end, let us already note,[1] which does not come only at the end of life but is deeply embedded in human consciousness all the way through. The Christmas story is beautiful because it affirms and celebrates the great good and eternal worth of all creation—of all that is embodied, of all that is involved in its embodiment. But if the Christian narrative were to end with Christmas it would not yet reach us in the reality of our being. The divine love that is ready to suffer birth in human form "must" follow through, if it is really love for creatures, for *us*. It "must" suffer life, not only birth; it "must" suffer death, too.

In a moment I shall take up the discussion of that *must,* which I have carefully placed in quotation marks in the foregoing. But first I would like to comment briefly on the subject of incarnational theology, in order to underline the point being made here. Am I mistaken, or do I detect in much of the theology that calls itself "incarnational" a hidden—or perhaps not so hidden—reluctance to dwell on the *cross* of Jesus Christ? Or, if not that, a tendency to find in the fact of incarnation as such a sufficient basis of the gospel? I should not quarrel with the assumption that the incarnation in itself, as the divine participation in creaturely existence, is already reason for the greatest wonder and rejoicing. If the human condition were no more problematic than that we are flesh, one might even concede that such participation on the part of our Maker is enough to constitute "good news." But our *problematique,* to speak at least for the human, is by no means just our enfleshment, our mortality, our finitude—and indeed the tradition of Jerusalem, as distinct from that of Athens, does not regard *that* as the source of our trouble, the thing from which we need saving! A theology of incarnation that does not go on to become a theology of the cross "heals the wounds of my people lightly." If we are speaking about God's assumption of our human condition (and what else could incarnation mean?), then we are speaking not only about Christmas but also about Good Friday.

The Friday event must be seen as the culmination of the movement of the Creator toward the creation. Here the decision to be God-with-us is brought to its final test. Gethsemane, that "cross before the cross," displays in the most dramatic and poignant terms the excruciating pain that such a final step entails: pain for the man who is our representative and priest; pain for the God whom he also represents. For this purpose, he says, he has been sent. It has been known to him throughout his short ministry of teaching and healing. It has been the destiny that he sensed long before hostility toward him had reached its frenzied height. "The Son of Man must suffer, be rejected. . . ." This "must" of the predictions of the passion, this *necessitas,* has been throughout his wanderings the pressing terminus of his earthly sojourn. But again we should note: it is only necessity so long as the free decision of God to seek such solidarity with humankind is affirmed. That is why, what Jesus of Nazareth struggles with at Gethsemane, that second Garden of Temptation, is not simply whether he will or will not submit to the execution that his human enemies have been planning for him, but whether he will or will not reaffirm the divine decision to be Emmanuel. Death as such, even the violent and truly horrible death of crucifixion, is not the primary issue here. Many have chosen, actually chosen, an honorable if torturous death in place of a life of compromise and quietude. The fundamental question of the Representative, the High Priest as the biblical writers dare to call him, is whether as God's deputy he will take this final step toward the world, or, to state the other side of the matter, whether as *our* deputy he will say yes to our creaturely condition, including the mortality that this implies. From neither side, neither the divine nor the human, can that step be taken easily, lightly, or as a matter of course. It is at least as hard for God, as God is conceived in this tradition, to identify Godself with creation fallen and distorted as it is for us, humankind, to say yes to our creaturehood (and each of us knows in his or her heart, in all the specificity of our personal histories, how hard that is!). The crucifixion, which is no glorious thing, as event, is nonetheless celebratory as symbol; that is, in our Good Friday remembrance of it, Christians celebrate the victorious decision of the Christ to traverse this final sad portion of the Via Dolorosa, to take this final step toward the world God loves. For all the pain of it, it is also a triumph over pain—the pain, namely, of the decision that has preceded it, the decision to go *that far.* When this is understood, the victory of the Christ is not reserved for Easter Sunday; it is already fully present at Golgotha. The third day, along with the other post-resurrection events (ascension, reign, and promised return), can only confirm, reveal, and illumine the scope and meaning of what has already occurred in the cross: namely, the fulfillment of the divine determination to follow the course toward which the divine pathos has been pressing and to participate unconditionally in the creaturely condition, to the end that it may be healed *from within.*[2]

I have commented on the passion narrative in this much detail because this kind of meditation on the central event of the Christian story is the presupposition of the main point that must be made in this chapter, namely, that what today we are calling the contextualization of the faith has its genesis and its foundation in an incarnational theology of the cross. The movement of God toward this world, understood in the light of the cross of Jesus Christ, is a movement into which all who profess this faith are drawn. Though the journey of the Creator toward creation has already, in the Christ, achieved its goal (yes, already), it is also a process, a becoming, a hope, a "not yet." That is not because God's loving solidarity with the world in Christ is less than it could be. No, as Christ's final word from his cross announces, "it is finished": nothing greater by way of divine compassion and solidarity could be achieved or imagined. But life goes on, the world goes on, history goes on. Eschatologically it may be said that the *end,* meaning the *telos* or "inner aim" of creation's redemption, has already been introduced into time in the middle of things (in media res), but time, *chronos,* has not come to an end. In a way, for faith, it has only begun, or begun *again* (as we might say, borrowing the thought from Elie Wiesel).This new beginning is the beginning of the church, the community of Christ's discipleship. The movement of the divine toward the world becomes now the necessity (the "must") under which all of us live who through the divine Spirit have found in the crucified and risen one new life and a new beginning. We, whose movement in one way and another had always been *away* from the world, whether into our own private little worlds or to some theoretic superworld of our own devising—we, through our "baptism into *his* death" (Rom. 6:1f.), are being directed toward the world where *his* life is being lived, hidden among the lives of those especially whom the world as such seems to have denied fullness of life (Matt. 25:31ff.).⁴

Discipleship of Jesus Christ is nothing more nor less than being sent with increasing insistence "into all the world"—or, in other words, embracing our freedom to manifest something like a new nonchalance about self and a new attention to the other. This movement toward the world, which is the gift and command of the crucified one, is the basis and motivation of the whole process of contextualization. For the world toward which we are sent is not a fixed and unchanging condition; it is rather a constant flux. It is in fact "the world" only as specific sets of circumstances, particular events and conditions, explicit combinations of people, races, ethnic groupings, extrahuman creatures, and processes, and the interactions of all these. It is the world—namely, God's beloved world—only as history, constantly unfolding, forever moving from one possibility to another, one problem to another. To name as "world" anything other than this ongoingness is to substitute for the specific reality toward which the love of God is directed a construct, an idea, an abstraction. The theology of the cross as faith's continuous commentary on the incarnating of God's suffering love for the world can only prove itself such by extending itself further and further into the actual. A theology of the cross that contented itself with a theoretical-theological contemplation of the cross of Christ, however spiritually satisfying that might be to those involved, would fall far short of the inner aim of this whole tradition. For that aim is not the meaning of Christ's cross in itself and as such, but its meaning for and application to the here and now. By definition, the theology of the cross is an *applied theology*. How *in this world of the here and the now* are we to perceive the presence of the crucified one, and how shall we translate that presence into words, and deeds—or sighs too deep for either? That is the question to which adherence to this theological tradition drives.

The Time and Place Dimensions of Contextuality

If, then, we speak of *contexts* today, and do so intentionally and on the basis of serious theological reflection (and not just because contextuality has become a cliché), it is because we have begun to recognize at long last that the beloved world in its actuality, as distinct from the mere idea of the world, manifests an astonishing variety and diversity. It differs not only from time to time but also from place to place. The world today is not the world of the Nicene theologians or of the Reformers (the biblical view of history is not cyclical, but linear); "there is a time, and there is a time" (Ecclesiastes 3). But it is also true that the world as it comes to us *here* in this place (North America, for instance) is not the same world as the one experienced *there* (in Africa, perhaps, or Indonesia).

The time dimension that is one of the two primary aspects of contextual thinking has long been part of the discourse of Christian theology, at least in the more sophisticated circles of academic theology.

Historical consciousness has been with us in the West throughout the modern period, and so responsible Christian thought since the eighteenth century has recognized—in a way that was not true of earlier epochs—that theological thought has constantly to be done with an eye to what time it is, and to be ready to adjust itself to historical change. It must do so not for the frivolous reason of seeming au courant, up to date, or immediately "relevant"; to the contrary, it does so in order to maintain, so far as possible, the continuity of evangelical significance that discipleship strives for throughout the ages. Even to say "the same thing," you cannot simply "say the same thing"; because language is also historically conditioned, as anyone knows who reads Beowulf, or even Shakespeare—or, more to the point, the King James Version of the Bible. For instance, if today we tried to commend the Reformation dogma of the peculiar and unique authority of Scripture (sola scriptura) by asking people to accept the idea of the Bible's direct dictation by the divine Spirit, not only would we go against the grain of every contemporary assumption about historical documents, but we would also put in the way of faith a barrier, a "false scandal," that would inhibit our contemporaries from appreciating what the Reformers and even the biblical authors themselves actually understood about the nature of Scripture's inspiration. Making sense of the concept of the holiness of Scripture in our time must mean assuming and teaching historical-critical method not as an end in itself, we hope, but as a means to better understanding on the part at least of Christians, as to why this collection of writings is sacred and authoritative. (I realize, of course, that there is an impressive following—especially in the United States—for a biblicism that deliberately refuses historical-critical method, but this has to do with another problem that comes into the present discussion only tangentially.)

While the time dimension of contextual theological thinking has to some appreciable degree affected the Christian community for the past century and more, the other main component of contextuality has been much slower in making itself felt. I refer to what may be called "the sense of place." By this I mean not only location, though that is certainly paramount, but also state or condition, as in the phrase "knowing one's place" or "the place of something or someone" (for example of government in moral questions, or of children in family decision-making). A *context* can be a certain geographic area, or a certain shared condition (gender, race, ethnicity, economic status, war). It is only lately, and at that only partially, that the discourse of the churches has begun to recognize that *place*—not only *time*—conditions the manner in which the Christian message is to be articulated and can be received. There is still, moreover, a conspicuous resistance to this aspect of theological contextuality usually on the grounds of its capitulation to relativity, or allowing the world, as one says, to set the Christian agenda.

But if the Christian message is intended for this world, if it is to be rendered in language and act that are in any genuine manner "address" (that is, being-spoken-to), then the specificity of contexts must be allowed to play a vital role in the theological reflection that serious Christian obedience and wisdom presuppose. Both Christian ethics and pastoral theology have recognized the veracity of this in a way that systematic theology has not. In ethics, unless one is given to a moral absolutism that makes itself ridiculous in our vastly changed and changing society, ethical principles and moral precepts that were binding upon past ages, such as the limitation of full human rights (for example, the right to vote) to male property owners, must be reconsidered in the light of more recent thinking and behavior on the part of both religious and secular segments of society. Ethical relativity is not introduced just as soon as this happens; for very often, if not always, the expanding or rethinking of the assumption of what is truly human must be seen, simultaneously, as an unfolding and flowering of the Christian faith itself; indeed, such expansion is very often inspired by Christian initiative. Similarly, in pastoral theology contextual thinking, by whatever name, has long—perhaps always—been practiced; for every sensitive pastor knows that what is pertinent to the life of one parishioner, say a person in mourning, is hardly the appropriate "word from the Lord" to another—such as the parent of a newborn infant. Preaching, too, when it has been worthy of the name, knows how to distinguish contexts: the comfort made mandatory by great catastrophe, such as the terrorists' attack on New York and Washington, is not appropriate, surely, as a perennial message and becomes quite inappropriate when, perhaps on the grounds of such consolation, congregations become smug about their own seeming innocence and victimization.

Systematic or dogmatic theology has been slow to learn the lesson of contextuality, especially its place-component, and one cannot avoid the conclusion that a (if not the) predominant reason for this lies in the character of the enterprise as such. The very adjectives *systematic* and *dogmatic* (or even the less blatant *constructive*) betray a predilection to permanency. It so easily happens that a (right and good) desire to "see the thing whole," to integrate, to describe connections, to honor the unity of truth, and so on becomes, in its execution, an exercise in finality. Who can devote his or her life to the contemplation of the wondrous indivisibility of God's truth and avoid, in the process, crossing that invisible line between theology and ideology that we discussed in the preceding chapter? Truly great theology (if that combination of words is not already idolatrous!) anticipates this danger at every turn, and builds into the enterprise a corrective principle. For St. Thomas that principle lies in the distinction between faith and reason, and it was dramatically accentuated for this saint of the intellect by his mystical experience, which caused him to question his whole endeavor as a schoolman and tempted him to regard his systematic work as "straw." For Calvin the distinction is expressed by the ontic distance between the Word of God and all human words and work, including that of theology. Barth followed Calvin in this. For Tillich, who in my view chose the better path, the thing that prevents the theological answer from assuming the status of the absolute is the human question, which is never silenced, and the situation, which keeps changing. Yet every one of these systems, and most of the others that could be mentioned, have functioned for the church as *theologia eterna,* their disclaimers notwithstanding. The extent to which this represents the hubris of the theologians or, on the other hand, the insecurity of the churches is a matter for discussion. But, wherever the blame may be placed, it remains that systematic theology (which on account of its holistic character tends to be the most influential of the theological disciplines in the churches) has manifested a perennial reluctance to open itself to the great *variety* of worldly contexts and has again and again resisted criticism from the perspectives of those whose worlds were virtually ignored or excluded in the great systems of Christian thought.

This is not a mere academic concern, for the excluded ones have not just been individuals or tiny minorities but whole populations, whole races, whole economic and other groupings. We have argued here that the theology of the cross drives to greater and greater contextual specificity and concreteness, for it is the ultimate incarnational theology, a theology that insists upon encountering the real world and not an ideational construct called "world" or "cosmos." And when, knowingly or unknowingly, theology identifies as the world or the human condition some particular *part* of the world, or some specific segment of human experience (for example, the experience of white middle classes in the United States toward the middle of the twentieth century), it not only severely limits the faith but courts the danger of turning the lively address we call gospel into a fixed and sterile formula—a frozen waterfall.

The history of Christian theology in North America amply demonstrates this point. Partly because we began as European colonies, partly because most of our founding denominations were based in Europe and continued, in some sense, to adhere to European authority structures, but also partly because we, as a people, lacked sufficient confidence in our own capacity for intellectual originality, European theological systems have dominated our Christian self-understanding. While we have produced a few theologians who dared something like "original thought" (one may think especially of Jonathan Edwards and Reinhold Niebuhr), we have been on the whole extraordinarily dependent upon European theological thought. To this day, despite the fact that the past thirty or forty years have seen the emergence of many sophisticated and insightful Christian scholars in the United States and Canada, theologies that are "made in Germany" or perhaps even in Britain, France, or Italy are given a certain weight that our indigenous scholarship cannot assume. Particularly in the case of Germanic theological work, there has been a kind of hidden assumption—at least among the teaching theologians on this continent—that it surpasses anything locally grown. (The problem is not limited to this continent. The Japanese speak of "the German captivity of theology." But as a largely European colony, we are especially prone to such behavior.) This is not to disparage theology done in Germany. It often bears an unusual stamp of authenticity and depth, which is not unrelated to the torturous history out of which it has emerged. The "contradictions" (Thomas Mann) in German history and culture represent, in my view, a heightened and sometimes a hysterical form of the duplicitous character of Western civilization as a whole. Out of the chaos of conflicting influences and characteristics that constitutes German history, great art and great thought have been born.

But it remains, all the same, that the Germanic context is not our context, and when North Americans rely as heavily as they do upon the insights of the wise who live and work within that quite different *hic et nunc,* they substitute for genuine theological struggle the bogus professionalism of applying to one context the questions and answers derived from the struggles of persons and communities in other contexts. There is nothing to be said against learning from others—indeed, today such learning must incorporate the theological work of the whole ecumenical church. But entering into the specificity of one's own time and place is the *conditio sine qua non* of real theological work. Without that *participatory* act and identity, theology inevitably lapses into mere doctrine. The world that the disciples of the crucified one are obliged to take seriously is first of all that world that is their own. To refrain from seeking to plumb the depths of one's own context is in all likelihood a sign of one's reluctance to enter the real world at all. While there is always a danger of becoming stuck in one's own, this usually occurs only where the penetration of the here and now is too shallow. If, with the prompting of the

Holy Spirit, Christians delve deeply enough into the crust of their own society and culture, they will discover, sooner or later, that it will be necessary also to widen their horizons to include that greater world of which their own is a small part. For—today especially, in this "global village" (Marshall McLuhan)—no one worldly context is ultimately isolatable. But this leads to yet another aspect of our reflections on the theology of the cross as contextual theology.

The Theology of the Cross and the Crisis of Planetary Justice

If we let a line four inches long stand for the whole human population of our planet, the populations of Europe and North American taken together account for approximately one-half inch of the four. Yet that half-inch, in economic and cultural (pop-cultural) terms, dominates all the rest. As Dorothee Soelle writes in her recent book *The Silent Cry: Mysticism and Resistance,*

> The fragmentation of the world into center and periphery is generally known. There is life that is said to be productive and worth living, and there is life that is economically useless. Twenty percent of humankind have the right to use, to exploit, and to throw away, while eighty percent are superfluous, the losers. . . . Living in the center of the fragmented world means there is nothing you cannot think of that cannot be produced and bought, accessed and possessed. . . . Far, far away from us, in some Third or Fourth World, there is a marginal sphere, the periphery.[5]

What such observations ought to tell us (and Soelle's is only one of countless such observations) is that any *deep and honest* analysis of our own context today must lead to a probing, a self-assessment, a judgment for which few churchfolk, not to mention citizens at large, are the least prepared. As is well known, the biblical (Greek) word for judgment is *krisis*. It is not short of a *krisis*, that is to say, a *crisis*, when members of the possessing, largely northern peoples of the earth confront openly, unguardedly, the data that pertains undeniably to their context, taken in its greater, planetary context. Our conventional theological assumptions, which as we have seen manifest an almost consistent triumphalism, simply will not suffice to take in the naked negativity—not to say condemnation—that this planetary crisis conjures up.

In consequence, we usually and regularly repress or suppress any truly relentless pursuit of truth where our own cultural analysis is concerned. If, traditionally, contextual theological thought has been rare in North America for the colonialist and other reasons adduced earlier, it is discouraged today by the heavy burden of guilt that such analysis is likely to inflict upon us. Rather than question the rectitude of our way of life, we will ignore incontrovertible economic, environmental, geopolitical, and other statistics, minimize the extent of our consumption and waste and its effects upon the biosphere, and consign to exaggeration and scare-mongering all those who demand of us a rigorous accounting and a change of lifestyle. As the aftermath of September 11, 2001, demonstrates, among other things, we are rather relieved when it becomes possible again to blame some other enemy for earth's malaise; for then we no longer have to face that subtle enemy that lives within our own corporate self.

Such a critique by no means implies that everything about our way of life is wrong or wicked. It does mean, however, that neither cultivated ignorance of what *is* wrong and wicked about that way, nor flag-waving defense of that way, can be tolerated—at least by Christians! For Christians are committed to a love of the world— that is to say, a love that, though it must certainly begin with the honest ownership of one's own specific context, cannot allow that specificity to become a myopic concern for one's own.

The contextualization of Christian theology on the part of all the possessing peoples of the planet today represents, in fact, a particularly excruciating task. In some ways, as a Christian in this so-called First World, I envy my fellow Christians in contexts less affluent, less developed (so-called), less technologically and economically smug; for I know that it is hard for the rich to enter the kingdom of heaven—or even to stand on the doorstep thereof and contemplate the glory that belongs to *that* sphere, so different from the glory of the kingdoms of this world. To contextualize the faith where *we* live—to follow the incarnate and crucified one into *this* world—is to submit oneself to truly daunting questions, literally to "the judgment *(krisis)* that begins with the household of faith" (1 Pet. 4:17). And all the more so because it is precisely *this* world, this sphere of the imperial peoples of the West, that rejoices still in the nomenclature *Christian*.

What shall we say about this Christian world of ours—this remnant of sixteen centuries of Christendom? What shall we think, as those who still want to claim this identity in some meaningful way, when, official protestations notwithstanding, our nations have allowed themselves to draw (in an albeit surreptitious way) upon the symbols and imagery of the Christian religion in their confrontation with the largely Muslim East? And what shall we say to one another in the churches when it is brought home to us again and again, by the ecologically vigilant, that it is in fact our religion that has given Western Homo sapiens the license to assault the earth and lay waste to its precious resources along with thousands of its species and natural processes? Is it *Christianity* that has taught us to love consumption and overabundance and waste? Is there some link between our trust in God and our astonishing prosperity, our being "First," our superpower-dom? Many avowed Christians think so, and they can count upon a whole hoary tradition of so-called Deuteronomic and puritan ethics to back up their argument. But can we, who have at least some niggling consciousness of the victims that have been created by our abundance, continue to draw upon that argument? Can we, who have had to face the racism, classism, sexism, homophobia, and other once-hidden realities of our "Christian" culture, still avoid the *krisis* that "begins with the household of God" (1 Pet. 4:17)?

To engage in contextual theological thought as an American or a Canadian today, in short, is to encounter questions for which our polite and decent Protestantism has not prepared us. I have argued here that the theology of the cross is by definition a contextualizing theology: if we pursue it in spirit and in truth, it will lead us more and more deeply into the world—the real world, not the world as a religious construct. If this theology has never been "much loved" (Moltmann), it is probably least loved *today* by the possessing peoples of this planet, for it wants them to become truthful about their own worldly condition, and about the manner in which that condition affects all other creatures and cultures. In such circumstances, it would be understandable if a theological seminary or a thoughtful congregation of the church were to settle for a theology of the cross that remained at the level of theology—a theology that did not drive to gospel or to ethic. But such a theology of the cross would not be, in fact, a theology of the cross. A purely professional theology of the cross is a contradiction in terms, an oxymoron. We need the vantage point of such a theology even to open ourselves, in our kind of context, to the questions that are there. Without some intellectual and psychic assurance that God, very God, participates with us in this submission to reality; that God, very God, is both the source of the *krisis* and the source of the courage we need to submit ourselves to the *krisis*—without this, we could not even begin, as First World people in this out-of-joint world today, to listen to the questions that must be asked of us, that are asked of us.

But beyond that listening, we are asked to think and speak and act in such a way as disciples of the crucified one that there may be, in the midst of this world that is "First," some insistent witness to the fact that, in the economy of God, "the first may be last." That, instead of assuming we have done our work as Christians and North Americans when we have urged the dispossessed to aspire more diligently to our level of alleged development, we have begun to act upon the belief that we ourselves must undergo something like *un*development.[6] For, as a Canadian scientist has calculated with as much scientific accuracy as can be applied to such an equation, if all the peoples of Earth were to demand of its total resources what we North Americans ask of it, it would require "four or five more Earths *right now* to supply that demand."[7] In short, what is being asked of us all—Christians and everyone else in our sphere—is a radical reorientation of our so-called values and of what we think is necessary to a good life.

But of Christians more is asked: we are asked whether we can rethink not only our manner of life but our faith itself. If it is *not*, after all, Christianity that has brought about the great instabilities of the creation, if it is *not* Christianity that has taught us how to pillage the earth and wage warfare against all who question or threaten our way of life and accept as given the inequality of classes and races and genders—if all that is not to be laid at the feet of the Christian faith but represents a misinterpretation and distortion of this faith, then *what precisely is Christianity, and to what would it lead, humanly speaking, if it were really "tried"* (G. K. Chesterton)[28]

chapter 3

Engaging the World

Discipleship as the Church's Journey toward the World

We have seen that the theology of the cross assumes a strong world-orientation and presses its adherents ever more insistently towards the actual world in which they find themselves—their context. Unlike religions that draw their converts away from this world, a faith informed by this theological tradition and posture constrains the community of discipleship to enter into its historical situation with a new kind of openness, attentiveness, and compassion. There is that in all of us—in some more conspicuously than others, but ultimately in all—that resists such a vocation. We are inclined to create for ourselves spaces apart, havens of withdrawal; for we know all too well that unprotected exposure to the world—to our here and now—is never painless, even at the best of times. Who can contemplate the kind of life undertaken by the great Christian activists of our epoch—Martin Luther King Jr., Jean Vanier, Mother Theresa, Dorothy Day, Helder Camara, and others—without feeling incapable of such vulnerability? Despite our admiration for such figures, we are apt to find more appeal in a religion that provides sanctuary from the world, or at least a reliable insulation against the world's insidious taunts, temptations, and revenges. As the cross of Jesus makes entirely plain to all who follow in his steps, those who seek great proximity to the world must be prepared to experience rebuff:

the world is governed by a strange wrath that is most vengeful against those who choose to love it. For, its complacency and conceit notwithstanding, the world does not love itself.

Faith in the crucified one means courage to love the world and to seek one's place in it despite both the world's indifference and one's own yearning for security and calm. I have always thought that the legend of the *Quo Vadis* ought to be in the New Testament (it might have more legitimacy there, say in the book of Acts, than some of what does appear), for it illustrates quite precisely the discipleship asked of those who follow the way of the cross. Whether or not such an event ever actually occurred is not the point. The point is that the early church found truth and sustenance in it, and so may we. According to the oral tradition, Peter, the "rock" (Matt. 16:18), the reputed cornerstone of the Christ's church, in a manner entirely consistent with his behavior as it *is* recorded in the Gospels (*and,* let us note, in a manner entirely consistent with the empirical *church* that he represents), is in the act of fleeing from burning Rome, where many Christians are undergoing the horrors of mad Nero's persecution. The old fisherman is moving with all possible haste along the Appian Way, lined with the tombs of patrician Romans, when suddenly he is apprehended by a vision of the Christ himself, heading in the opposite direction. "*Quo vadis, Domine?*" "Where are you going, Lord?" he asks. And the vision answers: "Into Rome, to be crucified again." Then Peter, once more humbled by truth, turns about and makes his way back into the flaming city and—according to tradition—to his own upside-down crucifixion.

What informs this legend, when it is not made the vehicle of mere hagiography, is a remarkable sense of the world-orientation of this faith. It is not the *suffering* of the impulsive disciple that is held up here as the goal that we should all emulate, but the indelible connectedness of this faith with responsibility in and for the city of Earth—*civitas terrena*—God's world. The risen Christ, in his eternal reign as in his historical sojourn, is always going toward this world, the world's rejection notwithstanding, and discipleship, when it is authentically so, is always a matter of being taken up into this world-directedness, despite one's own preference for security and peace.

The same thought is expressed in the last words of the risen Christ to Peter: "When thou wast young, thou girdest thyself and walkedst whither thou wouldest; but when thou shalt be old, thou shalt stretch forth thy hands, and another shall gird thee and carry thee whither thou wouldest not"—a reference, says the Johannine author, to Peter's martyrdom (John 21:18, KJV).[1] That suffering will accompany discipleship, that one will have to become a participant in the suffering of the crucified one—this is inevitable, in one form or another. Why, asks the writer of the first epistle general of Peter, should any Christian be surprised at the "fiery ordeal" that accompanies the companioning of the crucified (1 Pet. 4:12, RSV)? All the same, suffering is not the object of discipleship, only its consequence.[2] The object is greater and ever greater solidarity with the creation that God loves and, in Jesus Christ, seeks to redeem from within. As Bonhoeffer insisted in all of his writings, but more explicitly in his later works as he neared the final act of his own conformity with the crucified, the Judeo-Christian tradition is an extraordinarily "worldly" faith, which, if we are serious about it, will not provide for us—will in fact deny us—an escape from the terrors of finite existence but will instead beckon us toward an immersion in creation the like of which we should never have chosen on our own. The church, which certainly perpetuates that tendency of St. Peter to flee any such immersion, is also at its most real the place where men and women are themselves learning to be human, nothing more, nothing less, and therefore to be in joyful solidarity with other creatures, human and extrahuman. Faith, if it is faith in the God revealed in "Jesus Christ and him crucified," is a journey toward the world; if it is said that such a definition confuses God with God's creation, confuses theocentrism with geocentrism, one must answer, as a Christian, that *that* confusion seems to have been introduced by God himself, who will be loved only as one who loves the world (John 3:16).

In Yet Not of the World

But being in the world—being there more fully, more "attentively" (Weil)—is not yet a precise statement of the goal of discipleship, though it is its necessary precondition. It should go without saying (though probably it never does) that such an affirmation of Christian worldliness as Bonhoeffer urges does not mean that the Christian is in the usual sense of the term simply a *worldly* person, whose deportment is basically indistinguishable from the culture in which he or she resides.[3] The object of the Christian presence in the world—of discipleship—is to *engage* the world. A Christian community is not engaging the world when it merely *reflects* the world. By itself, proximity to the world, conformity to its standards and values, achieves nothing by way of worldly engagement. A religious body may be wonderfully accessible, open to its host culture, even manifesting a high degree of involvement with the great problems of the age and with those most victimized by those problems—in short, very much *in* the world. Yet it will not engage that world unless it remembers and in some degree embodies an alternative that is not already present in the world, at least in any obvious way.

The obverse is also true, of course: neither will the world be engaged if, while guarding vigilantly that which makes it other than, or different from, the world, a religious body refuses to enter its world with sufficient abandon to arouse the world's interest or curiosity. In biblical terms, the disciple community is called to be *in* the world yet not *of* the world—or (to turn the dialectic on its other end and so get both emphases straight in their essential tension and suggestiveness) not *of* the world, but most decidedly *in* it.

We may grasp a little more of what is involved here if we employ the metaphor of "text and context." The engagement of the world on the part of the disciple community entails a dialectic of textual and contextual awareness. By *text* in this juxtaposition I do not of course mean the biblical text in any exclusive and restricted sense. Text is here a metaphor for the entire perspective or vantage point from which, as a community of worldly witness, the church is being enabled by the divine Spirit to view and to enter into dealings with the world. It does not derive this text directly from its worldly context, but from the many sources (Bible, written tradition, oral tradition, prayer, and the *koinonia* of living discourse) that are opened to it as it tries to find its way into God's world and to bear its proper witness there. Its text in fact amounts to an alternative reading of that world—an alternative that at many points enters into conflict with the world's own reading of its story. Without this text the disciple community cannot engage in *dialogue* with its sociocultural context. Without remembering and constantly rehearsing the story of the world testified to in the deepest spiritual and intellectual sources of its life, the church simply enters into the existing discourse of its worldly context as one of the many participants—perhaps adding here and there a slight aura of what may be thought "religious" or "spiritual," but in the end contributing nothing substantive on the basis of which it would be accurate to use a word like *dialogue*.

In other words, in the metaphoric juxtaposition of the terms *text* and *context,* the definitive or operative component so far as the church's real engagement of its world is concerned is certainly the first term, *text*. The danger of those who overaccentuate *context* in this polarity is that they will lose track of the very thing that has driven them into this kind of proximity with the world in the first place. Perhaps they will find their worldly involvement so absorbing in itself that they will forget to ask after its rationale, its foundation, and its goal. Perhaps they will believe that it is enough to recall certain prominent features of biblical faith—the priority of love, the demands of justice and equality, the need for fairness and inclusivity, and so forth. In that case they may well achieve a certain amount of good in the world, and that goodness will be significant also from a Christian perspective. But if they forget or minimize their spiritual and theological foundations, their ethical involvement, however commendable, will lack the dimension of engagement; they themselves will sooner or later feel that they are without the wisdom and the fortitude needed to *sustain* their worldly involvement.

I am speaking, of course, about the dangers of the so-called liberal expressions of the Christian faith. Without writing off the whole impact of Christian liberalism, which has been so important in North American Christian history particularly, one must nevertheless recognize its potential and actual pitfalls. This is where the more conservative elements within all the churches have a certain legitimate complaint that should not be dismissed as "reactionary" and so forth.

But the dialectic of engagement also contains a warning against conservativism. It is no engagement of the world that holds so tenaciously to the text (whether that means the Bible, or historic confessions, or treasured doctrines and moral codes) that it fears to immerse itself too profoundly in its context. The conservative church can be compared, often, to that parabolic servant who was so concerned not to lose the coin he had been given by the householder that he hid it in the ground (Matt. 25:15f.). In the name of conserving the tradition (which always means some *particular* tradition and therefore one that should be tested in discussion with other, alternative traditions), self-styled conservatives frequently forget that the text is intended for the context—the coin will achieve nothing if it is merely preserved; it exists to be put into circulation. Circulating the coin of course involves risk. It is this risk that Christian conservativism wishes to avoid. It fears that its precious message (which, ironically enough, has in fact already been profoundly affected by various cultural contexts of the past) will be distorted if it is allowed to encounter the always-chaotic and always-enticing chatter of the marketplace. *Evangelism,* then, which in this camp becomes a special emphasis, regularly turns out to be the transmission of teachings gleaned from, or at least clearly influenced by, a quite particular *past* context, and often, as a result, inaccessible to all who must live without illusion in the present. A church that aims to engage the world cannot afford to cling to some previous formulation of the Christian message, the hearing and acceptance of which would make it necessary (for instance) for twenty-first-century persons, conditioned by a scientific outlook, to become early-nineteenth-century pre-Darwinians.

Engagement of the world occurs only where the bread of the gospel is cast on the waters of time and place—not carelessly, as pearls before swine, not just given away without any concern for its reception. Nevertheless, the evangelist is called to risk a real *sharing* of this precious thing, and that means to risk having it taken up into the souls and minds of others—taken up and altered somewhat, re-imagined. For that is what must happen if the Christian message as *I* tell it, as *we* (corporately) tell it, is to become existentially gripping for those whose stories are not mere replications of mine, of ours. Christian engagement of the world occurs only where the world's reality (the context) is allowed a real *function* in the hearing and for-mulating of the "good news." The impulse to control, which is never stronger in us than when it comes to our religious beliefs, must give way to a readiness to listen, to ponder the truth that may be repre-sented in the other better than in oneself—to believe, in short, that this is not a situation in which one is *oneself* the authority but one in which one knows oneself to be (in biblical language) *under Authority* (see Matt. 8:9).

In such a situation, the evangelizing community may be as much the recipient of the evangel as is the one being evangelized. Indeed, it is precisely as the Christian community engages in a give-and-take with its worldly context that it is itself brought once more to hear what authenticates itself as gospel. For gospel is not the *possession* of the church: good news must always be discovered and rediscovered by the church—heard again in all of its newness and goodness; heard, that is to say, in relation to the specifics of the here and now. The disciple community formulates its articulation of *good* news only as it experiences and seeks to comprehend the *bad* news that is just at this moment oppressing God's beloved world.

Kerygmatic and Apologetic Approaches

But at this point we must address the question that we have been begging all along, namely the ontological and epistemological ques-tions that underlies the concept of worldly engagement on the part of the Christian church—that is, to what extent, if any, does ordi-nary human *being (ontos)* and *knowing (episteme)* provide a link with "the word of the cross"? We have insisted (with, I think, good bibli-cal and theological backing) that the church is the bearer of a mes-sage that is intended for the world. Christians are called to engage their worldly context. But what can Christians assume about that world's capacity for being engaged, for hearing that message?

And here we encounter two quite different approaches, whose struggle can be traced throughout the history of Christian thought. Each cohort of the *koinonia*, each age of the church in its own time and place, and indeed each individual believer must come to terms with these two approaches—and probably not just once, but again and again; for in life, in history, nothing stands still. Let us characterize these two approaches by recalling their most recent—one could say, almost, their classical—confrontation during the previous (twentieth) century. This confrontation is illuminating not only because we still stand in considerable proximity to it and inherit its consequences in ways that we may or may not realize, but also because it represents in some way both the *classical* and the distinctly *contemporary* clash of the two approaches in question. While these two approaches have been present throughout Christian history, while we can see them struggling already in the Bible (consider for example the tension between Paul's words in 1 Corinthians 1 and 2 and on the other side his alleged speech to the philosophers of Athens on Mars Hill in Acts 17), while we observe them wrestling again at the time of the Reformation—say between Calvinism and Arminianism, and while we could note their quarrel in many places, even today, still, the historic meeting of these two approaches in the first few decades of the twentieth century is especially edifying. This is so partly because that meeting occurred within a highly secularized and nearly pluralistic world that was already moving beyond the modern into the postmodern—in other words, the world that we still inhabit—and partly also because the two approaches were thrown into a very clear light on account of the contextual realities, the cultural and political realities, in particular, that removed them from the realm of the academic and rendered them immediate and vital for the whole life of the church.

The two approaches were given in the course of this twentieth-century encounter the designations *apologetic* and *kerygmatic*.[4] First we should be clear about the terms themselves. Apologetic theology is theology seeking to explain itself to those who are not part of the community of faith, or who are on its edges—which, in some not incidental way, we all are.[5] The Christian *apologia* is at the same time an attempt to interpret, to correct wrong opinion, and to commend the faith. It hopes to achieve at least the beginnings of a commonality that will bridge the gap between belief and unbelief or disbelief. As such, it is not just a matter of method or technique, for its epistemological or methodological presuppositions are based on the ontological assumption that no human being is an *entire* stranger to the God Christians worship—the God to whom Augustine in his *Confessions* cries, "Thou hast made us for thyself, and our hearts are restless until they repose in thee" (a statement, let us note, that Augustine is making, early in his famous *Confessions,*[6] not about Christians only but about human beings simply as human beings).[7]

Kerygmatic theology, on the other hand, emanates from the epistemological decision (or perhaps the *pre-epistemological* decision) that there can be no real meeting between faith and unfaith. "What has Jerusalem to do with Athens?" (Tertullian). The point of the Christian witness is rather to announce, to "proclaim" *(kerysso),* the gospel *(kerygma).* Only the Holy Spirit can establish contact with the human mind, will, and heart; therefore the task of the church is not to try, vainly, to usurp the work of the divine Spirit but to get right to the point of proclaiming the gospel. The ontic assumption behind this noetic conclusion is that sin constitutes so complete an abrogation between God and fallen humankind that the human being manifests no remnant of innate God-directedness. Certainly (says the strict kerygmatist) the human being was created for communion with God, as Augustine insisted, but in its fallen condition its alienation from God is so great that no foothold for faith may be found in appealing to human rationality or experience.

How Contexts Matter in the Assessment of These Approaches

Now this manner of stating the issue (and we are speaking about the whole complex of subjects relating to the knowledge of God: revelation and reason, evangelism, preaching, Christian education, and so forth) can be greatly deceiving, because it can sound as though we were dealing here, in something like a purely theoretical and ahistorical manner, with two mutually exclusive ways of conceiving of the communication between the divine and the human. In the first, the apologetic, there is an inviolable connectedness, an ontological link of created being with the source of Being; in the second, the kerygmatic, there is alleged to be an unbridgeable gap, an ontic discontinuity that no human or religious art can overcome.

But in fact the debate between these two approaches always occurs (as does everything else) in a historical context, under certain quite specific cultural, economic, political, linguistic, and other conditions. When the debate is made a purely *doctrinal* one, which has so often happened in educational settings, it obscures the deeper reality that underlies this entire complex of problems that we call in a general way *epistemological* (relating to the nature of knowledge). How we think about knowing, too—*all* knowing, including the knowledge of God—is contextually conditioned. The debates about the knowledge of God always occur in historical contexts, and they are never *just* about the knowledge of God.

This was made very clear to all who followed at the time, or after the event, the greatest public outbreak of this historic debate in our epoch. The bare facts of the event can be told quickly enough. In the 1930s two Swiss theologians, both of them staunch members of the Reformed tradition, nearly came to blows over the seemingly innocent theological question "Is there a natural knowledge of God in the human being qua human being?" Emil Brunner, the Zurich professor, reacting strongly against the Basel-born theologian Karl Barth, whose early works emphasized a complete discontinuity between God and fallen humanity, issued a statement on the ancient subject of natural theology.[8] In it, he articulated the well-established Protestant position: namely, that biblical faith does not build upon a natural or innate awareness of God, but emphasizes divine revelation—unlike Catholic, Anglican, and other doctrine that in an Augustinian, Thomistic, or some other manner seeks links between human reason and divine revelation. Brunner was not willing to adopt a natural theology; but, over against the so-called fideism of Barth, he insisted that humankind, even in its sinful state, must at least be said to be "addressable." The human being qua human being, qua sinner, still has a "capacity for revelation" *(Offenbarungsmächtigkeit)*. Brunner abhorred as much as Barth the Thomistic practice of arguing for God on the basis of inductive reason applied to empirical experience. But, said Brunner, unless we can affirm that the human being, even in its fallen state, retains a certain potentiality for the reception of God, the entire Christian confession will be so based on extraordinary revelation and ecclesiastical authority that it will be like a foreign body in the midst of creation—like a rock thrown into the world from some unknown sphere. We *must* say, Brunner insisted, that there is at least a "point of contact" to which the special revelation of God in Christ can address itself. (The word he used was a comical-sounding German term, *Anknüpfungspunkt*—as if he had said that there must be a buttonhole for the button to fit into.) Humankind, Brunner argued, is capable of a general knowledge of God, to which the specific revelation of God in Jesus Christ can in some at least minimal way attach itself. There is a "general revelation" based on our creaturely experience and awareness that, though it is certainly not sufficient, constitutes a reference point for the specific revelation of God in Christ.

Against this, the great Basel theologian roared *"Nein!"*—that was in fact the title of the essay in which he countered Brunner's approach.[9] It begins with the ironic statement, "I am by nature a gentle being and entirely averse to all unnecessary disputes," but it ends by leaving poor Brunner practically cast out of the Reformed community. The rift between the two never quite healed.[10]

Now, what is too often overlooked when this story is told (and it is told frequently) is precisely the *context*. The rather bitter debate, which was of course not without its *personal* overtones, was occurring at a time in European history when tumultuous events were brewing—the 1930s. Nothing guaranteed the independence of the Christian faith to pursue its theological, ethical, and missiological course according to its own internal logic and need. In Germany particularly, where Barth was teaching, Christianity was being subtly co-opted by Nazi and para-Nazi organizations that had their own designs upon this ancient faith of Europe. Christian protest against

National Socialism was undertaken by a small minority only, and it was increasingly a persecuted minority, as we now know. Hitler and his chief lieutenants were, most of them, nominal Christians (Roman Catholic, mainly), but while they sought the church's support, they quite accurately perceived the church in its authentic expression (as in Martin Niemöller or Dietrich Bonhoeffer) to be an inveterate enemy of their project. Many today argue that it was in fact the object of Hitler and his strategists, after using the church (as they did with Pope Pius XII), to destroy it. The enemies of Christian faith, like Hitler's versions of Friedrich Nietzsche and Richard Wagner,[11] often have a greater sense of the incompatibility of biblical faith with certain human projects than do the Christians themselves. What was transpiring in Europe in the 1930s and 1940s was in fact the end, or at least the *reductio ad absurdum*, of the so-called *corpus Christianum,* and most Christians were entirely naïve about it.

Part of the strategy of the Nazi movement was to displace Christianity gradually through the subtle imposition upon ostensible Christian culture of the more ancient nature religions of the Germanic fields and forests. My best friend, a German pastor and theologian, tells of ceremonies and rituals in his childhood and youth, often connected with the so-called Hitler Youth Movement to which he belonged, and with festivals of seedtime and harvest and the like, that were part of this general attempt. Christianity in its majority expression in Germany not only did not raise questions about this synthesis of pagan and Christian ritual, but in the elections of 1933, confirming the chancellorship of Herr Hitler, some 70 percent of the *church* vote was awarded to the National Socialist element. And the so-called German Christian Movement *(die deutsche Christen)* blatantly endorsed the policies of the Nazi Party, including its racial program.

All of this must be considered when we ask why Karl Barth, the self-styled "gentle being" (Wilhelm Pauck compared him to a friendly bear), became so adamant, almost ferocious in his attack upon the truly gentle Brunner. It was because he considered Brunner naïve politically. The Zurich theologian, he felt, had no notion of the way in which his discussion of "general revelation," and "human addressability," and our "capacity for revelation," and so on could be taken up and used by the forces wishing to convey to a still officially Christian society the complete compatibility of Christianity with the old nature religions—namely, the allegedly indigenous sources from which the whole Nazi propaganda of the sacredness of *Blut und Boden* flowed; the basis, in short, of the racial *cleansing* that ended with Auschwitz and the death camps.

There has of course been much debate about the extent to which all this influenced Karl Barth's ire against Brunner and his complete rejection of natural theology, by whatever name. No doubt professional jealousy played a part. The fact remains, however, that the cultural atmosphere favored any theology that could legitimate, or *seem* to legitimate, or at a minimum offer no resistance to the nationalistic and racist project of the Nazi Party; Barth, the *kerygmatic* theologian par excellence, was the man of the hour—as he demonstrated in 1934 even more concretely in his nearly single-handed role in the composition of the Barmen Declaration—the charter of the Confessing Church.[12]

What this episode demonstrates so dramatically is the point that I have made before: *contexts alter meanings.* "There is a time, and there is a time" *and* a place, too. Those who do not know what time it is— as Brunner, possibly, did not know, or did not know with sufficient perspicacity—easily fall prey to the wrong witness, the wrong theology, the wrong gospel.

Does this mean that the kerygmatic approach is always the right one? No, certainly not! I believe, in fact, that one of the most unfortunate aspects of the exciting theological renewal that came out of that cauldron we call World War II is the way in which the kerygmatic position espoused by Barth and his friends, so heroic and so prophetic for the time and place, became in subsequent decades a kind of sacred epistemological and evangelical model for far too many otherwise intelligent Christians. The proclamatory stance, *especially in contexts where strong words of resistance are called for,* can be very, very effective. Directed against such an obvious wrong as the racist policies of the National Socialists, the Christian *"Nein!"* of Karl Barth can seem a veritable "word from the Lord"—a prophetic blast! But the world is not always so black and white as it was in the period 1930 through 1945. There came a time, in fact, when Karl Barth himself, who was never a victim of his own system or his own past, announced that now "all cats are gray." It was one thing to issue a clear, resounding, kerygmatic renunciation against Nazism; it was not so easily managed—not for Barth, at least—in relation to the Marxist state that came to dominate Western thought in the post-war, and especially the Cold War, situation.[13] When the Russian tanks rolled into Budapest in 1956, Karl Barth—much to the consternation of Reinhold Niebuhr and others—had no *"Nein!"* to shout against the oppressors. His avowed reasons for silence then can be argued about, and are, but the point (for our present purposes) is that even Barth's kerygmatism, though it was never exchanged for anything one could call apologetic theology, was not the wooden sort of fideism or revelationalism that is satisfied with unchanging doctrine and ethics. "There is a time, and there is a time" (Ecclesiastes 3).

The Theology of the Cross: Kerygmatic or Apologetic?

Finally we must consider the question of the knowledge of God in relation to the tradition that we are treating in these chapters. On the surface of it, one might think that the theology of the cross favors—if it does not actually demand—a kerygmatic approach to the question of communication between God and humankind. Remembering Luther's eighteenth and nineteenth Heidelberg Disputation theses, for example, there is at least a very strong suggestion that any attempt from the side of humankind to establish contact between the human being and God must fail. "It is certain that man must utterly despair of his own ability before he is prepared to receive the grace of Christ" (18). "That person does not deserve to be called a theologian who looks upon the invisible things of God as though they were clearly perceptible in those things which have actually happened (Rom.1:20)" (19)—seemingly a clear denunciation of natural theology *à la* Thomism. Such statements appear to discourage any attempt at Christian apologetics. Walther von Loewenich, in one of the most important secondary sources in any assessment of Luther's theology of the cross, while discussing Luther's doctrine of faith, asks, "Is there in man [in this doctrine of Luther] any point of contact for the divine?"—the very term that we encountered at the center of the great argument between Barth and Brunner: *Anknüpfungspunkt*. Loewenich feels he cannot give a direct and immediate no to this question, for it was, he admits, an existential question for Luther himself. In the Reformer, it is bound up with the term *synteresis*, which means preservation or "that which is preserved" (*syn* + *terein*). That is, it responds to the question whether, after Adam's fall and expulsion, anything at all was preserved out of his original consciousness of God or openness to God. Luther struggled with this question because on the one hand to answer in the affirmative seemed a concession to Pelagianism, which he felt was a grave danger in his situation; yet the founding spirit of his order—and the historic theologian he most respected, Augustine of Hippo—had upheld the belief that since, as he had said, God "created us for thyself," our human hearts are "restless" until they have found again repose in the divine. Loewenich concludes, however, that Luther could not, in the end, embrace the *synteresis*—and *precisely because of his theology of the cross:*

> For Luther the synteresis cannot have the significance of a divine attribute in man. Such a thing is unthinkable within the framework of a theology of the cross. The "reduced to nothing" [Heidelberg Thesis 18] is taken seriously. . . . [Unlike mysticism] the theology of the cross knows of no such [thing as a] spark of the divine [in fallen humanity]. . . . Luther would never think of denying that "Thou hast made us for Thyself." . . . [But] because the doctrine of the synteresis in the last analysis proclaims "the direct way" [to God] it is repudiated by the theology of the cross.[14]

Unfortunately, Loewenich does not explore the *contextual* reasons why Luther might have reached that conclusion. It could be pointed out, for instance, that Luther's whole approach to the question of the

knowledge of God was deeply affected by the fact that he was arguing for a critical theology that, were it pursued, would raise all kinds
of questions about the authority of the ecclesiastical hierarchy. If he
endorsed the notion that a remnant of God-knowledge remained in
fallen humanity, he *might* be endorsing the prevalent papal teaching
that the church has a natural claim on all humankind, since humanity is naturally and indelibly oriented toward precisely the God proclaimed by Catholic doctrine. Like Barth, Luther too was working
out his theology in a situation where even seemingly slight nuances
could be taken up and used against him or employed by the wrong
people—for example, spiritualistic enthusiasts *(die Schwärmer)*.
Again we see that these theological debates do not take place in a vac-
uum, but are affected on every side by existing realities, opinions,
and bids for power and preeminence.

Leaving to others the question of Luther interpretation at this
point, however, we may draw certain conclusions about the relationship of the theological tradition he named *theologia crucis* to the matter of knowing and communicating the Christian message. It is true,
I think, that there is a prominent and indispensable strain of kerygmatic theology where the theology of the cross is concerned. It is a
theology of revelation, a theology of grace, and a theology of faith.
The message of a crucified Messiah—as Paul insists in what is after
all the locus classicus of this theological tradition—is "foolishness" to
the wise and a "stumbling block" *(skandalon)* to the religious.[15] That
God, in the person of God's incarnate Word, takes our human form
and, in a life of complete identification with the creaturely condition, suffers with and for us: this is not the kind of message that
either reason or religious experience anticipates. Revelation and not
reason—whether in the contemplative sense of the Platonists or the
empiricist sense of the Aristotelians—is the epistemological presupposition of this message. I shall not think my way to it, nor are my
rational powers equal to comprehending it fully even when I have
heard this gospel.

And yet (there is, I think, always an "and yet" in Christian theological reflection), everyone for whom this message *has* achieved a

hearing, everyone who has found in this Word of the cross some vital response from the side of the transcendent to the deepest longings of his or her spirit, knows that this new awareness of God and of God's transforming love is not *just* "foolishness," not *just* an utterly foreign claim. It comes to us, not *only* as that which is new and strange—discontinuous with everything else we have thought and experienced— but also as something longed for, waited for—perhaps subconsciously, but still genuinely, sincerely. That it is different, surprising, unanticipated in its particularity cannot be denied: its unexpectedness is part of the joy of this hearing, of gospel. But once heard—at least then—its strangeness is like that of a quite new acquaintance in whom, nevertheless, we recognize an immediate potentiality for friendship. Perhaps even the kind of meeting where one feels a certain déjà vu—*"Haven't we met before?"*[16] Even Paul, in the passage immediately following his classical affirmation of this theological position, goes on to speak of a "wisdom" of the "depths" to which the apostle may appeal (2:6ff.).

Now a strictly revelationist or fideist point of view explains this by pointing out that it is all a matter of "sheer grace": the external grace that is the reality of the proclaimed Word is met by an internal grace, the Holy Spirit, who enables us to hear and receive what otherwise could only remain external to us. In other words, we contribute nothing; it is all the work of the divine, of grace. The human is excluded.

But while such an explanation may be thought a wonderful affirmation of the sufficiency and priority of grace, it seems to me (and the older I become the more it seems so) a rather artificial and theoretical way of sustaining the initiative of the divine in the divine-human encounter. Furthermore, one must ask whether it is not also a very time-bound emphasis. It is one thing to uphold such a stress upon the uniqueness of revelation in a more or less monolithic Christian setting. But in today's increasingly pluralistic and multicultural world, where one encounters not only in other faiths but even in seemingly secular settings thoughts and words and longings that seem tantalizingly close to the Christian's own spiritual longing, one is apt to think that it may well be a quite *human* thing to be, in Simone Weil's phrase, "waiting for God"—or in the metaphor of Samuel Beckett's more ironic yet profoundly spiritual play, *Waiting for Godot*. And wherever Christians are able to enact or tell with sensitivity and imagination their particular story of God's *finding them,* they often feel that the human condition, whatever its differences, betokens a sufficient sameness at the deepest levels of spirit and mind that their particular story as Christians is not as discontinuous with life generally as they might have thought.

And such a premonition is not without its theological rationale. For if, as we claim, it is the will of God in the Christ to seek solidarity with humankind—to be Emmanuel—then we must assume that the cross, while it is certainly (for us) the cross of Jesus Christ, is a symbolic statement about the human condition generally. Jesus' cross has its high significance for faith, in fact, because faith perceives it to be the closest God comes to us, where *we* are. To say this in other words, the reason why the cross of Calvary is not just an arbitrary symbol but a symbol and narrative to which men and women are drawn is because in itself and as such it depicts and speaks to something fundamental in our condition. Our ability to rise above our creaturely condition as "being-toward-death" (Heidegger) is a very limited or even illusory ability. Under auspicious economic, historical, and other circumstances, and given youth and health, we may seem for a time to be very great, nearly invulnerable! But in the end this image of ourselves cannot be sustained, and even at the height of our delusions of grandeur we know that about ourselves. We cannot quite ignore or turn away from the scene of the crucified Messiah because we know that we are, in some deep sense, "crucified people" (C. S. Song).[17] In the man on the cross we intuit a not-quite-forgettable statement about our own finitude.

This awareness, coming (for our time and place) not out of the high rationalism of the Middle Ages but out of the artistic, philosophic, and psychological investigations of the twentieth century and beyond, surely must also be seen to constitute a point of contact for the Christian witness. The mystery and otherness and discontinuity of that witness are not thereby undone; the kerygmatic element remains. But it is not a kerygma without potentiality for meaning even in the midst of a very secular, post-Constantinian world. Something like an apologetic link may be found here that, though it does ✓ not automatically turn into an argument for the entire faith (certainly not!), is perhaps at least a beginning, a small opening to the skeptical heart of contemporary humanity. As the art and literature of the past hundred years testify, post-Enlightenment humanity has acquired an exceptional awareness of its own vulnerability, degradation, and potential annihilation. The metaphor of crucifixion is not as inaccessible to us as it was to our Enlightenment forebears. There is a "cross of reality" visible in every honest news broadcast. It is in fact this everyday human cross that makes it both possible and necessary for us, as Christians, to develop a contextually sensitive *theology* of the cross. As Moltmann writes, "The more the 'cross of reality' is taken seriously, the more the crucified Christ becomes the general criterion of theology."[18]

In concluding his learned study of the history and theology of Jesus' crucifixion, Gerard S. Sloyan corroborates this point. The cross of Christ is even more pertinent and symbolically accessible today, he suggests, than it has been at other moments of human history, because the human condition as it now appears to many is indeed one of "crucifixion," metaphorically speaking:

> The cruel and inhuman way Jesus died has had a paradoxical twofold effect ever since. It has caused revulsion in some, making it in Paul's words a stumbling block or scandal. It has been strangely consolatory for others. Both the wretched of the earth and the more comfortable in their time of extremity—war, famine, illness, separation, death—have taken comfort from their faith that deity itself was acquainted with injustice, abandonment by friends, physical pain, and mental anguish. It is not likely that the Christian masses will soon desert a God who has experienced their pain. Christianity without the cross is conceivable among some race other than the present population of the earth. With this one, so beset by natural catastrophe and the evident effects of human sin, it is unthinkable.[19]

We must conclude, then, that the apologetic and the kerygmatic approaches are *not* an either/or but a both/and. Both adhere in the history and the theology of this tradition; neither is to be dispensed with as irrelevant or passé. They represent emphases—*emphases!*—that must always be reflected on by the church in its rehearsal of what it "professes." They are both present in the Scriptures, and they are both present in the history of doctrine. If the disciple community is familiar with this biblical and historical material, if its professional awareness of what is involved in this debate is serious and open, then it will know what is to be done in its here and now, in this context and in that. For when it comes to *confessing Christ,* as distinct from *professing* Christian belief and doctrine, it will always be one or the other of these two epistemological themes that will have to be emphasized. At Barmen-Wuppertal in 1934, I believe, Karl Barth and his cohorts in the Confessing Church *(Bekennende Kirche)* were being contextually sensitive and spiritually obedient when they said no to a too apologetic interpretation of this faith—when they became the adamant kerygmatists that they were. But there are other situations—and in my view, on the whole, the religious situation in the West at the present time is one of them—where the apologetic mode ought, with exceptions, to be explored more creatively than appears to be the case at present.

In short, these are not approaches that one can sort out theoretically and in advance. One may have a personal preference for one or the other; but a Christian is never just an individual person, nor is the Christian church all alone in the world. Our reading of "the signs of the times" are of the utmost importance for our conception and application of the manner in which God makes Godself known to humankind, and consequently for the stratagem by which we hope to engage the world into which we are always being sent.

Part Two

The Word of the Cross

Pope Innocent III Confirming the Order of Saint Francis
by Giotto di Bondone

chapter 4

The Crucified God

Which God?

In theology, as in most other human pursuits, it is not really possible to separate form from content, but with this chapter our focus shifts quite definitely from questions of method to questions of substance. *What* precisely do Christians believe? What do they believe about God, to begin with? More particularly, what conception of God emerges when we attempt to discern God through the lens of this tradition, *theologia crucis?*

In order to set the tone for the response I shall give to that question, I want to refer to an incident that seems to me one of the most illuminating moments in all of Christian history: the appearance of Francis of Assisi, the poor man of God, before the greatest ecclesiastic and political potentate of the day, the supreme pontiff, Innocent III. The event occurred early in the thirteenth century, and it was later depicted by the famous Florentine monk-artist, Giotto.

In Giotto's painting one has in visible form the contrast between *theologia crucis* and *theologia gloriae.* The truly innocent one, little Giovanni (Francis) Bernardone, the rich merchant's son, now clad in a plain brown robe, stands with a small band of similarly robed men, all of them in an attitude of evident awe, before the great Innocent—who is far from innocent in any conceivable sense of that term. Unlike Luther, Francis did not write about the theology of the cross, but perhaps he exemplified it more faithfully than anyone, including Luther.

So well, in fact, did the saint of Assisi intuit both the anthropology and the Theology[1] of this tradition that, given the power and pomp of Christendom in that age, his vision and style of discipleship were probably doomed from the start. For in his anthropology he exemplified the sheer creaturehood of humans (that is to say, the *shared* creaturehood of our species) and thus presented an offense to the high anthropology of classical culture as well as that of the emerging Renaissance; in his Theology he assumed an unhierarchic solidarity of the Creator with the creature, and was thus an offense to the high Theology of scholasticism that was the transcendent basis of the patriarchal establishment.

In his well-known series on *Civilization,* Sir Kenneth Clark writes about the fate of Francis and his vision of the Christian life in a way that must give pause to anyone with a modicum of historical imagination. Commenting on the great basilica that Francis's followers began to build shortly after his death, Clark writes:

> A strange memorial to the little poor man, whose favourite saying was "Foxes have holes and birds of the air have nests: but the Son of Man hath not where to lay his head" [Luke 9:58, KJV]. But of course, St. Francis's cult of poverty could not survive him—it did not even last his lifetime. It was officially rejected by the Church; for the Church had already become part of the international banking system that originated in thirteenth-century Italy. Those of Francis's disciples, called *fraticelli,* who clung to his doctrine of poverty were denounced as heretics and burnt at the stake. And for seven hundred years capitalism has continued to grow to its present monstrous proportions. It may seem that St. Francis has had no influence at all, because even those humane reformers of the nineteenth century who sometimes invoked him did not wish to exalt or sanctify poverty but to abolish it.[2]

 It is easy enough to claim belief in God. But the question that must always to be put to all such claims is, simply, *Which God?* What is your image of this God in whom you claim belief? What kind of company does your God keep? What does your God ask of you—if anything? And the real challenge, where belief in God is concerned, surely, is whether such belief can be held without presupposing or leading to a subtle yet entirely effective *dis*belief in the ultimate worth and meaning of life, creaturely life. So much religion is rooted in an implicit despair of creaturehood. God appears as the transcendent *alternative* to the ephemeral and transitory—as a Deus ex machina who rescues us from the impossibility of our finitude, or who dresses up creation as a kind of dress rehearsal for the glory that it cannot now contain (Innocent's papal court). Feuerbach's thesis that God is a projection, in reverse, of our own sense of failure and inadequacy as creatures cannot be written off. We are finite, we project an Infinite; we are mortal, we project an Immortal; we are mutable, we project an Immutable; and so on. We turn to "God"—a god made not in our own image but in antithesis to our self-conception—to escape the psychic fearfulness of our actuality. Both Freud and Marx—and still more profoundly Nietzsche—built upon this thesis, and Christians would do well not to dismiss it, because in the end it is doctrinally purifying.

And our Christian doctrine of God badly needs purification! For there has been an ambiguity running throughout the length and breadth of it from the beginning. This ambiguity is already recognized by the scriptures of the two Testaments, and perhaps there is finally no way of escaping it. Perhaps we just have to live with it. But it is one thing to live with it consciously, knowingly, and another to be uncomprehendingly at its mercy.

The ambiguity is this: Where deity is concerned, is our foundational assumption that of *power* or that of *love?* In homely terms, when we think "God," do we think the last word in sheer might, authority, supremacy, potency? Or do we think compassion, mercy, identification, grace, benevolence—*agape?* This, of course, is too simplistically stated, and I shall qualify it later. But for didactic purposes let it stand for the present. I am really asking for first thoughts. What does the word *God* (or its linguistic equivalents) first suggest to you? What comes nearly unbidden to your mind?

Now, if we are North Americans of a more or less Protestant blend, it may be that the thought that comes first to our minds derives from the second category, love; for we are nearly all of us products of the liberalization of Theology in the nineteenth century, even when we think we stand solidly in a more conservative doctrinal tradition. If that is the case, it is by no means without its problems; because what the Japanese theologian Kitamori called the "monism of love" in North American Christianity is indeed a highly problematic aspect of our religious context.[3] For the "love" we associate with God when we say, for instance (quoting 1 John 4:16), that "God *is* love" is frequently a dubious blend of sentimentality and pietism. If we loved our spouses or our children in the way that many of us say we love God, the unfortunate human objects of our love would quite rightly flee from us forthwith! For a love that involves no dialectic, no yes and no, no familiarity with hate, no suffering, no darkness but only light—such love is not the New Testament's *agape*. As Bonhoeffer stated the matter with his usual clarity, in the sentence "God is love" the emphasis is upon the first word. Love, as usually conceived, does not define God; God defines love.[4] And if the cross of Jesus Christ is the apex of God's definition of love, then the divine love has very little to do with the "luv" that is passed around so liberally in our contemporary context.

This quite modern way of picturing God, however, constitutes an exception to the historical norm. Perhaps it can be a useful exception, if it is not relegated to pure mawkishness; perhaps it is a corruption of the divine love articulated and depicted in the Scriptures; but it is an exception, in any case. For the dominant thought that human beings have entertained concerning God is certainly that of *power*. Even when love seems to color our *Gottesbild* (picture of God), it often turns out to be a love so perfect, so superlative, and finally so distant, that it is really being used as a synonym for power. God may be like a parent, but preferably the paternal parent, "the Father *Almighty.*" (Though, let us add in all honesty, given the Freudian potency of Momism in our culture, Mothers Almighty as well are not unheard of.)

It seems inevitable, almost natural, that human beings would think of God in terms of power. Whether we follow the disturbing logic of Feuerbach and locate that natural impulse in our consciousness of our frailty as finite beings or in more positivistic terms find its genesis in sheer awe before the majesty of nature and the elements—no matter how we explain its origins, the association of deity with ultimate power and authority seems an incontrovertible fact of history. Indeed, it would be hard to entertain the idea of a sovereign creator, a First Cause, a Prime Mover, and so on without having recourse to the attribute of power.

What I shall want to say on this subject does not *deny* the place of power in Christian Theology, but it does, on the other hand, seriously and deeply qualify and reinterpret what the power of God must mean if it is contemplated under the aegis of the incarnation and cross of Jesus Christ.

Love Qualifies Power

One thing that we must grasp if we are to appreciate the ambiguity of our Western Christian doctrine of God in its clearest light is that, over and above the seemingly natural inclination of the human spirit to associate God with power, principally, there is a purely historical-cultural reality that renders the psychic association of deity and omnipotence doubly complex. I am referring of course to the political functioning of the Christian religion over a millennium and a half. When religion is brought into the center of political power and caused to serve as the spiritual guarantor and cultic legitimator of the powers-that-are, the natural or psychic propensity to link God with power is given a new and subtle twist. God, then, is no longer merely the transcendent force behind the ever-changing scene of existence but an eternal sovereignty reflected in and radiating from the throne of earthly might and authority. Christian monarchies as well as ecclesiastical hierarchies have had vested interests in sustaining an image of God informed by power and a concomitant hesitancy about Theologies that draw upon love, justice, compassion, and other attributes that necessarily qualify the power motif. To say as the liberationists do that "God has a preferential option for the poor" is to suggest a Theology that is bound to be threatening to the rich and powerful.

It is instructive in this connection to listen to the testimonies of those who have been victims of the God of glory and power represented by Christendom. In his recent book *Constantine's Sword,* James Carroll quotes a Jewish author, Leon Wieseltier, who, writing in *The New Republic,* stated: "'No, "Jesus on the cross" is not a repugnant symbol to me. But the sight of it does not warm my heart, either. It is the symbol of a great faith and a great culture *whose affiliation with power almost destroyed my family and my people.*'"[5]

The implicitly polemical side of theologies that fail to affirm power as God's chief attribute is often not grasped by those who—often quite spontaneously—bring to the fore attributes that implicitly challenge the power motif. This was certainly the case with Francis and his associates. They had no idea of the extent to which their vision called in question the very thing the pope's court represented. To the contrary: when the guileless Francis—this Christian Parsifal—stood before the exalted Innocent, he and his simple followers imagined (so unsuspecting were they) that Almighty God Himself (certainly, Himself!) had deigned to bless their little enterprise, and they were so delighted in their innocence that they actually danced in the pope's august presence. They did not know the meaning of co-optation, nor did they suppose that their simplicity—their absurd dedication to "Lady Poverty"—constituted a direct affront to the age-old equation of deity and power, and specifically to the establishment of the Christian religion as the high priestly cultus of Western military supremacy and economic prowess. They were not the first victims of established Christianity's duplicity with respect to the nature of God, but they surely represent the most dramatic historical instance of ironic misunderstanding.

One wishes that Francis could have had Luther among his theological advisors—the early Luther, before he had himself become so embarrassingly involved with his own society's developing powers, the new nationalism. The sixteenth-century German monk's counsel would no doubt have robbed Christian history of the delicious irony of this thirteenth-century encounter, but at least Francis might have gone into his much-anticipated meeting with the great pontiff understanding somewhat better than he did what was really transpiring there. He would have known that there could be no melding of Innocent's God with his own; that however amiable the encounter, the theology of glory would not be able to accommodate the theology of the cross—certainly not in such a stark form as this, at any rate! Of course, it is quite possible that Innocent himself, a brilliant man and a sincere Christian, we are told, cherished a profound personal sympathy for the vision of St. Francis.[6] He is said to have had a dream in which the rule of Francis would save the church. (Giotto painted that, too.) But Innocent was, after all, the supreme pontiff. Whatever his own feelings, he had to uphold the establishment.

And that, surely, has been the dilemma of Christendom from its inception. At its best, Christendom was never without the realization of its inherent contradiction, perhaps even its apostasy. The self-knowledge that was present in a figure like Bernard of Clairvaux and surfaced again so movingly in John XXIII has always been there, just beneath the surface of the establishment. But establishment has its own logic, and so long as the guardians of that logic are—or can seem to be—in charge, it must be obeyed, even by the sensitive.

This, however, is what makes our present experience in the Christian movement so very interesting. Because the establishment has become unraveled or unconvincing in all but a few places within the precincts of what was Christendom,[7] the question now presents itself whether the disciple community will be able to overcome somewhat its ambiguity about God and at least allow its predilection for divine power to be qualified by a more consistent recognition of the manner in which love always qualifies power, no less when it is divine love than when it is human.

Paul, in whose thought the theology of the cross first assumed a distinctly Christian form, stated the matter with utter clarity in 2 Corinthians 12. Reflecting there on his famous "thorn in the flesh" (which, fortunately,[8] he did not identify more explicitly), the apostle relates his fervent attempt to be rid of this impediment. "Three times I besought the Lord about this, that it should leave me; but he said to me, 'My grace is sufficient for you, for my power is made perfect in weakness.'" And he concludes, "when I am weak, then I am strong" (vv. 8-9).

"My power is made perfect in weakness"—a statement that Paul puts into the mouth of God because he meant it not only as comfort in the face of his personal struggle but as a description of the God he served. Paul's God does not lack power. As Jesus is reported to have said to those who came to the Mount of Olives to arrest him, God could, if God would, send a whole legion of angels to defend God's anointed one (Matt. 26:53). But then the very object of God's power, namely, to reach down into the soul of the creature and judge it, cleanse it, befriend it, would have been forfeited in an instant. Those who wield the sword perish by the sword—a motto, surely, that applies to divinity as much as to humanity. A god who rules with the sword will not survive the revenge of his victims, however long it may be in coming. If God's object is proximity to us ("I will be your God and you will be my people"), if God wills to transform us through the power of "suffering love," then no application of power in the usual sense could possibly attain this object. Love, as Paul declares in the beautiful hymn of 1 Corinthians 13, "does not insist on its own way . . . [but] bears all things, believes all things, endures all things." We hear this scripture, usually, as the divine imperative under which we should live, and that is right. But we ought to hear it first as a description of the love that God manifests, voluntarily; for that is the presupposition of any such love that we might here and there, now and then, manage to live out. And what it makes very clear is that, wherever love is the objective and motive of the act, the act necessarily involves relinquishment of the impulse to pure power. Even in human love, when our love approaches something greater than the erotic or the filial, a certain sacrifice of self, of our natural *superbia,* is required, and most of the problems clustered around our human struggle to love come down to the immense difficulty we all have in letting go of self and the demands of self for preeminence.

Christianity makes the astonishing claim that God, who is pre-eminent in the only unqualified sense of that word, for the sake of the creature's shalom suffered—suffers—the loss precisely of that preeminence. In the words of Reinhold Niebuhr, "The crux of the cross is its revelation of the fact that the final power of God over man is derived from the self-imposed weakness of his love."[9] Not incidentally, Niebuhr's qualifying adjective is tremendously impor-tant here: "*self-imposed* weakness." Against Nietzsche, the pastor's son who complained so bitterly about the "feminine" weakness of the Christian God and his Christ, Niebuhr recognizes here that God's apparent weakness is the sign and consequence of a strength that is greater than mere brawn: it is the strength that is demanded of those who voluntarily forfeit their strength in order to be strong for the other.

The Trinitarian Presupposition of the Theology of the Cross

Students of the evolution of trinitarian Theology will have observed that what I am doing here involves an intentional application of the principle of divine unity in trinitarian thought or at any rate an insis-tence upon the unity of God's *work,* as in the dogma of coinherence or *perichoresis.*[10] That is, what we posit of the second person of the Trinity cannot be reserved for the Son only but applies in some quite definitive sense to the Father and the Spirit as well—*no matter how radical the consequence.* Otherwise, the integrity or unity of the god-head is compromised. Thus, if Christians confess that the Christ, the divine Son, "suffered,"[11] they cannot turn about and claim that suf-fering is impossible where God the Father is concerned. So that, for instance, when the author of Philippians declares that the Christ, though "in the form of God, did not count equality with God a thing to be grasped, but emptied himself, taking the form of a ser-vant . . . humbled himself and became obedient unto death, even death on a cross" (2:5f.), this must be taken as an indirect statement about God in the totality of God's being, and not merely as a statement about Jesus. In other words, the "emptying" or *kenosis* of the incarnation and the cross must be understood to apply to God in God's indivisibility. If Jesus Christ is the Revealer of God and not merely a subordinate who, finally, submits to the will of his superior (the Father Almighty), then the cross must be understood to apply to God's own being and acting and not only to that of the Christ.

It was with that assumption in mind that C. S. Dinsmore at the turn of the twentieth century penned the illuminating sentence, "There was a cross in the heart of God before there was one planted on the green hill outside Jerusalem."[12] It would be impossible to read the Scriptures of Israel without concluding, long before one had reached the end of them, that there is indeed "a cross in the heart" of Israel's God. It says more than one would like to admit about the supercessionism[13] of historical Christianity that so many Christians through the ages have been able to assume that suffering love, *agape,* appeared on the scene of God's dealings with humanity only with the advent of Jesus Christ. Luther was a better student of Scripture than most when, over against a whole philosophic tradition of Theological "aseity" (entire self-sufficiency) and ontic transcendence, he dared to speak about "the crucified God."[14] Following that same kind of Theo-logic, Dietrich Bonhoeffer, more strikingly still, wrote that while "Man's religiosity makes him look in his distress to the power of God in the world . . . the Bible directs man to God's powerlessness and suffering." And he added from the depths of his own suffering, "Only the suffering God can help."[15]

Such declarations constitute an enormous polemic against both the Theology and the Christology that has dominated particularly Western Christendom. To consider first the Theology, the power principle has been so prominent, so untouchable, that it has been nearly unthinkable for orthodox Christians to associate "God the Father" with the cross of "God the Son." It appears that the theologians would rather risk undoing the doctrine of the Trinity, which in the West always accentuated the principle of divine unity, than to suggest that God the Father suffered. Early in doctrinal disputations,

Christian orthodoxy had—in the so-called Patripassian controversy—rejected precisely that idea, and there are few in the history of
Christian thought who were ready to demur. Calvin, though a thoroughly christocentric theologian in most respects, continued, as
Barth demonstrated with force, to embrace a picture of God (the
omnipotent, omniscient, immutable, holy deity) strangely uninformed by Christology—as though, when he considered godhood,
the French Reformer were more beholden to pagan classicism than
to the biblical thought that he revered beyond any other source. One
of Barth's major contributions to Reformed theology is his insistence
that all of the great attributes (or perfections) that reason and piety
attribute to the divine being (omnipotence, omniscience, omnipres-
ence, aseity, immutability, holiness, and so forth) must, in their
Christian articulation, be brought under the lens of Christology.
What can one profess about the omnipotence of God, for instance,
if one considers it from the perspective of Golgotha?[16]

Luther, whose more random, less systematic theological reflection
could take many turns, nevertheless broke conspicuously with the
regnant Theological tradition and carried his christological point of
departure right into the heart of God: *Deus crucifixus*. If the central
fact of the newer Testament's witness is the passion and death of
Jesus, the Christ, then this fact must not become a mere addendum
to an a priori theism in which God is defined by a power and glory
that precludes any kind of qualification. If the crucified one is truly
representative of the God by whom faith believes him to have been
sent, then, however ponderous the transcendent power that reason
and religion have attributed to deity, the Christian God must be seen
as a suffering God.

Tillich's commentary on this subject, to which I referred earlier,
bears repeating: "One of Luther's most profound insights was that
God made Himself small for us in Christ. In so doing, He left us our
freedom and our humanity. He showed us His heart, so that our
hearts could be won." The passage goes on to recognize that the
human longing for a God of power and glory is very strong—which
is of course why so much religion and so much political ideology can

capitalize on it. We yearn for a God who sets everything to rights—indeed, who prevents wrong from occurring in the first place. But in such longings we overlook the fact that to have such a God we should have to relinquish our own freedom and become automatons who could only do right. And Tillich concludes that while in that case we might be happier (if happiness could still be used of creatures without freedom), we should have become beings quite different from what we are, "perhaps more like blessed animals." "Those who dream of a better life and try to avoid the cross as a way . . . have no knowledge of the mystery of God and of man."[17]

To illustrate: At the end of that fateful day, September 11, 2001, a day that bruised the spirits of us all, I was confronted by a woman—a good friend, in fact, but now quite distraught and almost belligerent. She glared at me, the representative of religion closest at hand. "Where was *God* in all of that?" she demanded. An avowedly unreligious person herself, she was apparently able, in that moment, to reach back into some previous flirtation with the God of power and might in order to find someone to blame. I refrained from saying to her that there were large numbers of people in the world—not in our immediate sphere but nonetheless fellow citizens of Earth and highly God-fearing in their own terms—who believed that God was precisely in charge of that whole plot against godless America, and who could look upon the dread event as a wonderful vindication of God's great glory and power. (Again one asks: Which God? Whose God?) I should have liked to explain to my friend the theology of divine Providence that emanates from this "thin tradition" we are considering; but it would not have been heard, for her fundamental assumption about deity (and in this she is entirely representative of her age) is that the term *God,* if the term means anything at all (which it probably doesn't), must stand for unequivocal power. Ergo, why doesn't He (yes, of course, He!) use it? This is the best argument for atheism known to our race, because of course the God of power and glory never has and never will set things to right in the manner that we, with our many and conflicting views of what right and just and true and good and beautiful would mean, could be satisfied. Thus, like my friend, many disbelievers have a permanent and very effective rationale for their high disbelief, and they are strangely self-satisfied (they manifest a high degree of what the Germans call *Schadenfreude*) whenever tragic or horrendous events occur that give them an excuse to berate and humiliate others who claim belief in God.

What such persons seem not to grasp, or even entertain, is that gods who prevent evil and set everything to rights can only do so by overruling the behavior of that one creature that creates more havoc than any other: ourselves. Ironically, those who most complain of God's failure to act godlike, that is, to exercise unmitigated power, are the very ones who are most affronted by any curtailment of their own freedom. They want the world to be what they want the world to be, and the only god they can abide is one whose will coincides perfectly with their own.

If we posit a God who both wills the existence of free creatures and the preservation and redemption of the world (and I take it that neither of these intentions can be dispensed with by Christians), then we must take with great seriousness the biblical narrative of a God whose providence is a mysterious internal and intentional involvement in history; a God, therefore, who is obliged by his own love to exercise his power quietly, subtly, and, usually, responsively in relation to the always ambiguous and frequently evil deeds of the free creatures; a God who will not impose rectitude upon the world but labor to bring existing wrong into the service of the good; a God, in short, who will suffer.

I said that statements like Bonhoeffer's "Only a suffering God can help" constitute a polemic against the dominant christological as well as the dominant Theological assumptions of the Christian establishment. The elaboration of the christological aspect of that statement must await another chapter (6), but in view of the trinitarian conception of the godhead that Christians embrace, we ought at least to notice it already in this consideration of God. Western Christendom in both its Roman Catholic and its major Protestant expressions has been welded to an atonement theology that has guaranteed keeping God the Father quite distinct from the suffering Son. For in the

Latin or Anselmic or satisfaction theory that the West has adopted in various forms almost without exception, the suffering of the Son is virtually at the hands of the Father, who requires satisfaction for the guilt and unholiness of the human race, for which the Christ substitutes himself. This presents a picture of God entirely different from the one that emanates from the theology of the cross. Anselm's Father God is still very much informed by the power principle. While such a God may be said to be motivated by a *desire* to forgive and love sinful humanity, this God is able to do so only indirectly through a transaction that, to say the least, calls into question the trinitarian unity of the godhead. There is in fact a tremendous gulf between the Anselmic conception of the atonement and the anguished cry of Bonhoeffer that only a suffering God can help. Anselm's *God* simply cannot suffer.[18]

A New Openness to the Suffering God?

The wide reception of the work of Bonhoeffer, as well as of Moltmann, Weil, and many others (including artists and writers like Georges Rouault, Shusaku Endo, Georges Bernanos, Flannery O'Connor, Rudi Wiebe, and many others) who in the past century have developed conceptions of a suffering God, raises an interesting question: is there a new openness to this Theology? I believe that there is, and I also think I understand some of the reasons for it.

The first reason is quite simply that the god of power has failed. The failure of the omnipotent deity to prevent or resolve evil and human suffering could be overlooked, so to speak, so long as people could be persuaded of a heaven in which their sorrows would all be healed. But with the increasing orientation of humankind (especially but not only in the West) toward the present life and our own earthly condition, a God for whom omnipotence was claimed could not be received as credible in a world where suffering both personal and corporate seemed interminable. It is not accidental that one problem has preoccupied Christianity in the past two centuries: the problem of evil. For if the thing you most wish to say about God is that God is absolutely and ultimately powerful, then in a world newly conscious of both its potentiality and its vulnerability, you will have to explain how such an omnipotent deity can tolerate the seeming triumph of evil, wickedness, and death. If Christianity has begun at last to consider the meaning of Paul's dictum that divine power is "made perfect in weakness," it is at least partly due to the fact that the conventional religious claim concerning God's limitless power ceased to persuade after about the seventeenth century.

But the move away from the equation of God and power has also had something to do with the sidelining of the Christian religion itself. Whatever else may be said about our de facto disestablishment, the good side of it is that the remnant of Christianity that remains is no longer obliged to mirror, in its doctrine, what is acceptable to the dominant culture and the policy-making classes. If, as I have maintained, the association of God principally with power has been profoundly affected by the functioning of the Christian religion as the cultic guarantor and legitimator of earthly power structures, then the removal of Christianity from that role, wherever it is true, means that Christians are at liberty (if they will take the liberty) to explore the dynamics of their own tradition without feeling bound to make their tradition serve the extraneous purposes of a perhaps moribund civilization.

The new freedom to explore the nature and meaning of God without looking over one's shoulder to see how one's Theology is being received by kings and governments and powerful classes is one of the most exciting realities of contemporary Christian theology. In the following statement of Moltmann, with which I shall conclude this chapter, we have a marvelous instance of what this new freedom can mean:

> To recognize God in the crucified Christ means to grasp the Trinitarian history of God, and to understand oneself and this whole world with Auschwitz and Viet Nam, with race-hatred and hunger, as existing in the history of God. God is not dead, death is in God. God suffers by us. He suffers with us. Suffering is in God.

God does not ultimately reject, nor is he ultimately rejected. Rejection is within God.

When he brings his history to completion, his suffering will be transformed into joy, and thereby our suffering as well.[19]

chapter 5

The Grandeur and Misery
of the Human Being

Created, Fallen, Lifted

How, under the aegis of the theology of the cross, ought Christian faith to view the human condition? In this brief response to the question I intend to develop a single thesis with three prongs: *The cross of Jesus Christ represents simultaneously a high estimate of the human creature, a grave realism concerning human alienation, and the compassionate determination of God to bring humankind to the realization of its potentiality for authenticity.* I will attempt to defend this thesis by elaborating on its three main components. We can think of these components as relating to the three basic foci of Christian doctrine: creation, fall, and redemption.

I would like to state in advance that my intention in this discussion will be to accentuate the priority of the first focus, creation, together with its echo or confirmation in the third, redemption. I do this for contextual reasons but also because I feel that Christian doctrinal history has not done justice to the positive assessment of human nature and destiny. In particular, classical Protestant anthropology has been too consistently fixed on the second focus, the concept of sin and the fall. There have been moments in history when such an emphasis was necessary and appropriate. But the power of this negative assessment of humanity, combined with humankind's own, often hidden, propensity to berate itself, has prevented both Christians and those observing them from appreciating the very positive statement that Christian faith in its whole witness makes concerning the human being.

"A Little Lower than the Angels"

The figure of a human being languishing on a primitive and ghastly device invented by a harsh regime to punish and liquidate criminals and enemies of the state seems hardly to symbolize a high anthropology. It is indeed possible that, over these two thousand years, the cross, the symbol by which Christianity is universally recognized, has conveyed to most people, including many Christians, a quite negative message: the sheer misery of human existence, the overt or latent violence of human beings in their dealings with one another, the terrible cheapness of human life. Seen at face value, simply as the depiction of a historical incident, perhaps represented in painting or sculpture or stained glass, the crucifixion of Jesus of Nazareth contains little if anything of what ordinary human imagination expects of high estimates of human life. Even when pious depictions of the cross present an idealized figure who seems not to be suffering in the least, the fact remains that this person is being put to death. And in the more realistic artistic representations of the crucifixion (above all in the spiritually profound work of Matthias Grünewald) there seems nothing to suggest human nobility. Looking at Grünewald's Isenheim Altarpiece in Colmar, France, or Rembrandt's etchings of the Christ, or Rouault's *Christ Mocked by Soldiers,* one is reminded of Isaiah's poem:

> He had no form or comeliness that
> we should desire him.
> He was despised and rejected by man;
> A man of sorrows and acquainted with grief
> And as one from whom men hide their faces
> He was despised, and we esteemed him not. (53:2-3)

The suffering servant and other older Testament passages that Christians have used to interpret this event, together with the newer Testament's own description of it, are almost calculated to discourage any heroics, ancient or modern. What is usually considered high anthropology cannot be found here unless the actuality of the crucifixion is deliberately falsified.

Faith, however, sees behind and beyond the brutality and ugliness of the crucifixion as such; it sees the glory *(doxa)* "hidden beneath its opposite" (Luther). The resurrectional-pentecostal perspective that is faith's presupposition sees in this scene of ultimate human degradation the ultimate identification and solidarity of the Creator with the creature. From that perspective the cross, as we have seen, is the last step on the journey of the Representative of God toward the world. God would go so far as this to seek the lost sheep, the wayward son, the stranger fallen among thieves, the alienated covenant partner. This, not the violence, not the wickedness, and not even the divine wrath against human violence and wickedness—this is the first thing and the last that must be said from the perspective of a theology that finds in the cross of Christ its critical point of vantage on the whole Christian account of life. No doubt certain other things have to be said between this first and last, but they must not displace this one crowning affirmation: namely, that if there is a cross at the center of this faith it is because the God who is our human source and ground cares infinitely about the creation and, especially, about that creature that is the creation's articulate center, steward, and representative. Whatever else Christianity may have to say about the human being, its *foundational* presupposition concerning humankind is irrefutably affirmative. This creature, both in its own right and because it is indispensable to creaturely well-being in its totality, is so significant, so wondrous a being, that its Creator will go to such lengths as these to reclaim it for its rightful life and its vital role in the scheme of things created. If the cross is understood as a statement about *God* (as I claimed in the previous chapter), then it must also and therefore be seen as the most astonishing affirmation of the grandeur of the human creature of God. This is a grandeur more extraordinary than that of the humanists. Humanism, which for very good reasons emerged precisely out of this Christian anthropological background, locates human grandeur intrinsically in the human as such. Biblical faith dares to claim that this creature is the beloved of Eternity itself—*not,* certainly, as a species *above* all the others, but as the priestly creature upon whose shalom the shalom of the whole is contingent. Clearly, a Theology that depicts the deity as a veritable "hound of heaven" in persistent, loving pursuit of this unique though tragically errant creature, a God who despite everything wills to be "our God," Emmanuel: such a Theology cannot but give rise to a high anthropology.

Now, besides the intrinsic doctrinal reasons for making such a claim, there are important contextual reasons for accentuating this first prong of our thesis. One such reason stems from an unfortunate tendency of historical Christianity itself, namely, its tendency to overstress the *second* anthropological datum illumined by the cross, that is, its representation of human distortedness or sin. This has resulted in a virtual loss within the various spheres of Christian orthodoxy of the biblical and especially the Hebraic/Jewish sense of the goodness of creation and the promise of human life. So seriously have Christians traditionally taken human sin and the fall that often, in their zeal for denouncing our wretchedness, they have forgotten that sin and the fall are only meaningful categories when they assume a positive condition in relation to which sin, fall, evil, death, and the demonic are negations. Throughout its historical sojourn, Christianity has seemed to many almost to glory in its negative assessment of the human condition and the dire prospects of the species: as if by stressing human *impossibility* it could enhance the *possibilities* of God—as in the old expression, "Man's extremity is God's opportunity." In many circles (and I am not only thinking of Savonarola and New England Puritanism and similar extremes), the more one could defile and denigrate the human, the more superlatively one could seem to glorify the divine. Thus, soon after the emergence of humanism from the ranks of the churches themselves, Protestant orthodoxy began to lament its humanist offspring—not because the early humanists questioned theism or the centrality of Christ (they didn't) but because the humanists, according to their orthodox critics, were giving off too positive an account of humanity. They didn't embrace "total depravity" with sufficient zeal. They didn't present damnation as the inevitable, inherited fate of the human being apart from the special act of divine election.

To be sure, nineteenth- and early twentieth-century Christian liberalism reacted strongly against orthodoxy at this very point. The liberals presented humankind in a far more positive light—in the case of modernism, so positive a light that one was left wondering why grace was needed at all, since nature and history seemed to be well on the way to perfecting the race. But liberalism did this precisely as a *reaction* to exaggerated renditions of Augustinian, Calvinist, and other historic systems on the part of latter-day orthodoxy. Instead of conducting its anthropology within the boundaries of biblical and Reformation thought, liberalism embraced the positive anthropology of modernity, which dismissed not only orthodoxy but much of the Bible itself as representing primitive and outmoded thinking. As Langdon Gilkey has written, "Liberal Christianity encountered modernity, accepted much of it, and now, instead of inspiring, directing, and renewing it, it has almost disappeared within it."[2]

It was therefore quite necessary for the so-called neo-orthodox theologians of the first part of the twentieth century (above all, Reinhold Niebuhr) to recover the biblical witness to sin; for in the meantime the entire modern vision had been rendered obsolete and misleading by the key events of the early twentieth century. When Niebuhr delivered his final Gifford Lectures in 1939, the bombs were already falling on the city of Edinburgh in which he was speaking.

This demonstrates once again how important *contextual* factors are in theology. Liberalism was right, surely, in cutting itself loose from the fatalistic and grim anthropology of Protestant orthodoxy, which had become not only moribund but also incredible to the mind of modern Western humanity. But the one-sided approbation of the human enterprise that liberalism then endorsed had within a few decades proved itself equally fantastic and incredible. Christianity must always work with both the first and the second foci of the thesis we are developing here—as well as, of course, with the third focus, which as we shall see incorporates dimensions of both the first and the second. When the church exchanges the dialectic of human grandeur and human misery for a more straightforward emphasis upon either the one or the other, it loses touch with the foundational tradition and becomes prey to the pessimistic *or* the optimistic assessments of humanity that are blowing in the wind.

Yet I would still insist that the high anthropology illustrated and affirmed by the cross as God's abiding commitment to the world must always retain a certain priority. For the dialectic of grandeur and misery (the terms are Pascal's) is an asymmetrical one. The two sides of the dialectic—the two polarities, the yes and the no—are not equal. The weightier of the two is the first, the grandeur, not because humankind in itself and as such is grand, but because it is God's creation, created for a purpose that entails and affects all creation. And this accent upon the first focus is confirmed by the third focus, redemption. That third term must never be treated as a positive that functions to negate once and for all the negation, so that we end with a Hegelian synthesis and no longer live in the Kierkegaardian tension of positive and negative. Still, redemption, eschatologically speaking, is the divine determination that "in Christ" the negative (sin, fallenness, estrangement), *has been, is being, and shall be overcome.* So that the final statement, the last word, that is being uttered about humanity in this tradition is, as Paul put it, wholly yes, not an ambiguous "yes and no" (2 Cor. 1:17f.)—this from the side of Christian eschatology.[3]

But there is another reason, contextually speaking, why it is necessary today (at least in *our* context) to accentuate the priority of this high anthropology that stems from the theology of creation and redemption. I refer to the fact (and I think it must be acknowledged to be a sociological fact) that in contradistinction to the spiritual climate of the first part of the twentieth century, that situation to which Reinhold Niebuhr addressed himself so responsibly, the image of the human that dominates our present civilization is precisely *not* a high one but one that is devastatingly and even dangerously low. The Promethean image of the human *(imago hominis)* that informed the modern conception of human capabilities—perhaps strangely, perhaps predictably—proved to be very short-lived. The rhetoric that it created—the rhetoric of progress and success and mastery and utopian futurity—achieved, of course, a life of its own. It is bound to be regurgitated and even exaggerated well beyond its heyday, precisely in inverse proportion to the demise of the image itself, and especially by those social elements most dependent upon that image. But while this rhetoric still abounds, it is patently unconvincing. The programmed optimism of the affluent, consumer-driven West is by no means the real thing![4] There is simply no comparison between the optimism of nineteenth-century industrialism—as symbolized for instance by the Crystal Palace of Prince Albert—and the slick commercial bravado of today's television hucksters. The "future shock" that Alvin Toffler correctly analyzed as part of the present-day Zeitgeist in the most so-called developed societies is a palpable reality. It only takes a passing reference to one of the great instabilities with which we all live today (for instance, terrorism, AIDS, the depletion of the ozone layer and global warming, and the recurring prospect of economic collapse) to conjure up in the minds of most ordinary people a vast and fearsome darkness that has no place any longer for such a bright vision of human potentiality as inspired the whole project we call modernity. Against the image of "Man the Master," recent cultural history has placed that of "Man the Bungler," hoist by his own petard.

Now it would be much too easy for Christians in such a context to utter a snide, "I told you so!" And many do. But that, I think, is both to betray the profundity of the Judeo-Christian tradition and to miscalculate the meaning of *gospel* in our time and place. For the great temptation of our contemporaries (and it can be documented in hundreds of ways) is to give in fatalistically to the seeming impossibility of our situation. As Elie Wiesel in *The Town beyond the Wall*[5] insists, the real sin of the present is not that of pride (*superbia*, hubris) but that of sloth (acedia, apathy, ennui, escape, indifference). Since the problems are so overwhelming and since we humans are so haphazard and inept (especially by comparison with the clever machines to whose perfection we have devoted our best efforts), there is nothing we can do to direct a process that has been out of hand now for at least a century; therefore let us, where possible, cultivate *private* happiness and let the world proceed as it will.

This is not Prometheus; it is Sisyphus—as Albert Camus, decades in advance of his time, declared.[6] In the churches we had become so accustomed to attacking human pride, and so determined to eliminate from our own house any show of difference and originality that we hardly know how to take in the sloth, the passivity, and the capitulation to mediocrity that has come over our society. We seem paralyzed by a pervasive sense of our own banality as a species. On every side we are reminded that we *are* the problem: humankind (especially the male of the species) is the Achilles' heel of the biosphere. Science does not hesitate to announce—indirectly, for the most part—that the world would be better off without the human component. If our species were to disappear, says E. O. Wilson of Harvard, a leading expert on biodiversity, "the earth would flourish," but if the ant species were to disappear, "there would be catastrophe."[7] The conclusion that even unreflective people regularly if quietly draw from such pronouncements, as from the whole seeming success story of technology, is that the human species at best is a very second-rate affair and probably a detriment to life in the larger sense.

In the face of this kind of working fatalism[8] of our context, it is imperative for Christians (as for others who can do so honestly) to counter such defeatism—not, please, along the lines of a mindless celebration of everything human but in a sane and nuanced way, a way that remembers that we are dust yet remembers also that we are dust fashioned into life by the Creator of all things. As Pascal put it, "Man is only a reed, the feeblest thing in nature; but he is a thinking reed."[9]

Gospel today, it seems to me, must have something to do with the recovery of the high anthropology that is the presupposition of the cross of Jesus Christ. The Christian ethic, about which we shall concern ourselves later, must surely accentuate human responsibility, under God, rather than the kind of moralism that feels constrained to warn humankind at every turn about the limitations and dangers of all its thoughts, words, and deeds.

Is it strange that the cross should inspire such an anthropology and ethic? Only, I think, if the cross is too undialectically interpreted as the symbol and reality of human alienation and wickedness. To be sure, Golgotha does affirm (with Jesus' earlier teaching) that "for mortals [what is asked of human life] is impossible," but more strongly still it insists that "for God all things are possible" (Matt. 19:26). And the cross of Jesus is above all God's *dispensatio* (economy, strategem), however much it may also be of humankind's instrumentality. What it tells us of human capabilities is that we are capable of great evil. But what it tells us of God's capability for us— *pro nobis*—is that great good may come even out of our evil intentions and acts. As Joseph tells his brothers at the end of that extraordinary biblical saga, "'Even though you intended to do harm to me, God intended it for good, in order to preserve a numerous people, as he is doing today'" (Gen. 50:20).[10] And Luther, recalling this and many biblical stories in which humiliation seems a necessary prelude to exaltation, writes: "The gospel is nothing more than the story of God's little son, and of his humbling, as St. Paul says, 1 Cor. 2:2: 'I determined not to know anything among you, save Jesus Christ, and him crucified.'"[11] The cross is good news *for* humankind even while it is a stark reiteration of the bad news *about* humankind. This leads to the second prong of the thesis.

"Fallen"

The cross of Jesus Christ expresses a grave realism concerning human alienation. The crucified Christ represents (re-presents) the ultimate yes of God to the human creature, and therefore to creation as a whole. But the crucified Christ also represents the ultimate no of the human creature to its Creator, and therefore also to its own creaturehood. We shall consider this dual representation of the Christ in the subsequent chapter; for the present, we limit ourselves to recognizing what this means for Christian anthropology.

"Whatever else the cross may tell us," wrote the late Hendrikus Berkhof, "it certainly proves that we cannot stand God and that He must be eliminated if he comes too close to us."[12] The cross gives the lie to all theories and sentiments about humanity that find an easy continuity between the so-called religious longings of the human species and the God and the human revealed in the crucified one. One may agree with all that apologetic theology from Augustine onward has claimed concerning the restless heart of the human creature, which longs for reunion with its ground and source. It will be remembered from an earlier chapter that I do, in fact, favor a modified apologetic theology for our present context. But (to repeat) there is no *easy* continuity between religious longings, needs, and gropings, and the divinity and the humanity that are revealed at Golgotha. It is beyond question, I think, that human beings are religious by nature (I suspect that Bonhoeffer was premature when he announced the end of *homo religiosus*). The new "spirituality" that is much discussed today must be taken seriously as a fresh (though by no means novel) expression of the religious impulse. But biblical faith and the best of the Christian tradition (including the apologetic side of Augustine and Tillich) are well aware that this same religious impulse is a deeply ambiguous phenomenon. It did not take Karl Barth to remind careful readers of the Bible that religion is something that God for the most part hates. Religion combines egocentrism and other-directedness in a very deceptive—often a very cunning—manner. No representation of the religious impulse in Scripture is more illuminating, parabolically, than the myth of the Tower of Babel (Gen. 11:1ff.). The desire *for* God is subtly interwoven with the desire to *be* God— as so much of the "new" spirituality once again demonstrates.

There is that in the human, however it got there, that resists and rejects the God who is (to use Tillich's well-known expression) "God-beyond-God" or in Martin Buber's similar term the God who is "more than merely God," that is, the God who transcends our idols, our imaginings, and (yes) our Theologies. Consistently and with great poetic skill, the Scriptures of both Testaments demonstrate that humankind from the mythic Adam of the first Garden to the historical Adam of the second Garden, Gethsemane, "cannot stand God." Even Jesus (as he must do, because he is behaving here as our priest, our representative) pleads with God to "remove the cup," to take away the destiny that is his vocation. And in between the two gardens every one of the prophets tries valiantly to resist his or her calling. Israel itself, as the name suggests, "struggles with God," "contends with the Unnameable"—and for the very understandable reason that its election is an election not to privilege but to a responsibility, a priestly and prophetic existence, that can never be devoid of pain. The late Paul E. Scherer, regarded by many as the greatest preacher of his era, used to point out that in the newer Testament the kingdom of heaven is customarily depicted, poetically, as a great feast, a bounteous banquet—*from which, ironically, everyone wants to stay away*. St. Paul himself, the most articulate and fervent apostle of the early church, could only be brought into the sphere of Christ's lordship kicking and screaming and only remained within it because of a "necessity" (*ananke*—destiny[13]) that, he said, "is laid upon me" (1 Cor. 9:16).

One wonders why, in North American Christianity, all this was lost—or was it ever present? The most successful churches on this continent are those that present Jesus and the divine kingdom as the most desirable sort of "product" that one could ever want to acquire. Where is the Good Friday—or, indeed, the Easter—motif? The Gospels record that upon the arrest and condemnation of Jesus, all his followers "forsook him and fled," and the resurrection at least in the earliest account (that of Mark) produced in its first witnesses not Easter-lily jubilation but "terror and amazement" (Mark 16:8). How does it happen that the whole population of the United States of America manifests, according to the assumptions of megachurchianity, a strong compulsion to get as close to Jesus as possible? What a marvel!

The theology of the cross, which from beginning to end is unattractive to popular religion, does not forget this flight from God, this No! to God that is unmistakably and centrally present in the event at the center of the Christian narrative. I have been at pains in the first point to emphasize the *affirmation* of human life that this event stands for. But that affirmation is rendered innocuous and banal when it is not held in dialectical tension with the reality that it confronts: namely, the reality of human alienation, distortion, and fallenness—the adamant, perpetual denial and rejection of the God who "must be eliminated if he comes too close" (Berkhof). An affirming, celebrating, accepting Christian message that knows nothing of the impossibility over against which such an affirmation is made, a gospel ("good news") that knows nothing of the bad news that is always the presupposition of the good, is not only a matter of "cheap grace," it is finally just incredible—because there is sufficient self-knowledge and sufficient truthfulness in most people to realize that they are not quite acceptable and cannot be easily accepted, nor life easily celebrated. Most of us know deeply that we are not the "very nice people" that we project publicly. I am generally rather skeptical where human motives are concerned, but I find that there is, on the whole, enough rudimentary self-knowledge beneath the surface of bourgeois smugness to ensure that—to be concrete—when people see films like *American Beauty, In the Bedroom, Midnight in the Garden of Good and Evil, About Schmidt, The Hours,* or so many of the other films that emerge now from the Hollywood that used to be the chief factory for our high estimate of ourselves, they are at least slightly unsettled by the mirror that is being held up to their way of life.

The truth that the cross of Christ embodies about us is certainly that we are loved by God, but that we are loved as prodigals, as problematic creatures, as beings whose alienation from God, from one another, from ourselves, and from the inarticulate creation is so great that we will accept love only on our terms, when it corresponds with our desire to be affirmed without asking of us that we become authentic and without requiring of us any depth of commitment comparable to the love that is being shown us. There is a great deal of "cheap love" in our society, and its cheapness lies in the assumption that real love is all "come hither" and no "go away." The rhetoric of love conditions us to expect of our loves, including their sexual aspects, such untarnished bliss that no area of our life is more strewn with unhappiness and turmoil. We did not learn what the ancients who collected the wisdom literature of our tradition knew—that (as an eastern proverb insists) under the conditions of existence "the line between love and hate is as thin as a razor's edge."

I venture upon this thorny topic because I want to introduce in the most memorable way possible the fact that the sin we are considering when we contemplate this second side of the revelations of Calvary is precisely what the tradition of Jerusalem has always maintained it is: broken relationship. Alienation! Estrangement! The brutal death of Jesus of Nazareth is not to be attributed to some heavenly blueprint intended to make up for the guilt of the race, à la Anselm. It is not *God's* vindictiveness, *God's* "plan." It is the work of human beings who are entirely and accurately representative of human behavior whenever and wherever the spontaneous and unmotivated love of God comes close enough to them to judge their unloveliness and shame.[14] If in the last analysis, *after the event,* faith is enabled to see in this terrible sequence of human hate the will and hand of God, that is not to be construed as something divinely predetermined. To be sure, the early preaching of the church proclaims that Jesus was "delivered up according to the definite plan and foreknowledge of God" (Acts 2:23), but this affirmation of divine involvement in the cross should not be equated with straightforward manipulation from on high. It must be seen within the biblical teaching of God's "sovereignty," which never abandons the dialectic of grace and freedom in favor of either human voluntarism or divine determination. That Jesus Christ was crucified was no more the direct will and plan of God than that a million innocent children should have been slain in the Holocaust. To put forward the events of Holy Week as a kind of divinely predetermined Omeramergau play whose author and director is none other than Almighty God is to have substituted for biblical faith a fatalism that *may* belong to Stoicism, but not to the tradition of Jerusalem. Afterwards—but only then—faith is allowed to see the hand of God in this human tragedy. "He maketh even the wrath of men to praise him" (Ps. 76:10, KJV). But it is still human wrath that has done the thing; it is still human wrath—the nihilism and vengeance of the fallen spirit of humanity—that the God who created ex nihilo has to work with. And no kind of Theology, no high-minded desire to uphold the sovereignty of God, can be allowed here if it has the effect of distracting human attention away from the reality of our own distortedness by making God the puppeteer who pulled the strings of Christ's executioners. (I shall return to this when we consider more fully, in the next chapter, the so-called Latin theory of the atonement.)

What is important anthropologically in this second of the three foci of the cross of Christ is that the hamartiology it depicts is strictly *relational*. It has become fashionable to use this term, and its status as a cliché unfortunately detracts from its importance. All the same, what it stands for is vital. No word in the Christian vocabulary is so badly understood both in the world and in the churches as the word *sin*. Christians have allowed this profoundly biblical conception, which refers to broken relationship, to be reduced to *sins*—moral misdemeanors and guilty "thoughts, words, and deeds," especially of the sexual variety, that could be listed and confessed and absolved. Anyone who wants to trace the decline of Christianity in the West would do well to study the history of reductionism associated with this little word. There has been no more effective way of erasing the profundity of this term, which refers to a quality of relationship, than to quantify it. The result is a petty moralism that no longer speaks to the great and abiding conflicts of human persons in their complex intermingling.

One wonders how, looking upon the cross of Jesus Christ, with its whole narrative treatment in Scripture centered in the morass and malaise of human relationships—the relationship of Jesus with his uncertain and vacillating disciples; the relationship of the priestly class to the charismatic religion of the Baptist and the prophetic religion of the Nazarene; the relationship of Rome to its subject states; and all the personal relationships encompassed in these greater categories—one wonders how, with this narrative as our window into the reality that biblical faith expounds, Christianity could ever have ended up with an ontology of substances and quantities and moralities and not of relations. Sin as a substance, quantifiable, measureable; grace as a substance, eatable, drinkable; forgiveness as a substance, certifiable, doc-

umentable. Even the three so-called theological virtues as substances—faith, hope, love—things that are not things, cannot be
possessed, cannot be transferred.

Only the most amateurish science thinks that life is about substances. And Christian faith is about life! The negative reality, the
human inauthenticity that the cross of Jesus Christ depicts, this second focus, is not the sort of passive nonbeing that is just the absence
of the good—in short, a lack of substance; it is an active nonbeing, a
refusal, a rejection, a no to the other: the other who is God, the
author of life; the other who is the neighbor, the partner of life; the
other that is creation itself, the context of life. It is this relational
understanding of sin that has to be grasped in the churches today,
and that can be grasped if there is any serious attention on the part
of the teaching ministry to the theology of the cross. In fact it can be
grasped much more easily and immediately by people today than in
the classical and medieval periods, because, as all the literature, art,
drama, film, psychology, psychiatry, sociology, and intellectual discourse of our period make plain and even the natural sciences confirm, any system of meaning that wants to receive a hearing today has
got to deal with and, one hopes, illumine the complexity of the
between-ness that is to be found in all life. The substantialistic ontology that Christianity borrowed from Hellenic and Hellenistic culture and philosophy, profound as it may be in a Socrates or an
Aristotle, is not where we live today. But the recovery of relationality
in Christian teaching and preaching is not a concession to modernity
or to postmodernity; it is a recovery of the original Hebraic and early
Christian ontology, and in the end it may be as critical of contemporary views of human nature and destiny as it should always have been
of the tradition of Athens.

Toward Authenticity

The third focus on anthropology present in the cross comes from the
perspective of redemption, and I expressed it in my initial thesis in
this way: *The cross reveals the compassionate determination of God to
bring the human creature to the full realization of its potentiality for*

authenticity. This focus, as I have already said, reaffirms and makes central the first dimension of the cross, its affirmation of the human. It assumes that there *is* a potentiality for something highly affirmable in the human creature as God's creation. Whether we see this potentiality as something that was once actualized and then lost, or as something always being actualized and always being lost, or as pure potentiality never yet actualized—this no doubt makes some difference. But it is not the great difference that it has been made out to be by quarreling factions in Christian history. I do not see how a twenty-first-century educated person could maintain a historical fall after the manner of Christian fundamentalism; but I do see how someone like William Golding, whose novels always circle around this subject, could apply the idea of the fall to historic progressions such as the transition from Neanderthal man to homo sapiens; and I do see how someone like Paul Tillich could see the fall mirrored in the transition from "dreaming innocence" of childhood to adolescence. And above all I know that something like fallenness belongs to the best and deepest reflections of our species about itself—for instance, Albert Camus's novel *The Fall* or Franz Kafka's story "Metamorphosis." Christianity that is worth its salt—that is, that can claim any connection with the Scriptures and the great expositions of this faith throughout the ages—*must* deal with the distortedness that the myth of the fall commemorates as well as the nostalgia for Eden, so to speak, that is never very far removed from human experience and history.

So it is true that this third focus recapitulates in itself both of the preceding foci: it reaffirms the affirmative first focus (there *is* something eminently worthy of redemption in this creature), and it assumes as well the negating second focus (redemption is *necessary* only because this creature is living a contradiction of its essence).

It is in this latter sense that I have used the existentialist term *authenticity;* for it is still, I think, the best way to speak of what the Bible calls "righteousness" and the doctrinal tradition "original righteousness" *(justitia originalis)* and the Reformers "justification." The object of divine grace in the life, death, and resurrection of Jesus

Christ is the justifying of the human. But today most people do not understand this language, really, as Tillich wrote,[15] and partly we do not understand it because the post-Reformation Protestant dogmatists gave it a very legalistic (forensic) connotation.[16] *Faith*—understood as assent to orthodox teaching, combined with obedience to religious duties and moral precepts (and so "quantified")—became the legal currency by which believers met their share of the debt owed to God on account of their "unrighteousness." Faith was (in terms borrowed from Scripture) "reckoned to him [or her] as righteousness" (Rom. 4:3). Of course, in Protestant theology above all, no human being *could* pay the debt; the debt, namely, the great weight of guilt accumulated by the children of Adam and Eve from the beginning, could only be paid by the innocent second Adam. But faith, in this forensic understanding of justification, constituted our appropriation of Christ's once-for-all payment of this debt, almost as if it were our becoming registered members of the bank and drawing upon this account. Thus the forensic understanding of justification, combining with Anselmic-Calvinistic conceptions of the atonement, presented a conception of the religious life that was in fact very accessible to the middle-class capitalism that accompanied the rise of Protestantism. An economy that dealt in debts and payments and loans and interest and so forth could understand this language and, if it did not in fact invent it, at least contributed greatly to its currency.

So powerful has this conception of justification been in Protestant orthodoxy that liberalism felt it had almost to jettison altogether the Reformation teaching "justification by grace through faith." It is indeed very hard to retrieve this central teaching of the Reformation, but the existentialist category "authenticity" can help.

Joseph Sittler, the American Lutheran theologian and poet-preacher who perhaps more than anyone else in our continental context grasped and, for many, helped to recover basic insights of Luther, spoke of justification in the following homely way: A carpenter who enters a hardware store in search of a new hammer picks up the various items that are offered him and hefts them, as though he were driving a nail. He knows by the way that the hammer moves under his impetus (does it deflect to the right or the left? Does it seem balanced, properly weighted?) which of the hammers he tries is "just." A hammer is just when it is capable of doing the thing that hammers are meant to do. Its justification means the appropriate casting and molding and weighting of it, so that it will "hit the nail on the head." Similarly, *justification* is the righting of the human person so that he or she will behave humanly—will become, so to speak, himself or herself,[17] will be, as Bonhoeffer put it, a human being, pure and simple, nothing more (not a god), nothing less (not a devil, not a "happy animal"). "By grace you are justified, through faith." By grace you are being humanized, made human, made *truly* human. You are being liberated from the demeaning attempt to rise above your humanness and the equally demeaning desire to slink out from underneath the possibilities and responsibilities of your humanity: the sins of pride and sloth, Prometheus and Sisyphus. God wills that you be human: *vere homo—truly* human.

The idea of authenticity helps to interpret this. Divine grace does not intend to make me into someone else but to make me the self that I am before God *(coram Deo).* This self is "a new creation," because it has not been actualized heretofore. It has been a potentiality, a remembering and a hoping of which I have never been wholly unaware, but it has been prevented by another, strong impetus within me—what Paul called "the old Adam"—that urges me to rise higher than human or sink lower than human.

When Tillich wanted to describe justification by grace through faith in nontheological language, therefore, he preached a sermon he titled "You Are Accepted."[18] The progression of ideas in the sermon runs as follows: (1) You are certainly not acceptable (sin). (2) You are accepted, though unacceptable (grace). (3) Accept the reality of your acceptance (faith). The "justifying" or "authenticating" of the person, in other words, entails, beyond the knowledge of our actual *in*authenticity, a self-acceptance that is consequent upon our gracious acceptance by God. Many of us regard this as Tillich's finest sermon. He wrote it when he became sixty years old, and in the corner of the manuscript he penciled in the words "For myself."[19] This demonstrates one very important aspect of the notion of justification, without which it becomes a travesty of religious presumption and legalism: namely, that it is a process. The authenticating of human beings, insofar as it happens, goes on and on and on. There is never a time when the Christian can say, "Now I am authentic. Now I have arrived." Among the pioneers of our faith, no one understood this ongoingness better than Martin Luther, who wrote:

> Christian living does not mean to *be* good but to become good; not to *be* well, but to get well; not being but becoming; not rest but training. We are not yet, but we shall be. It has not yet happened. But it is the way. Not everything shines and sparkles as yet, but everything is getting better.[20]

chapter 6

Jesus Christ—and Him Crucified

In the question of the person (Christology) and the work (soteriology) of Jesus Christ, the *theologia crucis* has both its beginning and its center. We have seen that this tradition must be rescued from a *too narrow* concentration on the Christ and the cross of Christ; for the theology of the cross touches every aspect of Christian faith and life. But there can be no question that this is the focal point of the entire tradition.

As in the previous chapters, I have no intention here of recapitulating what I wrote in the three-volume work that is the *background* of this smaller study. That work can be consulted easily by anyone wishing to pursue my interpretation of the subject further.[1] In the present text, I intend to concentrate only on the key aspects of Christology and soteriology as they seem to me to present themselves under the aegis of this theological tradition. I will state and discuss seven propositions. Taken together, they constitute the basic assumptions that I bring to the consideration of the one Christians call "the Christ," the Messiah of God.

1. The Foundational Confession

The foundational confession of Christian faith is its confession of faith *in Jesus as the Christ.* Christianity stands or falls on this confession. One does not have to be a fundamentalist to agree with Paul's insistence upon this point—as for example in his diatribe against "other gospels" in 2 Corinthians 10–11 or Gal. 5:6-10. I can see no reason why anyone would deliberately claim a Christian identity apart from his or her conviction that Jesus of Nazareth is the bearer of ultimate significance for his or her life. The fact that many people who are statistically or nominally Christians do not hold this conviction or hold it only rhetorically or hardly give it a thought does not alter the assumption. The church will always—and *should* always— open itself to individuals who need it, for whatever reasons, but as church, as a faith, as an intentional movement, it is centered in this confession. As a culture-religion, the established religion of Western societies, Christianity has had to serve the various religious and secular interests of its host societies. Human beings are religious, and if Christianity is the only or the most prominent religion in a society— as it was, in the West, for many centuries—then it will perforce become the locus of that society's cultic and cultural needs, and these may relate to the Christ only tangentially. But serious Christianity has always assumed the centrality of the confession concerning Jesus, and in our time Christianity is being thrown back upon this foundation—to the extent that those who find no meaning in it also find less and less reason to retain association with organized Christianity. Today, with both secular and religious alternatives to the traditional Christianity of Western peoples, those who remain in the churches are increasingly conscious of the need to examine and understand this central confession of their faith.

The theology of the cross is quite evidently, even unqualifiedly, a christocentric theology. Such an affirmation should be taken literally: that is, this tradition is *centered* in the Christ; it is not fixated on Christology in an exclusivistic manner—that is, it is not christomonistic. We have already seen that the theology of the cross reaches into every aspect of Christian faith and life. But its point of departure is Jesus as the Christ. This is not necessarily true of the *theologia gloriae;* in fact the theology of glory usually prefers a *theocentric* point of departure, based on speculation concerning the grandeur and glory of the deity. It is hard—it should be impossible, really—to base Christian triumphalism on Jesus. It can only be done, in fact, by ignoring or transforming the actual witness to the historical Jesus that we have in the Gospels, especially the Synoptics. It is far more easily managed to build a theology of glory on an unspecified and abstract conception of deity. Luther recognizes this when, in the key theses of the Heidelberg Disputation, he identifies the *theologia gloriae* with speculation about *God* and insists upon the suffering of the crucified Christ as the only authentic point of departure for Christian belief.

2. The "Thou" Factor

It is necessary to distinguish carefully and perpetually between Jesus Christ and doctrine concerning Jesus Christ. The foundational confession of Christian faith (the previous observation) is that *Jesus* is the center, the "cornerstone," *not* that this or that Christology or soteriology constitute that *fundamentum.* Far from being a merely rhetorical distinction, this distinction is of the essence of this theological tradition. For the one thing on which all Scripture and responsible christological tradition agree is that Jesus was and—as the risen and reigning one—is a living person, and *person,* in the tradition of Jerusalem, cannot and must not be reduced to descriptions of, or accounts of, or reflections concerning person. The commandment against the making of graven images applies to God and to all living beings, and (what has rarely been recognized!) graven images are by no means limited to *graphic* images. It is also a graven image when living beings, divine or human, are defined in language—in propositions, doctrines, creeds, etc. God infinitely transcends our theologies. Jesus the Christ cannot be contained in statements about Jesus the Christ.

In Martin Buber's well-known categories, the Thou whom Jesus is must not be reduced to It,[2] and doctrine, no matter how inspired it may be, remains It—an objectification of its living Subject. Just as any human person transcends the descriptions and images of that person, whether we are speaking of historical writing or literature or simply the images that people have of those around them, so Jesus transcends the church's conception and images of him. The mystery of the person Jesus of Nazareth may of course be *pointed to* by Scripture, doctrine, creed, sermon, hymn, religious drama, etc., but he may never be captured by any of these. Nothing is more abhorrent to prophetic biblical thought than is idolatry, and the idolatry of doctrine is among the most subtle of all idolatries. What Paul Tillich insightfully identified as "the Protestant principle," meaning the guiding methodological assumption of classical Protestantism, applies here with exceptional rigor: nothing that is finite must assume the posture of the infinite; nothing that is conditional must be accepted as though it were absolute; nothing that is penultimate may be put forward as if it were the ultimate. *Jesus* is our foundation, not ideas or images or doctrines about Jesus.[3]

This is part of what is entailed in Luther's concept of the "hiddenness" of God: precisely in God's self-revealing, God conceals Godself. If, for Christians, revelation consisted of the disclosure of explicit doctrines or dogmas or truth claims, there would be no "hiddenness" about it. The whole point would be straightforward disclosure and the strictest possible articulation and preservation of the truths thus disclosed. But if, on the contrary, one says that God reveals Godself supremely in a living *person,* the inherent and inviolable mystery of that person means that the revealing simply *is,* simultaneously, a concealing. And this should not be difficult for thinking persons to grasp, for *every* human being who gives him- or herself to us in love and trust is for us at the same time the most known and the least known. The very depth of our knowledge of that person prevents us, when we are acting in good faith, from reducing him or her to an image or characterization. The mystery of personhood defies strict definition—a matter of frustration in most relationships but simultaneously the very essence of our attraction to and relationship with the other. A human being defined is a human being dismissed.

Even the words of Jesus himself do not exhaust the meaning of the Word *(Logos)* that John's Gospel insists that Jesus is. No matter how illuminating the teachings of Jesus may be, they remain the teachings *of Jesus;* the Teacher himself, in his unique subjectivity, his thou-ness, remains the subject and indispensable center of what he teaches. The disciples cannot take the teachings and leave the Teacher; as they themselves are reported to have said on at least one remembered occasion, "To whom would we go? You have the words of eternal life" (John 6:68). The words of eternal life have their reality and effectiveness, their power to grasp and convict and comfort, only because they are "Your" words. This leads directly to the third observation.

3. Doctrinal Flexibility

There will always be a certain necessary flexibility in doctrine (specifically, in this case, in Christology and soteriology), and this flexibility must be expected, allowed, and even celebrated. For faith in its Christian sense is engendered in people through their encounter with the Spirit of this person Jesus. And, as in all meeting between person and person, each individual brings to this encounter—the genesis of Christian faith—experiences, characteristics, foibles, problems, needs, hopes, anxieties, and so forth that are unique to that person. It is natural therefore that different feelings and articulations of the meaning of the person Jesus will occur. They have occurred from the very beginning. The four Gospels and the epistles of Paul already testify to this diversity. Paul's picture of the Christ is not that of John; Mark's witness to the Christ differs from Luke's; and so on. The differences do not (at least in my opinion) add up to gross inconsistencies or contradictions; on the contrary, I think these various testimonies serve to give us a quite well-integrated picture of the one at the center of this story. The witnesses that were *glaringly* different (such as those that did not take the flesh-and-blood reality of Jesus seriously) were excluded from the canon precisely because of their conspicuous divergence from the witnesses that had gained authenticity in the church.

All that is true. But there are, all the same, real differences already in the biblical testimony to the Christ, and there could be no alternative to such an outcome so long as the New Testament intended to insist, as it does with great consistency, that it is the *person* Jesus who stands at the center of the faith that it professes. "*I* am the way, the truth and the life," declares John's Jesus, and in that single statement the writer of that Gospel grasped and exemplified the principle to which I am referring here. We may call it the I-factor, or (alternatively) the Thou-factor. If *Jesus* is the Truth (capital T), then nothing less than Jesus (including statements *about* Jesus, or even statements *of* Jesus) can assume the posture of ultimate truth. Only if Christianity were to define itself propositionally, by basing itself on specific truth claims that can be articulated in precise and unchangeable language, could it avoid flexibility of doctrine. To be sure, some historical forms of Christianity have done and do precisely that—or attempt to. But the price they pay for it is the reduction of revelation to the disclosure of religious data—ergo to data that is forever fixed in time *and*, ironically, bears all the earmarks of the historical situation in which its expression was fixed (which is why, for example, American fundamentalism, in its dogma of creation, must forever project a scientific worldview that belongs to pre-Darwinian or anti-Darwinian science). When such reductionism of revelation prevails, faith, which in Reformation thought as in biblical thought is a *relational* category (*fiducia,* trust, faith *in*), becomes instead assent to specific truth claims (*assensus*). *Thou* has been exchanged for *it*. Faith becomes faith or belief *that* something is true, not faith *in* one who has revealed himself as trustworthy, faithful.

4. A False Dichotomy

This acknowledgment of the relativity of christological doctrine does not imply that such doctrine is insignificant or incidental to faith. The modern mind, prompted by a very simplistic appropriation of scientific method, tends to assume that there are only two possibilities, absolute and relative, and that anything that cannot claim the status of the absolute is *merely* relative—and of course, that relativity is bad. Popular religion is especially victimized by this assumption; there-

fore, in the face of the relativity that is obviously all around us and
within us today, popular religion puts forward its truth claims with
all the more vigor as absolutes. This religion is popular, in fact, precisely because it offers absolutes in an age of overwhelming relativity. But the absolutes require of their adherents fantastic and
sustained credulity (which is not to be confused with faith biblically
understood); and therefore communities pursuing this approach to
religion necessarily become guarded communities—frequently,
indeed, communities of such insidious watchfulness that they cannot be sustained for any length of time, but end in splinter groups
and factions.

Any theology that bases itself on the theology of the cross is
bound to be modest about its own claims; for it is faith, not sight—
it points toward an ultimate reality that it can by no means contain.
Its understanding is quite strictly a matter of "standing under," and
so of awe and adoration at what infinitely transcends its capacity to
describe. In other words, theology written in this "key signature"
always deals in relativities. That is the nature of this "modest science"
(Barth).[4] To claim anything greater for itself would be to move
straightaway into quite a different key—the key, namely, in which
the theology of glory is played.

This necessary relativity of doctrine, however, does not *necessarily*
devolve into mere chaos and license. Obviously enough, a thing may
be relatively closer or relatively more remote from its object. Living
"under authority"—*under* an Absolute that one knows perfectly well
one cannot possess, transcribe, or even fully comprehend—such a
consciousness, when it is genuine, imposes upon one a greater
responsibility for faithfulness than when one imagines oneself to be
in possession of absolutes.

Thus Christology and its inseparable companion, soteriology,
constitute for the Christian community (certainly for its theological
wing, but also for the whole community of faith) an immense spiritual and intellectual responsibility: This community must try to
understand and to articulate the presence and the meaning of one
who, by definition, defies the community's power to understand and

to communicate yet who nevertheless *(nevertheless!)* requires this of his witnesses. Under such a necessity the disciple community is aware that it must labor very hard—intellectually, spiritually—if it is to be as faithful as possible to the Truth that Jesus is. It cannot possess this Truth, but it can and must seek to be oriented toward this Truth. It cannot claim the status of the absolute for its Christology, but it can and must assume full responsibility for its relativities.

In practice this means adherence to certain very concrete tasks: *first,* ongoing biblical research and contemplation; for even if the Bible itself participates in our same human relativity (and it does), its relative proximity to the Event that is our center (at least that!) means that it must be taken with utter seriousness. *Second,* concern for responsible relativity means a constant dialogue with the whole tradition—the great councils, the writing theologians, the controversies and heresies, the historical consequences of this or that expression of belief, and so on; because we can assume that those who have gone before us also wished to be faithful, and we can learn from their attempts and even from their failures. *Third,* the assumption of responsibility for our relative truth has to mean listening to the present-day church in all its ecumenicity, variety, and struggle. None of these aids, these checks and balances to our own obvious biases and limitations of knowledge and wisdom, will ever deliver us from the status of relativizers, because they themselves also participate in that status. But they at least prevent mere arbitrariness and unchallenged subjectivity, and they offer a larger vision of the ultimate mystery than we as the present cohort of disciples can have within the confines of our own time and place.

In the end, of course, all of our Christology and soteriology—with everything else theological—is fated to fall short of the truth that it seeks to understand. It can only hope and pray that its *relative* appropriation of truth will be taken up by the divine Spirit—the Spirit that is able to make use even of our errors. It was, I think , with some such understanding as this that the young Karl Barth wrote: "The Word of God is at once the *necessary* and the *impossible* task of the minister."[5] Human words, even the words of Scripture, can only point. But point we must—while believing and hoping that God, who permits this risky business of theology, will use our strictly relative testimonies to be vehicles of the absolute that only the triune God is.

5. Faith as Presupposition of Christology

Nearly everything that I have said thus far could as well fall under the category "theological method" as under the heading "Christology." I have remarked before that in this modest science, content and method cannot be kept apart, but when it comes to this center— Jesus Christ and his identity and his work *pro nobis*—we have to be very clear about what we are trying to do, ergo about our method. This clarity is demanded of us because Christology is not only the foundation of our whole Christian edifice but also the place where the limitations of our understanding and faithfulness as Christians (and specifically as theologians and teachers of the church) show up most blatantly. Imagine that we, ordinary human beings who are hardly able intelligently and faithfully to describe our own spouses, our own children, our own close friends, and who invariably in fact *misrepresent* them, weaving graven images around them—*we* are asked to comprehend and communicate knowledge of *this* person, whom in fact we find indispensable to our very existence and in whom we believe the very ultimate Truth of all existence is revealed—concealedly revealed, revealedly concealed! Clearly, as Jesus said to his disciples upon the departure of the one who came to him by night asking for eternal life, "for mortals it is impossible" (Mark 10:27).

And just here (to make the main point toward which I have been struggling) is where the theology of the cross has its main impetus and message: namely, in faith's recognition of its terrible inadequacy and utter dependency when it comes to this center and core of its object, which is no object but a living Subject (Barth[6]). This is why the very first thing that Luther and his interpreters (for example, von Loewenich[7]) have to say about the theology of the cross is that it is a theology of *faith*. And again one should add (so as not to make our faith too grandiose in itself, which would invite the theology of glory in through the back door): "faith, *not sight*" (Heb. 11:1). Even more than Theology proper (that is, the doctrine of God), Christology confronts us with the limits of our analytical capacities. Indeed, in a real sense "God" is a thought natural to the human, perhaps the aboriginal thought: an idea, a concept, a feeling for which the human has an almost innate capacity—as Anselm argued in his *Proslogion*. Whether this is because we were created that way (as theists believe), or because our very finitude and contingency drives us to such a thought (as Feuerbach and nontheists think), God does seem to come automatically into the heads of most human beings, even those who deny the reality. But the *Christian* belief in God is from the start bound up with this specific human being, this particularity, this historical man, this story, this unique individual. The abstract is replaced by the concrete.[8] The speculative is replaced by the historical, by text, by the collective memory of the community, by the *testimonium Spiritus sancti internum*. And so, like every concretization of universals, the particular called Jesus of Nazareth confronts us with a "givenness" that we cannot immediately appropriate by reducing it to theory and abstraction. Human beings theorize endlessly about God, about deity, and we soon come up with generalizations that seem on the surface of the thing remarkably adequate: God is the Supreme Being, omnipotent, omniscient, omnipresent, immutable, infinite, absolute, ultimate, prime mover, first cause, etc., etc. Yes—and precisely in so defining and naming deity, we can in some quite interesting way effectively dispense with the mystery of deity! As with our relatives and friends, to define God is to dismiss God. This has been the tendency, especially, of the so-called civilized peoples of the earth, who then proudly distinguish themselves from the people they call, ironically, "primitives," who insist on living with the mystery. One suspects that our Western concepts of God are the answers that we give to depth experiences that are too basically unsettling to remain undefined, unnamed. Better name it straightaway—otherwise what control can we claim?

But by contrast with such answers as hover about the word *God* and its linguistic equivalents in abstract religious discourse, Jesus as the Christ, the supreme Revealer of God according to Christian faith, confronts us with questions. We give answers to these questions too, of course, and often our answers (our Christologies) *become* the (idolatrous) object of our belief. But the Spirit that "proceedeth from the Father and the Son" continues to unsettle our answers, and we are brought again and again into the presence of the one who asks *us* questions—the one who *is* for us and before us an unanswerable and living question.

I suggested in my trilogy that it is not accidental that the first Christologies of the newer Testament are *the questions* that are so frequently put by and to and about Jesus: Who do people say that I am? Who do you say that I am? Who is this that even the wind and the waves obey him? And so on. Faith, in the true sense of the term, begins with this encounter with the *unknownness* of Jesus and the *unanswerability* of these and similar questions. He is the stranger, the one who does not fit—and yet makes an undismissable claim upon those who meet him, whether in the flesh, as in the encounters of the New Testament itself, or in the Spirit, through the witness of the Scriptures, the church, preaching.

And it is just here (I repeat) that what Luther called *theologia crucis* has its genesis: namely, in this same sense of a revealing that is also a concealing, a concealing that is also a revealing. In all of the encounters of Jesus with the various figures portrayed in the Gospels (not least of all with the disciples themselves, Peter especially, perhaps) such a paradoxical exchange takes place. Those who are met by Jesus are held by the impression that they are being met by something more final, more luminous of the ultimate, than his seemingly ordinary humanity as such could account for. There is a sense of something of infinite significance being disclosed, yet at the same time they know that they are not able to *receive* this something, to take it and to *have* it—because it is not, after all, a something, not tangible. It is inseparable from the giver. If it is utterly mysterious, transcendent, it is a mystery concealed beneath its opposite—mere humanity. We are held by it precisely because we cannot appropriate it—cannot accommodate it to our accustomed schematization of reality. As the Mary Magdalene character in Andrew Lloyd Webber's *Jesus Christ Superstar* sings: "He's a man, he's just a man, and I've had so many men before," but "I don't know how to love him."

This paradoxical experience (revealing/concealing) is not just the *beginning* of faith, but faith's continuing character—at least, when faith is understood within this tradition. The theology of glory grasps at the revealing and resists the concealing. Because there is a theology of glory at work in every one of us, we know very well that desire. Every time I address myself to this subject, I am seized by the ambition to state everything definitively, finally. I should like to make the ultimate statement about the Christ. And every time I try to do so, I am brought up short again by the sheer impossibility of doing that—impossibility and absurdity. The theology of the cross (as I had to conclude in my first book on the subject) *cannot be a wholly satisfactory, wholly integrated statement about our human brokenness in relation to God; it can only be a broken statement about our brokenness—and about God's eschatological healing of our brokenness.*[9] Still, I have never tackled this subject since I wrote that book thirty years ago without hoping that now, at last, I could see the thing whole, straightforwardly, clearly. The drive to mastery is perhaps never so great as when we try to master theology. Christian theology—particularly Christology—is perhaps a peculiar and poignant instantiation of the original temptation: the temptation to *have* instead of continuing to live vis-à-vis this Thou who is not have-able.

We know this temptation already in our relationships with one another. We want to *know* others unambiguously: we want to have them, possess them. That desire is deeply if unconsciously present in the sexual act. After all, it is uncomfortable, even threatening, to live with their unknownness, their unknowability, their frustrating transcendence. We create images of them in order to escape the terrible hiddenness of their being. In fact, of course, what we are trying to do is to get free of them. We reduce them to images—images that last for years and years, graven images—because as they are, in all their mystery and duplicity and contradiction and unpredictability, they deeply unsettle us. We objectify them because to live subject-to-subject is unbearably taxing emotionally. Who can do it twenty-four hours a day? It is perhaps natural to create of them—of our nearest and dearest even (oh, especially!)—caricatures of themselves, exaggerations of certain qualities, or simply figments of our imagination. Yes—for the theology of glory has as much to do with our behavior toward our own kind as toward our Maker. The theology of glory is indeed, all things considered, the natural theology—under the conditions of human fallenness. For in the insecurity of our anxious creaturehood, our only hope seems to be the creation of a *manageable* environment, and that means managing in particular those all-too-human variables that constantly remind us of what Alfred Lord Whitehead called "the livingness of things."

So Jesus, the living variable of Christian theology, when it is true to its mandate, continuously assails the theologian and the church with the great fact of his livingness. And whenever this happens, theology has to be a theology of the cross. The glory of ultimacy, of finality, of definitiveness is denied. The theologian of the cross can only point, in an awkward way—like John the Baptist in Grünewald's crucifixion—to a crucified Christ who in death is more alive than the living.

6. Christ's Dual Representation

Any responsible pointing toward this center of the faith must take seriously, and try to do some kind of justice to, the claim of the tradition concerning Jesus' dual representation, namely, his representation of God and his representation of the human. This is the major *christological* problem of the subject, and the great *errors* of developing Christology have all consisted in some kind of refusal to develop *both* sides of the Christ's identity. It is almost a foregone conclusion of christological discourse that it will get stuck in divinity or humanity. But make no mistake: by far the greatest temptation and error of Christendom has been its tendency to dwell too exclusively on Jesus' representation of deity. Popular conservativism on this continent always creates the impression that what has been lost or was always understated was the so-called divinity of Christ. But the history of doctrine demonstrates that the greatest threat all the way through has been the loss of Christ's real humanity—and therefore of the whole concept of incarnation and the reality of Jesus' suffering and cross. From the beginning—and especially after its establishment in the fourth century—Christianity was tempted to accentuate the "very God of very God" of Nicene and Chalcedonian Christology. In the early church, once it had gone beyond the bounds of Judaism, it was only or chiefly the school of Antioch that kept Alexandria and other centers from ending with a nondialectical affirmation of Jesus' godhood. The early church must have been under tremendous internal and external pressure simply to announce "Jesus is God"—an announcement that one can hear twenty-four hours of every day in North America, in effect rendering null and void the whole doctrine of the Trinity that was in its origins the attempt precisely *not* to end with what H. Richard Niebuhr rightly called our continental tendency toward "Unitarianism of the second person."[10]

The theology of the cross—as exemplified in Luther, in Kierkegaard, in the early Barth, in Tillich, in Jürgen Moltmann and Elisabeth Moltmann-Wendel, in Alan Lewis, in Mary Solberg, and in many others—by no means minimizes Jesus' representation of God. But since it sees this representation under the guise of what is opposite to deity as commonly conceived, it maintains throughout a strong hold on the real humanity of Jesus Christ. It understands this unique representation of God as occurring hiddenly *through* this genuinely human life. Jesus' representation of God is faith's *conclusion* to its strict observation of Jesus' representation of true human being. One glimpses the God whom Jesus represents as one follows the human life that he leads, the relationships he forms, the responses he makes to power, to weakness, to illness and death, to sin, to the demonic. In christological doctrine, this theology assumes—as in the life of the Christ as such—that the prior concentration is upon the actual living, teaching, suffering, and death of Jesus. Only when that which can be seen has been seen does faith find itself (perhaps despite itself!) concluding that "very God" has been in this life and death from beginning to ending—like the centurion who at the cross was moved to say, "Surely this was a Son of God" (Matt. 27:54). The transcendent significance of Jesus of Nazareth—his being the Christ of God, the revelation of the Absolute—is *inductively,* not *deductively,* communicated. Jesus is ultimately significant not because the church says that he is significant but because, here and there, now and then, faith perceives this significance in and through and behind what it sees and hears of this person.

The Chalcedonian teaching concerning the two natures of the Christ was, I think, an understandable and historically necessary outcome of the evolution of christological doctrine, but it was also a very historically—that is, contextually—conditioned outcome. The early church already in its biblical witness felt that it had to maintain two things in its testimony to Jesus as the Christ: *first,* that he was certainly a fully human being (thus the Gnostic accounts of his life that indulged in fantastic feats that could not be attributed to human capabilities were rejected), and *second,* that in and through his humanity faith knows itself to be met by the ultimate—by very God. The Gospels and epistles of the newer Testament maintain this in one way, largely under the form of the relational ontology discussed in the previous chapter; but as soon as the Christian movement entered the Greco-Roman world, it had to translate this into the ontological terms prevalent in that world, which were not relational but substantialistic.

Unfortunately, the church has never overcome its captivation to that substantialistic ontology—partly because it was that ontology that informed from start to finish the great concilliar decisions regarding the godhead and the doctrine of Christ's person, and these have remained definitive. Still today we are fighting in the churches over the extent to which the substances of humanity and divinity are to be seen in this person, which dominates, which is "the real Christ," how the two natures come together in one person, and so on.

What I have wanted to do in my more sustained discussions of Christology is to free Christology from the substantialistic ontology of classical orthodoxy and to state what I believe the New Testament intended by holding onto those two affirmations. My object has been to express this dual representation in *relational* terms. Such terms not only do away with the absurdity of mixing two incompatible "ingredients" (divinity/humanity) in one living being. They also retain the theological and anthropological dimensions of the biblical confession concerning Jesus Christ without capitulating on the one hand to liberalism's loss of the divinity principle nor on the other hand to conservativism's exaltation of that principle to the point of courting docetism. The informing concept in this relational Christology is that of *representation*. Without wading into the murky waters of substantialist ontology, it is possible to keep hold of the biblical witness to the God-relatedness of Jesus by saying that Jesus is for faith God's representative, that his life is one of a unique relationship with God, a relationship that enables him to relate to us—to humanity—in a manner that is also unique. Simultaneously, his exceptional solidarity with humankind gives him the possibility and the right to represent us before God. Precisely in his true representation of God, Jesus moves inevitably ever closer to humanity—to the point of a complete identification with the human condition, the cross; precisely in his true representation of humankind—of *true* (that is, authentic) humanity—Jesus moves inevitably closer to God, the God who (in Augustine's language) has created us for himself, so that our hearts are restless until they find their consummation in communion with God.

In stating the matter in this way, I am of course not using biblical language, but I believe that it is possible to retain, in some such manner as this, the basic biblical confession concerning Jesus Christ, namely, that he is at the same time a fully human person and the person in whom faith glimpses that which is infinitely beyond the human. In a world where the substantialistic thought of the classical period seems increasingly artificial and forced and where relationality is better and better understood as the essence of what it means *to be,* we are perhaps in a better position today to grasp the dual representation of the biblical testimony to Jesus than was the case heretofore.

The great frustration of classical Christology has been the difficulty it has in retaining both the divinity and the humanity principle without ending with a person who is less than fully integrated, if not in fact a type of split personality. With the relational category of representation, grounded in an *ontology* that is relational, it is possible to avoid such an undesirable outcome. After all, without making anyone a split personality, we may without difficulty speak of the dual representations in which the lives of most people are steeped. Parents represent to their children the adult world, with its demands and its opportunities; at the same time, they represent their children *to* that adult world—in the form of school teachers, physicians, sports organizations, and so on. In democracies, those elected to represent their constituencies in the high courts of government simultaneously (one hopes!) represent the decisions and actions of government to their constituencies. Most of us play these dual or even multiple representational roles, and far from being split or disintegrative, one side of our representational life *enables us* to actualize the other side. I could not represent my children to the adult world were I myself not thoroughly involved with the lives of my children; nor could I represent the adult world to my children were I withdrawn from society with its many problems and possibilities. So I say: Jesus' profound relationship with God is what drives him increasingly toward communion with humankind, and at the same time his deeper and deeper solidarity with and compassion for humankind turns him ever more intensely toward God. It may be called a dual representation, a priestly mediation, but its duality is in fact a necessary and mutually sustaining unity.

So if I am asked, "Do you believe in the divinity of Christ?" I answer: "Yes, otherwise how could he have been so wonderfully human?" And if I am asked, "Do you believe in the humanity of Christ?" I answer, "Yes, otherwise how could he have been so profoundly oriented toward God?"

7. Soteriology

In view of its contextual grounding, the theology of the cross aims in its soteriological reflection to take with great seriousness the human condition from which salvation is needed. To begin with, we must recognize that it is the soteriological side of Christology that this theology accentuates. Once Luther wrote, "Christ is not called Christ because he has two natures. What is that to me?"[11] In this he was giving characteristic expression to his dissatisfaction with christological speculation that has no real relation to the human condition and predicament. The question of Jesus' identity is not unimportant for him or for this whole theological tradition, but its importance is dependent upon its application to *us,* to "me." All theology can become merely theoretical, nonapplicable, nonexistential. This can also happen to the theology of the cross. But a theology of the cross that speculates in an abstract way about the meaning of the theology of the cross (and this is not unheard of) betrays the contextual, salvational, and ethical orientation of this whole tradition. When the soteriological dimension of Christology is one's point of departure for the whole subject, however, it is less likely that one will become bogged down in christological speculation. For the theology of the cross, Christ's *person* is significant because of the *work* that he is perceived by faith as having done *pro nobis, pro me.*

Now, if it is to the human condition that this work must be seen to speak, then this theology cannot and must not be allowed to substitute for concrete historical and contextual reflection a theoretical once-for-all preconception of what the human condition is. There *is* no "human condition" if by that we mean something eternal and unchanging. There are of course recurring themes, possibilities, problems, scenarios. If this were not the case, we would not understand Shakespeare's plays, let alone those of Sophocles. But as these works of literature convey to us, there are also significant differences between human contexts. The fact that ancient works of literature have to be *studied* in order to be understood at depth is evidence of their differing contexts. To be human is to be mutable, to change; it is to be historical; it is to be involved in flux.[12] The human condition experienced by George Eliot's characters in her novel *Romola,* set in fifteenth-century Florence, is very different from the human condition of people in present-day Beijing or New York or Toronto. Even a quantitative factor like life expectancy introduces qualitative changes that must be taken into account whenever the question is asked: What is it that we must be saved *from*—and *for*? If earlier ages of Christendom were particularly fixated on the afterlife and heaven, it was at least in some considerable part because *this* life was for most people extraordinarily brutish and short. But in a context in which the average life endures well into the late seventies and it is not unusual for people to live to be ninety or a hundred, offering heaven and immortal life as the answer to earth's sorrows speaks in a direct way only to the infirm and the aged—if even to them! At least in the "developed" world, the astonishing postponement of mortality that has taken place in the twentieth century and beyond means that life itself—not death (not, at least, in the same immediate way)—has become the great question. Or, to speak more accurately, the extension of finite existence has meant that the great questions about this existence that have always been there have now become more urgent. The question of people in developed societies today is not "Is there anything after death?" but "Is there anything *before* death?"

What the theology of salvation must address if it is going to speak to an age (or at least to a context) that is as it were condemned to life is whether life is *purposeful*. There will of course always be many other general and specific problems to which, hopefully, the Christian message can and must speak. But it is the great responsibility of the church in every age to try to discern the overarching predicament, the question behind the questions, that is the situational backdrop of all human striving. Western Christendom has in fact been quite adept at this discernment, all things considered. As I argued in my trilogy, the early church realized (intuitively, I think, rather than through a definite kind of investigation) that the great dilemma of its epoch was the one that Tillich named "the anxiety of fate and death," and therefore its soteriology was a theology of liberation from the power of fate and death. The medieval church certainly more deliberately discerned that human beings in the European Middle Ages suffered most conspicuously from "the anxiety of guilt and condemnation" (Tillich's second anxiety category); accordingly, Anselm and

others gave them a soteriology of forgiveness based on substitutionary sacrifice and accompanied by the rituals of a sacerdotal church.
Christian liberalism in the nineteenth century began to sense that
the human condition had to be interpreted now in terms of "the anxiety of emptiness and meaninglessness"—though unfortunately it
only went a little way into this darkness before it brought forth its all
too superficial light![13]

Atonement theologies come to be in response to perceived or partially perceived human anxieties and epochal dilemmas. The problem with atonement theologies is that they are sometimes so
perceptive and brilliant that they last beyond their appropriate
time—and, at the same time, they are perpetuated longer than they
should be because too few Christians have the courage to enter into
the new, emerging darkness and prefer to rely on the old light of
entrenched soteriologies. Both this positive and this negative factor,
I think, must be drawn upon to explain the astonishing persistence
of the Latin or Anselmic/Calvinistic theory of atonement. As
observed earlier, much of the West got stuck in this theory—and it
still is. This is partly because the Latin theory of substitutionary
atonement is indeed a powerful one, which found its way into every
nook and cranny of ecclesiastical life in the Western hemisphere—
into prayers and liturgies, into deeply emotional hymns, into art,
into scriptural interpretation, and so forth. But the persistence of
substitutionary soteriology has a more subtle basis: as tried and true
doctrine, which on occasion can still speak to human guilt, it is able
to function as an ideational refuge from the far more dominant anxiety of our epoch, that of meaninglessness and emptiness (to use
Tillich's language). The latter, manifesting itself in a pervasive sense
of purposelessness, superfluity, boredom, escapism, etc., is so profound and perplexing and unsettling an anxiety that few Christians
have been courageous enough to plumb its depths. Despite its exploration in the artistic and literary works of almost a century, to say
nothing of the investigations of psychology and sociology, the anxiety of meaninglessness and emptiness remains for the general public,
including the churched, a virtually uncharted depth—and one intu-

itively, legitimately, feared and repressed. Yet until the depths of the human predicament have been plumbed, in any age, there can be no response to that anxiety from the depths of the Christian gospel. We have kept on repeating the Anselmic soteriology, then, because in considerable measure we fear entering this very dark place that is the present with its deep suspicion of purpose. "What are human beings *for?*" (Wendell Berry).[14]

It is particularly difficult in our North American context to enter this darkness, because our culture is so determinedly fixed upon the utter meaningfulness of our entire exercise in progress, in happiness. The mere acknowledgment of such a *problematique*—for instance, acknowledgment of the fact that one in every four Canadians is "clinically depressed" or that suicide accounts for a very high percentage of deaths among our young—requires more courage than most North Americans can muster. We are a people in despair, but it is a covert despair—a despair that will not and perhaps cannot admit of itself.[15] And precisely as such it is, as Kierkegaard argued more than a century ago, the very depths of despair, the sickness unto death: "The specific character of despair is precisely this: it is unaware of being despair."[16] Surely the first step toward a meaningful articulation of Christian soteriology in our context would be for the churches to try to become spheres of truth, places where people can give expression to the anxiety of meaninglessness and emptiness—without being utterly debilitated by the experience. It is unfortunate that our churches are, on the whole, places where people feel constrained to be even more hidden than usual.

The greatest theological task of our times, I think, is to bring forth out of things old and new a soteriology that can actually speak to the anxiety of meaninglessness and emptiness. There have been some attempts at this, but on the whole it is still to be accomplished. Theologians during the classical age of the church found a way to address the anxiety of fate and death: they presented Christ as the liberator from these destinies over which men and women seemed to have no control. In the medieval period ways were found to address the anxiety of guilt and condemnation: the Christ was presented as the one who assumes the great burden of our human guilt and so frees us to live more fully. There will never be a time when the themes presented in these two atonement types are wholly irrelevant, because the anxieties they address are perennial. *Nevertheless,* until the postmodern, post-Christendom church has found a way of addressing this third and most complex and damning anxiety, that of meaninglessness and emptiness, we will not have spoken to the predicament that is dominant here and now—and into the foreseeable future. Moreover, so long as we continue to confine Christ's atoning work to the assuaging of the older anxieties of fate and guilt, we will serve only to postpone our whole civilization's encounter with the great question that with all its technical and scientific ingenuity it begs: *"To what end?"*

The theology of the cross is essential to this task—indeed, it may even be thought to have been waiting for just this moment, just this *problematique,* to assume the prominence that it has. If, in the face of the one who suffered,[17] we cannot see a Redeemer who shares precisely our questions (What is it all about? What are we for?), then surely we have lost any theological imagination we might once have had. If, in the word of dereliction from the cross ("Why have you forsaken me?"), we cannot hear the anguished cries of millions of our contemporary abandoned and our own deeply repressed cries as well, how shall we ever expect to find in this person one who takes our despair upon himself and gives us in return hope? In so many ways, hard as it is to answer convincingly under any circumstances, the anxiety of meaninglessness and emptiness is the very anxiety to which the word of the cross speaks most directly. By comparison with the correlative possibilities here, the anxiety of fate and death and the anxiety of guilt and condemnation seem almost to require contrivance, not to say manipulation, to become the predicaments to which the message of the cross speaks immediately and directly. No one could deny that death and the anxiety of finitude are real, but to cause the death of Jesus to assuage the anxiety of death does require, to say the least, a certain ingenuity. And even when the ingenuity succeeds, how does the person freed from the bondage of death cope with the bondage of *life,* which can be far more intimidating? And then, while Western theologies have made a wonderful case for the cross as God's answer to human consciousness of guilt and condemnation, the question still remains: how does the one now released from guilt face the still more perplexing question of what this freedom is *for*?

The despair that arises from a repressed anxiety of meaninglessness and emptiness (or however else it may be designated) has been lurking beneath the other dominant anxieties all along. But today it is no longer in the background; it is in the foreground—at least in the allegedly developed societies, whose very development, involving as it does a certain postponement of death and a relativization of guilt, has left whole classes of society open to the devastations of profound thought concerning our meaningfulness as a species.

Theologies of glory have been productive of soteriologies that can seem to bring closure to the human predicament: eternal life in place of death and fate; forgiveness in place of preoccupation with guilt. But no theology of glory will be able to bring closure to the question "What are people for?" For that anxiety, the only answer that will suffice is the participation in our lives of a God who shares the question, whose Presence gives us the courage of hope.

Part Three

Church of the Cross

Christ at Emmaus
by Rembrandt von Rijn

chapter 7

The Church and the Cross

A Suffering Church?

What kind of ecclesiology—what doctrine of the church—emerges from the theology of the cross? There can only be one answer: the *theologia crucis* gives rise to an *ecclesia crucis*. Indeed it could be said that the whole purpose of this theology of the cross is to engender a movement—a people—that exists in the world under the sign of the cross of Jesus Christ: a movement and people called into being by his Spirit and being conformed to his person and furthering his work. A cruciform people.

Now this can sound very pious. And one has to acknowledge straightaway that much of the Christianity that *has* taken the cross seriously has left the impression that the ecclesiological consequence of the theology of the cross is the existence of an especially devout community of belief, conscious of the need to suffer, and rather too smugly certain that *its* suffering renders it particularly beloved of God. Not only a certain type of pietistic Lutheranism, but various sectarian groups that have emerged out of, or in reaction to, state Lutheranism, give evidence of a good deal of this sort of cross-conscious piety. Karl Barth (with perhaps too much Calvinistic smugness) attributed this to "Nordic melancholy," seeing it as a blend of the almost-natural "world sorrow" *(Weltschmerz)* of a people living a good deal of the time in the cold and the dark and a Christianity that expects to inherit eternal life only if life in this world is sufficiently gloomy: "No cross, no crown." One has a rather kindly if bemused portrayal of this kind of religion in the famous story by Baroness Blixen (Isak Dinesen), "Babette's Feast." There are certain equivalents of this dour piety in the religion of most northern peoples, including my own Canadian people, and on the whole it is not more objectionable than the blasé optimism of dwellers in more hospitable climates.

An ecclesiology that manifests such world sorrow is certainly able to *use* the theology of the cross—and it has and does. But I think it has often been a misuse. It is quite correct in perceiving suffering as a mark of the church, but its error is in its introversion and subjectivization of this suffering. In what follows I shall elaborate on that contention.

To begin with, we have to reckon with the fact (and it is a fact) that there is more in the New Testament about the suffering of the church than about any other single theme or issue of ecclesiology. Not only is this theme prominent in the recorded teachings of Jesus ("If any would follow me, let them take up their cross and follow"), but it is a recurrent subject in the epistles, particularly those of Paul. For example:

> Therefore, since we are justified by faith, we have peace with God through our Lord Jesus Christ. Through him we have obtained access to this grace in which we stand, and we rejoice in our hope of sharing the glory of God. More than that, we rejoice in our sufferings, knowing that suffering produces endurance, and endurance produces character, and character produces hope, and hope does not disappoint us, because God's love has been poured into our hearts through the Holy Spirit which has been given to us. (Rom. 5:1-5, RSV)

Or again:

> For what we preach is not ourselves, but Jesus Christ as Lord, with ourselves as your servants for Jesus' sake. For it is the God who said, "Let light shine out of darkness" who has shone in

our hearts to give the light of the knowledge of the glory of God in the face of Christ.

But we have this treasure in earthen vessels, to show that the transcendent power belongs to God and not to us. We are afflicted in every way, but not crushed; perplexed, but not driven to despair; persecuted, but not forsaken; struck down, but not destroyed; always carrying in the body the death of Jesus, so that the life of Jesus may also be manifested in our bodies. For while we live we are always being given up to death for Jesus' sake, so that the life of Jesus may be manifested in our mortal flesh. (2 Cor. 4:5-11, RSV)

Or again, this time from 1 Peter:

Beloved, do not be surprised at the fiery ordeal which comes upon you to prove you, as though something strange were happening to you. But rejoice in so far as you share Christ's sufferings, that you may also rejoice and be glad when his glory is revealed. If you are reproached for the name of Christ, you are blessed, because the spirit of glory and of God rests upon you. But let none of you suffer as a murderer, or a thief, or a wrongdoer, or a mischief-maker; yet if one suffers as a Christian, let him not be ashamed, but under that name let him glorify God. For the time has come for judgment to begin with the household of God. (4:12-17, RSV)

Passages like these describe a Christian life so foreign to the average North American congregation—and indeed, so foreign to the vast majority of Christian churches throughout Western Christendom—that it is hard for us to appropriate them or even to hear them. "Beloved, do not be surprised at the fiery ordeal that is coming upon you." It would be difficult, on this continent, to find even one Christian congregation that could immediately identify with this statement, except among African American congregations here and there, or perhaps among small churches comprised of indigenous peoples, or perhaps in certain gay and lesbian communities—in short, among minorities, who may for this reason be more truly Christ's church than the others. As for the average Protestant,

Catholic, or Orthodox church, the prospect of a "fiery ordeal" is far from the minds of the people gathered for worship of a Sunday, unless, after September 11, 2001, they leap to the conclusion that America is suffering today because it is Christian—and that is a conclusion having neither scriptural nor sociological foundations. Such passages of Scripture as I have just cited, and countless others could be added, have indeed been heard in the churches—certainly among those churches that follow a lectionary. But they are heard and not heard; they pass over the heads of congregations without making any existential impact, because they seem completely discontinuous with the church as we have known it or with the life most of us lead from day to day. If anyone actually hears them, such scriptural statements can be attributed without much mental exercise to Christian beginnings; few are likely to think of them as belonging to the essence of the church.

Yet these and similar pericopes of Scripture describe a motif that is far from incidental to the New Testament's understanding of the meaning of "church." I repeat: no other single ecclesiological theme receives the attention that the suffering of the church receives in our textual sources. For centuries theology has maintained that the true marks of the church are the four that are named in the Nicene Creed: "one, holy, catholic, and apostolic church" (unity, holiness, catholicity, and apostolicity). Each of these *notae ecclesia* can find some biblical basis, but none of them can claim a fraction of the attention paid to the theme of the church's suffering in these sacred writings. They are all latecomers on the scene of Christian ecclesiology. The earliest and most prominent manner of discerning the true church and distinguishing it from false claims to Christian identity was to observe the nature and extent of the suffering experienced by a community of faith. Why? Because, of course, as Paul makes clear in the passages I quoted, if you claim to be a disciple of the crucified one you must expect to participate in his sufferings; if you preach a *theology* of the cross, you will have to become a *community* of the cross. Anything else would represent a kind of hypocrisy. A purely doctrinal or theoretical theology of the cross is a contradiction. This theology is only authentic—only "for real"—insofar as it gives birth to a community that suffers with Christ in the world. Nowhere does Christendom's difference from the New Testament church show up more glaringly than in the fact that the birth of Christendom in the fourth century c.e. brought about a species of Christianity that with rare exceptions could be practiced without any threat or hint of its being a process of identification with the one who was "despised and rejected."

It is only within the last sixty or seventy years, and only among a minority, that there has been any serious attempt to come to terms with this persistent theme of the Scriptures—a theme prominent in the newer Testament but by no means exclusive to it. In fact, it is there in the *newer* Testament because it is there in the older. Think of the suffering servant passages of Isaiah, of the prophetic tradition (especially Jeremiah and Lamentations[1]), of the wisdom literature (especially Job): the theme is already fixed in Hebraic faith that the people chosen by God to represent God's way and will among the inhabitants of the earth will suffer in their pursuit of this vocation. And I think it behooves Christians today to admit finally that if some of us have at last begun to grasp this reality of our identity and our mission, it is because the whole people of Israel has suffered so excruciatingly in our own time—and, what is worse, has suffered on account of a climate of spiritual suspicion created by Christendom itself. On account of the Holocaust of the Jews, sensitive Christians have had to ask not only how their faith could have contributed to such an event but also why the Christian faith in its established form has been so conspicuously devoid not only of any sustained suffering but of the very contemplation of that biblical theme.

In terms of a recognition of the importance of the biblical theme within the precincts of Christendom itself, it is again necessary to look to Europe during the period of the Second World War. That great cauldron of human chaos and revenge brought to the fore some few Christian witnesses who were able to recognize in the "fiery ordeal" that Fascism had brought upon the world some parallels with the earliest Christian communities. Dietrich Bonhoeffer's writings,

especially his first major book, *The Cost of Discipleship,* were a
poignant and searing cry to his fellow Christians in both Europe and
the West in general to realize at last that the discipleship of Jesus
Christ is a serious business; it is not all the sweetness and light of
Sunday morning ritual, confirmation at age twelve, pretty weddings,
solemn funerals, the pageantry of state occasions. It is a quest for and
a witness to truth in the midst of societies that lie, for authentic
goodness in the midst of societies that reward duplicity, for true
beauty in the midst of societies that celebrate kitsch and sentimentality. Above all, it is a call to obedience in the midst of a society *and
church* that offer "cheap grace." For many of us it was Bonhoeffer's
work more than any other that caused us to consider anew—or for
the first time, really—this unmistakable claim of the New Testament
that the discipleship of Jesus Christ entailed suffering.[2]

But of course it was not Bonhoeffer alone who recognized this out
of that devastating ordeal prior to, during, and after World War II.
Countless German and other European Christians who were
harassed, imprisoned, tortured, or killed in the camps of that regime
left their testimonies to the *meaning* that they found in their sufferings because they could understand them as participation in the suffering of the church that is its baptismal and pentecostal birthright:
Edith Stein, the brilliant Jewish woman who had become a
Carmelite nun, killed at Auschwitz; Martin Niemöller, the renowned
preacher of Berlin/Dahlem, one of the first Christians to be imprisoned by Hitler; Helmut Gollwitzer, one of the great theologians of
the immediate past, prisoner of war for five years in Russia; Simone
Weil, daughter of a secular Jewish family who became deeply Christian, one of the outstanding philosophic minds of our age, hounded
by her times and by the Spirit of God to identify increasingly with
the victims of poverty and oppression; and many others.

And then, beyond this testimony from Europe, the post-war
period saw the emergence of theologies that came to be in the face
not of war and overt violence so much as in consequence of the subtle oppression of economic, racial, class, and gender systems that quietly stifle human possibilities and destroy hope. Out of the sufferings

of the progeny of African slaves, the poor of the world, women, those harassed because of ethnicity or skin pigmentation or sexual orientation, and other great or small divergences from the dominant and policy-making majorities of the planet, there have arisen new expressions of Christian faith that have been able to remain within the faith despite its majority expressions because they recognized their own condition in the biblical depiction of God's people as a people of suffering. The various theologies of liberation have their own particular stories to tell and their own causes to uphold, but they can relate to the theology of the cross at least in this: they can find in the biblical testimony to a suffering church a genuine point of contact with their reality.[3] Unlike the churches of the possessing peoples of the earth, for whom the New Testament's description of a suffering church remains an anomaly or a merely historical narrative, the communities that have given us these theologies speak from experiences that place them far nearer to the scriptural account of the people of God than are we dwellers in the developed nations of the Northern Hemisphere. And they have helped some of us to notice and to try to appropriate this much neglected theme of the church as a community of the cross.

The Character of Christian Suffering

If I were asked to state in a single thesis what this theme is all about, I would borrow a sentence from the first Christian theologian who talked about it more than anyone else, Paul: "While we live, we are always being given up to death for Jesus' sake, so that the life of Jesus may be manifest in our mortal flesh" (2 Cor. 4:11). In what follows, I shall elaborate on this thesis in two observations: (1) The end (*telos*—inner aim) of the suffering into which faith is plunged is *life*-oriented, not death-oriented. (2) This suffering is a necessity that comes with faith, but it is not merely a foregone conclusion, as though it were predetermined or destined; moreover, it has more to do with the suffering that is outside the community of discipleship than with our own personal or ecclesiastical suffering. I want to expatiate a little on each of these subthemes.

Its Orientation toward Life

It seems to me very important to distinguish Christian suffering from the phenomenon that Sigmund Freud named the *Todestrieb*—literally, the drive to death, or, as it is usually stated in English, the death wish. There *is* a drive to death in human nature under the conditions of historical existence, as is evidenced by the high rate of suicide in countries that, from every external point of view, offer unusual opportunities for self-development. Sartre claimed that the reason why most of us suffer from acrophobia (fear of heights) is that in such situations we have actually to *decide* at the semiconscious level not to jump! In other words, there are situations when the fascination with nonbeing—what Keats called "half in love with easeful death"[4]—is accentuated, rising far enough into our consciousness that we have actually to suppress it.

Earlier in my life, I read a good deal of the martyrology of the early church. I would have to say that these accounts often come very close to ambiguity precisely at this point. One frequently senses in the souls of those being put to the test the extremity of the tension between their religious convictions and their psychological confusions. They may speak humbly or perhaps heroically of their faith, for which they are ready to die, but their words and actions also betray a kind of dogged determination to have their day with the lions. Combined with a highly personalistic and sometimes even a romanticized pietism that desires (as Paul once put it) "to depart and be with Christ" (Phil. 1:23), the *Todestrieb,* which on biblical grounds is more demonic than divine, is often only slightly concealed by the martyr's excessive zeal for the "crown" beyond the "cross." Even though the acts of the martyrs are later, rather idealized accounts of these events, they sometimes attest to the genuine humanity of those charged with judging the persons accused. Certainly some of these judges were on the side of life; they are appalled by the prospect of having to condemn decent, law-abiding, and often young people to death. Yet the prospective martyrs seem determined to go all the way—their youth, family, rationality, and all the rest abandoned in favor of the apparent glory of a martyr's death. Time and again, one's sympathies are with the judges, who in many cases were persons both of fairness and compassion. It is not for nothing that the early church had to warn its members not actually to *seek* martyrdom!

Obviously that warning did not imply a negative judgment against those who had been martyred already. The same church can acknowledge that "the blood of the martyrs is the seed of the church" (Tertullian). But the warning against seeking martyrdom indicates a recognition on the part of the church that martyrdom is by no means always "for the right reason"—a telling phrase from a modern literary source (T. S. Eliot's play *Murder in the Cathedral*)[5] that treats exactly this same problem. Christianity, so long as it remains true to its own sources, cannot embrace any of the heroics of death, including those associated with war or various causes, because its orientation is toward life. Life should not be easily or lightly thrown away. Christianity has this life-orientation from its parental faith, Judaism, a religion that, unlike *many* other religions of the human species, never succumbs to the subtle whisperings of death—*even when it is hounded to death and rounded up by death and shipped to factories whose sole product was the transformation of the living to the state of death.* One of the most astonishing facts of human history, surely, is that a people whose whole recorded history is one of suffering at the hands of other, more powerful peoples manifested and still manifests the most intense and jubilant commitment to life—a people whose most cherished motto is "To life" *(l'chaim).* Christianity did not and does not embrace that type of life commitment with the consistency of Judaism, for Christianity has been intermingled with other strains of human longing and frailty; but there is enough of a memory of the life affirmation of the children of Abraham and Sarah in this "grafted on" community of faith (Rom. 11:17ff.) to resist, on the whole, the pull of oblivion that is the answer to life's trauma entertained by many, including not only a few contemporary cults but many ancient faiths (such as, some would say, that of ancient Egypt).

For biblical faith, death is "the enemy" (1 Cor. 15:26)—as the

Apocalypse also insists (Rev. 21:4)—"the last enemy," waiting for its final eradication by "the Lord and Giver of life." This is why the theology of the cross must never become, or seem to harbor, a glorification of death. And this is why, when the cross *has* been turned into such a glorification, it is right that it should be resisted—as some feminists and others in our time have done. To the surprise of many, Jürgen Moltmann began his book on the theology of the cross with the sentence, "The cross is not and cannot be loved."[6] With this short sentence, Moltmann writes a great question mark over all cross-inspired pietism, heroism, and sentimentality, such as one has in many much loved hymns ("In the cross of Christ I glory," "I shall cherish the old rugged cross," etc.). To such sentiments one wishes to say a qualified yes, but always with this caveat: be careful! The symbol at the center of our faith must not be turned into an apotheosis of death, including the death of Jesus. Golgotha, rather, is a courageous *facing* of death and a *confrontation* with death—with "the enemy." Here God confronts the enemy and oppressor of life with a view to death's eschatological overcoming. This enemy, like all great enemies of life, can only be overcome from within. This is the permanent truth of the ransom or classical theory of the atonement.[7] Death must be faced, undergone, entered into—if it is to be challenged, defeated. Hence the *second* sentence of Moltmann's book on this theological tradition reads: "Yet only the crucified Christ can bring the freedom which changes the world because it is no longer afraid of death."[8] What Paul calls "the sting of death" (1 Cor. 15:55-56) is removed in faith through the grace-given courage to confront death's mockery of life openly. (We shall return to this theme in the final chapter.)

This, however, constitutes no camouflaging of the grim *reality* of death. The theology of the cross "calls the thing what it actually is" (Heidelberg Disputation, thesis 21). Death is death, not sleep, not an automatic translation into the realm of the immortals, not the after-all quite beautiful thing that the funeral industry on this continent has so cleverly made of it. Death is real. For biblical faith it is perhaps even God's creature and servant, like Satan. At the very least it only has its reality and its (penultimate) power within the *providentia Dei;* that is, it has its purposes. Like the Bible's other negatives—evil, sin, the demonic—death too can serve, under God, life's positives. Where would love be without death? It belongs to the heart of love to know that the beloved like oneself is mortal, that we love only under the conditions of *chronos* and mortality. Genuine love, as distinct from mere infatuation or passion, contains a large measure of compassion borne of the recognition of our common finitude. So death is not *wholly* despised in this tradition—which is why we do not end up with a dualism, life/death, good/evil, darkness/light, and so forth.

The great objection of the Bible is in fact not to death in itself and as such; it is to the power of death over life—a power given it not by God but by *us,* by human beings, who in their state of "finitude in anxious self-awareness" (Tillich)[9] are fixated upon death. This anxious preoccupation with mortality detracts from our capacity fully and joyfully to enter into life. If you like, God's problem with death is not death itself but our human fascination with and temptation to and anxiety concerning death. Not death but our death wish or (which is the other side of the same thing) our nervously deliberate avoidance of the thought of death: that is the thing that the gospel of the crucified one wants to eradicate. And we do not learn this only from the resurrection accounts; it is there all the way through the biblical witness. The cross, which through the illumination and spiritual power of the resurrection becomes for us "gospel," *is* gospel, good news, because it frees us from the *bondage* to death and decay that is our spiritual condition. It does this through confrontation—through causing us to face and to enter into the negating reality that, because it is repressed in us, exercises an inordinate influence in our lives. The power of death—"the sting of death"—is a power that it has chiefly because it is so deeply concealed in our psyche. When Paul in Romans 6 writes of our baptism into Christ's death, he surely has in mind precisely this debilitating concealment and the profound need in all of us to be able at last to bring to consciousness this confining, draining, subconscious awareness of our total vulnerability, our nothingness, that we expend so much psychic energy holding down. The God of Israel and of Jesus the Christ wants *life* for us, and we are kept from life on account of our preoccupation with death and all that death stands for by way of life's negation. So, says Paul, we are thrust down beneath the waters of baptism—we are brought that close to death—so that we may at long last face it and see through it to the life that is God's gift for us. We notice that death, here liturgically enacted in the baptismal rite, is only the means to another end:

> Do you not know that all of us who have been baptized into Christ Jesus were baptized into his death? We were buried therefore with him by baptism into death, *so that as Christ was raised from the dead by the glory of the Father, we too might walk in newness of life.* (Rom. 6:3-4)

What we should pause to consider here is that this kind of neurotic fixation on death—which is "the sting of death"—must be applied not only to individuals but to whole societies. Our society, perhaps more than any other in history, is engaged in a massive denial of death. (And remember that for biblical faith *death* does not just refer to the termination of life, biological death, but stands symbolically for a whole Pandora's box of fears and negations that become particularly virulent when they are repressed or denied.) This was the point of one of the most insightful books written in our era, Ernest Becker's *The Denial of Death*. The more fixated the human spirit is upon its mortality, its vulnerability, its nothingness or apparent insignificance, the less capable it is of participating freely and joyfully in the life that it has been given. And this condition is most grievous, most overwhelming, when it is covered up with a show of shallow positives. Individuals whose sense of well-being depends upon a rigorous silencing of every thought of their own mortality are very difficult and sometimes dangerous people to be around. But what of a whole society whose well-being—whose way of life—depends upon the constant reassurance that the happiness it seeks is in no way threatened by the limitations that creaturely life places upon us? Such a society, says Becker, could be problematic, especially for those in its immediate sphere of influence or those within its own midst who are beyond pretension, the reality of whose condition precludes repression. When an entire culture is held in the grip of a worldview in which death is allowed no voice, death's power over life is immensely increased.[10] Such a society is greatly in need of (shall we say?) liberation, and at least in this respect the ancient atonement theology called the "classical theory" or *Christus Victor*[11] ought to be pondered anew by Christians who ask what their mission might be in this highly developed society of ours—this society that perennially searches for "the enemy" *outside itself* because, perhaps, it half recognizes how painful it would be to confront the enemy within.

Faith in the crucified one, which means both trust in him and conformity to his death and life, delivers us from the sting of death—not as a once-for-all deliverance but as an ongoing liberation. Or, to say the same thing in another way, such faith frees us from the kind of *self*-preoccupation and morbid anxiety that hold us back from the abundant life that the Creator intends for our creaturehood. And such faith is brought about (if I may put it in this no-doubt childish way) when the divine Spirit takes us by the hand, so to speak, and puts us into the company of the crucified one, where we are caused to face, finally, our utter vulnerability, mortality, and impermanence but in the company therefore of one who befriends us and shows us that this ending is also a beginning, that *this* death is the entrance into newness of life. Luther, as usual, understood all this when he said:

> The fear of death is merely death itself; he who abolishes that fear from the heart, neither tastes nor feels death. . . . The dream I had lately will be made true: 'twas that I was dead and stood by my grave, covered with rags. Thus am I long since condemned to die, and yet I live.[12]

So, in summary, the theology of the cross takes death very seriously—unlike, for instance, the Socratic tradition, which thinks of death as the soul's release from the body—but it does not glorify either death or dying. Because of the commitment to life on the part of the whole tradition of Jerusalem, this faith has more in common with Dylan Thomas's "Do not go gently into that dark night" than it has with some modern psychological schools that urge death's acceptance—schools that may be more Stoic than Christian. Even Jesus did not "go gently." There is no Hamletian "to sleep, perchance to dream" in the passion narrative. The literature of the Judeo-Christian tradition (so long as it remains the *Judeo*-Christian tradition) takes death so seriously as the end that it can only counter this ending by a beginning that is *not* found tucked away within this ending in some natural way but must be introduced de novo as God's possibility for us, not a possibility residing already within us. Grace and not nature counters this ending.

But it *is* countered. And its countering is already *anticipated* existentially and eschatologically whenever trust in the God of Golgotha takes us beyond the incapacitating fear of death and offers us some semblance of new life—some new courage to live *(Mut zum Leben)*. As the negative in biblical thought is *always* present for the purpose of serving the positive (think of the role of Satan in Job), so death is there in order to enhance life and the beauty and joy of life, and in some sense death has to be gone through before life can be experienced in something approximating its fullness. Just as light presupposes the experience of darkness, and love of lovelessness and aloneness, and hope of despair, and faith of doubt, and so on, so life becomes the miracle it is only as we confront its antithesis. But the end, always, the bleakness of the *means* notwithstanding, is the positive pole in this dynamic—the yes, not the no. Therefore a pietism of the cross that ends by basking in unrelieved, morbidly enticing sorrow must certainly be seen as a contradiction and misrepresentation of the theology of the cross.

Suffering as Consequence of Obedience

The second generalization of my opening observation was that *the suffering of the church is a necessity that is laid upon faith but not as though it were an unavoidable fate; moreover, this suffering has more to do with the human situation outside the community of discipleship than it does with our personal or corporate condition as church.* Now to elaborate.

There are those who complain of Christians that they are much too interested in suffering. They ought to be listened to! Nietzsche was one of them; the great contemporary Jewish author, Elie Wiesel, is another; and one can hear this complaint also from some Christian feminists. The source of the complaint is of course related to the first point that I have been making, namely, that there are some forms of the church that manifest a certain fixation and glorification of suffering. But the objection also relates to the fact that the connection between true faith and suffering seems to be so deterministic, allowing for no decision on the part of the faithful. Feminism has been especially critical of this, because such a theology has been used to persuade women of their duty to accept their lot as long-suffering wives and mothers, in much the same way as this theology has been used to keep enslaved races or economic groupings from complaint or revolt.

It is true of course that both the newer Testament and some very important theological traditions accentuate the theme of *necessitas* in relation to our theme, the suffering of the church. When these traditions are informed ones, they make once again the important connection between Christology and ecclesiology. The Christ, too, as he is presented in the Gospels, was conscious of a necessity carrying him ever closer to his passion and death: "The Son of Man must suffer and be rejected"—the so-called predictions of the passion. The suffering of the church is seen and should be seen under this same *necessitas.*

However, over against those who feel that such a necessity is the equivalent of a kind of fatalism, let it be remembered that Jesus in the Gospels is conscious not only of this "must," which he clearly associates with the will of God, but also of the fact that he himself is left to decide the matter. He is not simply born to suffer: he is born as one whose gift for compassion and justice will probably in the natural course of events lead to great suffering, but he is not presented as one following a script written by Another. Were he such a one, he could in no way be considered (as Paul considers him) the second Adam—the only other human fully free, like the first Adam, actually to *choose* not to sin *(posse non peccare)* (Romans 5). Jesus' decision for the cross, which he makes only with the greatest difficulty precisely because he is perfectly free *not* to make it, is a voluntary decision on his part, and this same volition belongs, in some real measure, to the community that Jesus calls the body of Christ *(soma Christou)*. The suffering of the body of Christ is therefore by no means a fate, and where it is genuine (as in the case of Bonhoeffer, or of Simone Weil, or of Martin Luther King Jr.) the element of choice is prominent and vital to it. The church does not *have* to suffer, as if there were no other possibility—indeed, the fact that the historic church has so regularly and characteristically managed to *avoid* suffering ought to set to rest any insistence that Christians always and necessarily suffer.

However, whenever the church has made good its claim to Christ's discipleship, it has at least known the *call* to suffer. And again let me repeat (because it can never be said often enough): called to suffer not because suffering is good or beneficial or ultimately rewarding (I think Paul can actually be criticized a little for giving that impression in Romans 5), but called to suffer *because there is suffering*—that is, because God's creatures, including human beings, are already suffering, because "the whole creation groans."

The point is: the suffering of the church is not the goal but the consequence of faith. For faith, we said, is that trust in God then frees us sufficiently from *self* to make us cognizant of and compassionate in relation toward the other—in particular, the other who suffers, who is hungry and thirsty, who is imprisoned; the other who "fell among thieves"; the other who knocks at our door at midnight in need. The church is a community of suffering because it is a community whose eyes have been opened to the suffering that *exists*. The first assumption of this ecclesiology is not that the church should suffer but that it should be (in Simone Weil's sense) "attentive"— namely, attentive to the suffering that is simply there and that is usually bypassed by the world, as in the parable of the Good Samar-

itan. The Bible assumes that human and creaturely suffering is
perennial and manifold. If the church does not see this suffering and
if, seeing it, it does not take the burden of it upon itself, then its
whole life must be called into question.

This is why Luther insisted that among the so-called marks of the
church there is only one that is indispensable—only one whose
absence would automatically call into question everything else
claimed by such a church, including its unity, holiness, apostolicity,
and catholicity. As von Loewenich writes:

> Luther lists cross and suffering among the marks of the church.
> In his book *Of Councils and the Church,* 1539, Luther counts
> seven marks by which the church can be recognized, and he
> would prefer to call them the seven sacraments of the church,
> if the term 'sacrament' had not already taken on a different
> meaning. . . . As the seventh mark of the church, Luther men-
> tions "the holy possession of the sacred cross" . . . suffering; a
> church of which that cannot be said has become untrue to its
> destiny.[13]

This seventh mark of the church, surely, is one that ought to exercise a good deal of critical guidance today as the churches struggle to
overcome their internal conflicts and their penchant for excessive
concern over their own institutional survival. Surely the only survival
in which the church as *Christ's* body can be interested ultimately is
the survival of God's groaning creation. The whole ethic of justice,
peace, and integrity of creation, which the World Council of
Churches tried two decades ago to make central to ecclesiastical and
ecumenical concern, is not a mere addendum to Christian faith and
life but stands at the center of our identity as communities of
Christ's discipleship.[14]

I do not wish to be heard to say that the condition either of the
individual Christian or of the Christian community as a whole is of
no great concern to this tradition. Against any such claim, the whole
high priestly prayer of John 17 would have to be read: "'I am asking
on their [the disciples'] behalf,'" Jesus prays. "'I am not asking on

behalf of the world, but on behalf of those whom you gave me, because they are yours'" (v. 9). We all suffer, individually and corporately. To be human is to suffer. Some of our suffering is integral to our creaturehood; without it we could not become fully human.[15] And some of our suffering as Christians and as churches is integral to our becoming mature disciples of the Christ—it belongs to what the tradition named *conformitas Christi* (being conformed to Christ). One dimension of the suffering of the church, therefore, is its appropriation and internalization of the pain involved in being identified with the crucified one—what the Reformers called its "continuing baptism" into his death.

But this side of the suffering of the church can be badly distorted if it becomes interesting in itself. It is for this reason that I claimed at the outset of the chapter that where the theme of Christian suffering *has* been acknowledged in certain Christian (especially Lutheran) traditions, it has too often been marred by introversion and subjectivization: "See how I suffer, see how we suffer, life is a cross," etc.

The necessary corrective to this kind of melancholy self-preoccupation on the part of Christians and churches is their being made newly conscious of the suffering that lies *outside* their own persons and communities. Surely if it is truly Jesus Christ whom we follow, that is the direction in which we must move; for in the scriptural sources we never hear of a Jesus preoccupied with his own pain. Even on the cross itself he is conscious, chiefly, of the pain of others—of the thieves on either side, and of the pathetic little group of his followers standing beneath the cross, devastated.

Christians, we have maintained, are those who through confrontation with death are given a new freedom from the sting of death and so a new freedom *for* voluntary service to others. Surely if this claim has any truth in it, then it is not our own suffering but the suffering of the world beyond us that must claim our attention. Indeed, is not the whole purpose of our liberation from excessive personal anxiety the creation within us of a new consciousness of and care for others? Just here we encounter the transition from theology to ethics. The theology of the cross is intended to give rise not only to an ecclesiology of the cross, but to an ethic, the essence of which is the attentiveness to human and worldly suffering that is made possible in those who have been and are being delivered from self.[16]

The completion of ecclesiological doctrine under the aegis of the *theologia crucis* is thus relegated to the discussion of Christian ethics. This, unfortunately, has been avoided too often in Christian thought concerning the nature of the church. Ethics have too often been appended (tacked on) to ecclesiologies arrived at without much reference to the worldly calling of the church. When this happens in the name of the theology of the cross, however (as it sometimes has), an enormous contradiction has been perpetrated. For a church that has its being in its ongoing identification with the crucified Christ is, under the very terms of that ongoing identification and not as a second step, thrust into solidarity with the suffering creation. When therefore we turn in chapter 9 to the question of ethics in the framework of this theological tradition, we shall be resuming this discussion of the church under the cross.

chapter 8

The Theology of the Cross
and the Crisis of Christendom

Religion in the Postmodern World

It is almost a public consensus today that both religion in general and
Christianity in particular are passing through an extremely difficult
and critical period. To speak first, and briefly, of religion, I would
characterize the crisis as it is perceived from *inside* religion as one of
overwhelming temptation to fundamentalism. In the face of the
ubiquitous and (I believe) irreversible secularization of global consciousness,[1] in the face of the attendant questioning and depletion of
many religious traditions and communities in the West, and in the
face of the pluralistic clash of cultures and cults globally, the religions
are tempted to articulate themselves in increasingly doctrinaire, militant, and simplistic forms. The apologetic—or at least the dia-
logic—dimension that has been present to one degree or another in
all of the great religions of humankind (and for that reason they may
be called "great") is in very serious jeopardy. Facing the apparent
impasse of dialogue with a world defined by what Jacques Ellul called
"the Moloch of Fact"[2] (or we might say today the great god Information!), the religions seek refuge in authoritative dogma that purports
to transcend scientific Fact yet reflects, ironically, the secular world's
same dogged enthrallment with Fact and Data. Since scientific secularism (which in its most simplistic expressions could even be called

the religion of Fact) has also created its own version of hell (for many of its facts, so far as humankind is concerned, have turned out to be terrifying ones), the religions most adept at promulgating *countervailing* facts of dogma have been able not only to get a hearing but often to achieve quite spectacular numerical successes.

But this success is a very ambiguous success, because its foundation is fear and its modus operandi retrenchment, ghettoization, and sometimes aggressive or violent defensiveness. It does not bode well for the future of civilization when religion (or quasi-religious ideology) establishes itself on such a foundation and sustains its life in such a manner. We have just emerged from the toils of a political ideology (doctrinaire Marxism) that carried the logic of true belief to the extreme, and religious history is replete with similar warnings. To be sure, human fear and foreboding have always been part of the apologetic backdrop of religion, for it is a fearful thing to be human, and we seek to assuage our fearfulness in whatever ways open out to us. Religion has undoubtedly counted on and frequently exploited that need. But the great religions (and this too is why they may be called "great") have never depended upon this inherent human fearfulness for their whole appeal. They have all manifested, sought, and found positive points of contact with the human spirit and human culture. Without such positive links with human experience, neither religion nor secular ideology can endure. Lacking such links, an ideology whether sacred or secular may be able for a time—perhaps even for a long time—to maintain itself through sheer power (power based largely on its connections with political structures able to use it), but its lifespan will not likely surpass that of the sociopolitical structures with which it exists in a symbiotic relationship. The great religions have outlasted empires and nations because, whatever their relations with political structures and the needful masses may have been, they were able to engage some vital dimensions of what is noblest and most compelling in human experience. Their appeal was not confined to the amelioration of need, to the soothing of present anxieties, or to the seeming demand of the public for extraneous or heteronomous authority. They could enter into dialogue and struggle with the highest and best in human culture and could win the respect, if not always the allegiance, of those who represented in their varying contexts the most determined and courageous quests for goodness, beauty, and truth. Never forget that the Christian faith has been profound enough to address and captivate a mind as penetrating (and as devious) as that of Augustine of Hippo, to mention only one such. Something comparable can be claimed, I believe, for all the religions of humankind that have endured long enough to be thought great.

That is why the present drift toward what is called (for better or worse) "fundamentalism" in all of the world religions (and *notably* in the three so-called Abrahamic faiths) must be understood as *temptation*.[3] It may seem a triumph when religion, which Nietzsche and other architects of modernity and its postmodern displacement declared obsolete and dead, achieves the kind of comeback that some analysts see occurring in certain contemporary contexts. But it is at best a Pyrrhic victory. Pyrrhic victories are superficial triumphs that cost too much—that incur too many losses. What is *lost* in many apparent religious gains today is the profundity of the religious tradition itself and its capacity to speak to the depths of human reason, experience, and longing. Too many of the *quantitative* triumphs of religion are purchased at the cost of their quality, their depth, their worthiness. What is called, uncharitably, the "dumbing down" process in religion and society has to be taken very seriously by all, whatever their religious affiliation, who sense in their faith a capacity to grasp and challenge the most profound aspirations and visions of humankind. It is bad enough (it is appalling!) when religion is allowed to become the inspirer and propagandist of racial, ethnic, sexual, and political ideologies, as is the case today within all of the world religions. But it is just as pathetic (and in the long term far more damaging) when, partly in order to achieve or retain a place for itself in the public sphere, religion is ready to reduce itself to the most unnuanced and sloganized expressions of doctrine and morality. In doing this, it *may* be successful for a time in commending itself to an unthinking, oppressed, or frightened majority, but it will repel the thinking minority upon whose thoughtfulness religion, in the last analysis, depends.

What pertains to religion in general (this temptation to perpetuate itself through doctrinal reductionism and religious simplism) pertains also to Christianity. But as Christians living inside the remnants (or perhaps the ruins) of Christendom, we are obliged to look more closely into our own crisis.

Christian Disestablishment

To do so we must begin with a sober recognition of the fact that our religion, which has been the established cultus of the West throughout most of its history, exists today in a state of varying degrees of disestablishment. I trust it will be understood that I am using the terms *establishment* and *disestablishment* in their broadest sense. The nearly monopolistic hold of the Christian religion on the Western world in the past has not depended upon the de jure (legal) establishments of the European flagship of Christendom. In the United States, Canada, Australia, New Zealand, and other European satellite societies, despite the earlier efforts of some denominations to establish themselves, our normal form of Christian establishment has been what Peter Berger and others have called "cultural establishment"—that is, the identification of Christianity with the dominant cultural and moral values of society at large. In the end this form of establishment has proved the more durable and the more perplexing to sort out.

As a process, the disestablishment of the Christian religion in the West has been occurring for at least two centuries, but it is more obvious in those older, mostly European societies where establishment has been a matter of law and where, accordingly, disestablishment has been more straightforward. Legal relationships are always more easily terminated than are informal or merely conventional relationships. In North America—and particularly in the United States (that nation's vaunted sense of the separation of church and state notwithstanding)—the near-equation of Christianity and culture has blurred the reality of Christian disestablishment to the extent that in some parts of America, particularly the South, one can have the impression that the Christian establishment has never been so firmly in place. But this is illusionary, and in spite of the efforts of many Christian groups in the United States (and some in Canada) to ✓ reinstate some facsimile of Christendom, the process of its winding down is, I believe, irreversible.

It can be argued, of course, that the reductions experienced by the once-mainline Protestant churches of the United States are counterbalanced and even greatly outweighed by the growth of what used to be called "sectarian" Protestantism and ethnic, charismatic, and other elements within the Roman Catholic communion and therefore that Christendom, far from winding down, is simply assuming another form among a different segment of the population. Such an assumption seems to inform, for instance, the recent and much-discussed work of Philip Jenkins.[4] That assessment, however, relies far too heavily on quantitative considerations—specifically, on religious demographic statistics. In religion, as in politics, statistics are useful for some limited purposes, but by themselves they convey little of analytical, to say nothing of historical and theological, significance. The demise of Christendom is not just about the loss of numbers; it is about the loss of influence—including the influence of this faith among the intellectual, artistic, and critical elites that such analyses as these regularly dismiss on account of their minority status numerically. Christians of the type assumed by the theology of the cross do not expect these elites to *endorse* the Christian faith, but they do ✓ hope that Christianity will be sufficiently stimulating to such representatives of the "high culture" to be taken with some measure of seriousness. When Christianity is no longer noticed by the critical elites, if only for purposes of argumentation, or when it has become for these elements so entirely predictable as to be understood a priori (for instance, to be written off as "the religious Right"), then it must be supposed that the process of disestablishment has run its full course. Perhaps we are not *quite* there in North America just yet, but in Canada at least we are very close to it, and in the United States *most* of the continuing interest in Christianity shown by the intelligentsia is strictly of the observer variety that rarely involves itself with faith sufficiently to be thought engaged at the level of spirit and intellect. Such engagement is not occurring when the Christian religion is being analyzed by sociologists and journalists and statisticians; if it is not part—at least a small part—of the concern of philosophers, historians, novelists, filmmakers, artists, and others who must deal with the *content* and not only the quantifiable facts of belief, then its adherents should wonder about the worldly status of their faith. At the very least they should *not* continue to behave as if nothing had happened! Christian disestablishment in the West (not only in Europe, where it is unavoidable, but also in North America, where it is overlaid with the bric-a-brac of "culture religion") is a reality—the fundamental religious reality with which all serious and thinking Christians must contend.

The Changing Profile of Global Christianity and Its Relevance to the Discussion

The aforementioned work of Philip Jenkins has drawn attention to the fact, which he believes Northern Christians have almost totally ignored,[5] that there has been a dramatic quantitative shift in Christian population statistics toward the Southern Hemisphere: "By 2025, 50 percent of the Christian population will be in Africa and Latin America, and another 17 percent will be in Asia. Those proportions will grow steadily."[6] When this type of statistic is combined with two further observations, both of which Jenkins accentuates, it raises significant questions for any discussion that, like the present one, argues for the demise of Christendom. One of these observations concerns the *character* of the Christianity that is growing in the South: much of it (though perhaps not as much as Jenkins implies) is by Western standards very conservative both theologically and morally—to the point, he maintains, of eventually rendering dialogue between the Northern and Southern Christianities extremely difficult.[7] The second observation is that on a global scale Christianity and not (as is often assumed) Islam is the largest religion on the planet and will become so increasingly: "Christianity is going to continue to be the world's most numerous religion, at least until the end of the twenty-first century."[8]

Leaving aside questions relating to these generalizations as such, our concern here is their pertinence to the subject of this chapter, namely the "humiliation" (Albert van den Heuvel) of Christendom and responsible Christian behavior in relation to that occurrence. The linkage of impressive growth statistics in the South with affirmation of a still more dominant global Christianity, *plus* the suggestion that this victorious global faith will be in the nature of a "Counter-Reformation" (his term), virtually annihilating liberal forms of the faith, not only appears to call into question any idea of the end of Christendom but provides marvelous fuels for the fires of *Northern* conservatives who wish to believe both that Christianity is on the increase *and* that the Christianity of the future will be their kind of Christianity! Jenkins writes:

> The moral and sexual conservatism of Southern believers is music to the ears of North Americans or Europeans who find themselves at odds with the progressive leaderships of their own churches. When they suffer an ideological defeat at home—when, for instance, a new denomination approves of same-sex marriages—conservatives are tempted to look South and to say, in effect, "Just you wait." History is on the side of the Southern churches, which will not tolerate this nonsense.[9]

Though Jenkins himself does not openly betray any bias toward conservative Christianity, he uses the language of "the Next Christendom" *almost* as though no questions needed to be asked about the whole concept of Christendom—as if Kierkegaard, to mention only one of Christendom's inside critics, had never lived or, more to the point, as though "the first Christendom" (his term) did not in itself cast grave shadows over the very idea of another such.[10]

As a Northern Christian of a critical Protestant stance, one is tempted in the face of this analysis to exclaim, "Been there, done that!" If it gives comfort to crusading Christian conservatives to think that the future still holds a longed-for triumph of the Christian religion, then they had better think again about the actual history of Christian triumphalism in Western (Northern) experience. Do they really wish to become an intolerant, authoritarian, violent religion, ready to go to war not only with Iraq but with Islam and many other religious alternatives that can now no longer be nicely confined to specific territories? Do they really want a biblicism that is basically uninformed by historical and linguistic research and that dismisses not only complex modern scientific theories like evolution but even much of the ordinary science on which our daily lives are now based? Would they welcome a moral ethos in which not only gays and lesbians but also divorced people were consigned to hellfire, and the psychologically ill were considered demon-ridden?

To speak of the next Christendom without raising such existential questions arising out of the first Christendom is patently irresponsible. As I shall say in a moment, I do not believe that Christendom was all bad, but does it represent a desirable model of the Christian movement—a faithful way of being the church of Jesus Christ? Whatever may be said of Christendom, it behooves Northern Christians to remember that *we have been Christendom* for a millennium and a half. If out of that experience and at a point (namely, its ending) where we can engage in some more objective assessments of the course of it, we can still say that we would welcome yet another Christendom, then wisdom would have to conclude that history teaches the human race little or nothing! And none would agree with that judgment more than would the most thoughtful Christians of *the Southern Hemisphere,* for they have been and continue to be the *victims* precisely of Christian nations and empires—including the economic empires of today.[11]

As for the so-called liberal Christians of the North—and that would have to include many who like myself are by no means unambiguously pleased to be called "liberals"[12]—the confronting question is not only whether we are ready to endorse the language of a second Christendom but whether we are able to appropriate the *critique* of

Christendom that has been present in the most faithful theological and historical analyses within the churches for over a century and, beyond that, whether we are prepared to explore any radical alternatives to the Christendom model of Christ's church. For us, the question is not whether we like or dislike, approve or disapprove of, the kind of popular Christianity that is emerging in Africa, Asia, and Latin America and also in powerful movements in our own midst; the question, rather, is whether we can mount any truly viable and faithful alternative to it—and remain confident and enthusiastic about that alternative even when it is strictly a minority Way, which it almost certainly always will be. It solves nothing in the Northern churches to say that in the South Christianity is thriving. We in the once-powerful, now-reduced churches of the West must work out our future in relation to our own peculiar past and present, from which there is no turning back to some earlier religious mentality or form of church and society.

Disestablishment as Opportunity

Beyond believing that Western Christendom's displacement is real and irreversible, I am bold enough to think that this process is actually providential. For I am convinced that Christendom—which means the dominion not of Jesus Christ but of the Christian religion—was a "misunderstanding," as Brunner said, if not "a mistake" (which is what Franz Overbeck thought it to be) from the outset. This is not tantamount to saying that nothing good came of it. Such a generalization would be childish. There can be no doubt that the Christian religion introduced many modifications into the developing civilization of the West—influences for good that at every level of society should be counted as gain. With its high regard for human rational capacity the Christian religion ameliorated the reign of the chaos and capriciousness in public life; with its sense of balance between the individual and the group it guarded against the tyranny of elites and the chaos of individualism; with its relative openness to minorities it softened the tendency of majorities to exclude and oppress; with its sense of justice and morality it helped to build civil codes of behavior that compare favorably with those of other cultures; with its feeling for beauty in color and sound and language it created a climate in which art might flourish. Sometimes I have said, in jest but with didactic intent, that if all that Christendom achieved was to give us Johann Sebastian Bach, it was worth the effort! The point is: to celebrate the end of Christendom is by no means to overlook the good that accrued to the West because it was profoundly influenced by this particular religion. We may even use the expression "Christian civilization" to refer to the West, provided we do not load that term with an overdose of approval!

But however good and desirable Christendom at its best may have been as civilization, it was *not,* in my view, an appropriate expression of the Christian faith. There was something incongruous about it from the outset and always. If one reads the newer Testament and most of the literature of the pre-Constantinian church without the dubious benefit of establishment hindsight, one cannot but conclude that between that early vision and what came to be after the fourth century of the common era there is an abiding hiatus, if not an irreconcilable conflict. Surely Jesus as he is presented in the Synoptics and John never dreamt of anything remotely resembling the Holy Roman Empire or the United States of America as a Christian nation. I cannot even attribute such a thing to Paul, or Irenaeus, or Tertullian, or the second-century apologists. The Acts of the Apostles frequently remarks on growth in the numbers of converts, but at its height Christianity prior to Constantine could not possibly have accounted for more than 10 percent of the population of the Roman Empire; as for power, it had none beyond its own internal persuasiveness.

From a somewhat different angle, one may ask whether the Christian faith as we have it in the newer Testament and the pre-establishment writings of the church was in any way *designed* for such a role as, under and beyond Constantine, it was required to play. Certainly some of its emphases suit or can be made to suit the necessary goals of empire. In particular its strong emphasis on the principle of unity can serve and has many times served the need of imperial peoples to maintain a sufficient integration of vision and peoplehood to withstand the natural and historical forces of disintegration that are always present. Believing in one God means that rival claims to ultimacy, whether heavenly or earthly, are held in check—and that was certainly a great need for Rome, as for most imperial cultures, because empires have usually been comprised of a variety of peoples, tribes, ethnic groupings, and races, each with its culture and its cultus. A religion that celebrates not only one deity but the unity of all living things *under* that one deity can be a boon to strong governments—especially when they are under duress, as Rome in the fourth century was. One could also in this respect think of certain key aspects of the morality outlined in the Gospels and epistles—especially the epistles. Read from the perspective of power (which always means power threatened by internal questioning and potential revolt), epistolary scriptures that exhort the obedience of slaves to masters, and women to men, and children to parents, and (above all) the citizenry as a whole to "the governing authorities" (Romans 13) can seem a veritable gift from above; every imperial people in the history of the Christian West, not excluding the Third Reich, has been eternally grateful for this apparently divine sanctioning of its endeavor to control and regulate. Even the biblical laws against such things as adultery, homosexuality, sexual promiscuity, divorce, insubordination in relation to parents and other authority structures, and so on: all of these can be used by dominant cultures to great advantage, because these types of behavior represent deviation from the norm and the potentiality of chaos. So yes—at some levels of assessment, Christianity *was* attractive to empire, and without protest from the leading lights of the Christian faith themselves, all such advantageous elements could be (and were) accentuated, while other aspects of this faith could be downplayed or simply neglected.

The latter, however, include almost everything that most serious Christians would consider essential to Christian faith: the primacy of love; the demand for justice, especially toward the underprivileged; the insistence upon forgiveness (not just once, but seventy times seven!); the equality of all human beings, without reference to race, culture, gender, and all else; above all, I think, the insistence upon a continuous and prophetic orientation toward truth and a concomitant vigilance against hypocrisy, subterfuge, and oversimplification. None of these things (and I have not tried to exhaust the list) are natural allies of power, and while a few very unusual persons of power in history have tried to incorporate some of these qualities in their political visions, most have ignored them or relegated them to the explicitly cultic—"Let the churches look after that!"

I must conclude, then, that if some highly intelligent and honest advisory committee had sat down with Constantine to consider what religion might help him cement together his rapidly disintegrating imperium, the Christian religion would not have been chosen, despite some of its (almost peripheral) advantages. Since in fact Christianity *was* chosen, what had to occur if it were going to function in the manner that empire needed it to function is simply that a great deal of it had to be effectively jettisoned or reinterpreted in purely spiritual terms or relegated to the few who could manage to take it very seriously—which means, practically speaking, the monastic communities. The truth is, surely, that Christianity was never designed for the imperial cultus that it became and that it could only serve that end by becoming (as Søren Kierkegaard said so blatantly and so brilliantly) something else altogether.

What we are called upon to assess today, however, is not primarily whether Christendom *was* wrong, a contradiction, a misunderstanding, a mistake, but rather whether it *is* wrong—that is to say, whether we should attempt to perpetuate, refurbish, or reinstate that manner of being the church—or what counsel we might humbly offer Christians in the Southern Hemisphere who may be tempted by the Christendom formula.

Surely we have had enough Christendom to know that it was an aberration, a mutation. To seek to impede the process of disestablishment or to reverse it, and to attempt in the face of all odds to win the whole world for the Christian religion is not only foolish; it is disobedient! For at this juncture in history the Christian movement is being offered by divine Providence an *opportunity* that is unique in the church's experience. The Christian faith is being made free from its Babylonian captivity to political, cultural, racial, and (yes) religious structures to the end that it may be and become what in essence it is: salt, yeast, light—a vigilant and prophetic diaspora in the midst of a global society that will from now on manifest immense multiplicity and the intermingling of peoples, cultures, and cults. Christians ought to embrace this possibility. Instead of waiting passively for the final waves of the long process of disestablishment to wash over us, we should seek actively to direct the process. The message of the divine Spirit to the churches is "Disestablish *yourselves.*" Do not wait for it to happen *to* you, but take hold of it, give it some purposeful direction, seek the possibilities that open to you as the Christendom way becomes impossible. Endings are not always tragic; they can also be new beginnings. Christianity is being liberated *from* the burden of folk religion, of legitimating secular powers, of being the moral police force of our society. This means that, so far as we are willing, we are being liberated *for* the kind of adherence to our own authoritative sources, our own spiritual and ethical vocation, and this is a kind of freedom that throughout its long centuries Christendom rarely tasted and could never for long sustain. In a word: the end of Christendom could become a new beginning for the Christian Movement.

Such a welcoming approach to the end of Christendom is, however, very hard to communicate within the churches. At one level, especially in North America, the difficulty of actually embracing disestablishment stems from the propensity of a people reared on the mythology of success to view any relinquishment of Christian preeminence as failure. Christianity has known enormous power, wealth, and prestige. For fifteen or sixteen centuries we have been living in the houses of emperors and kings, conducting prayer breakfasts in the courts of the mighty, commanding the allegiance of the masses, baptizing, marrying, and burying practically everybody. Are we now expected to play second fiddle to something else?—perhaps to share the stage with a whole cadre of other cults?—perhaps even

fade into the background altogether, and just wait for those few cer-
emonial occasions when somebody will ask us to bless a spaceship or
pronounce a benediction at a university convocation? A society that
✓ respects success as much as ours (and this means success that can be
measured quantitatively) finds it nearly unthinkable to countenance
reduction of any kind. Witness the panic throughout society whenever there is any hint of an economic slowdown. With few exceptions
the churches manifest this same neurotic need to seem to grow and
to succeed.[13] The typical approach to congregations when they find
themselves dwindling, even after all the tricks of the church-growth
technicians have been tried, is to seek at the earliest opportunity
other dwindling congregations, amalgamate, and make as much
noise as possible in order to avoid (for a time) facing the fact that
dwindling is now part of our ecclesiastical reality. At the present
time, there are fifty-two large and magnificent Roman Catholic
church buildings in the city of Montreal up for sale to the highest
bidder because they are no longer viable as churches. Some will be
turned into condominiums, some to concert halls, some to muse-
ums, and many, like many before them, simply demolished, the land
on which they sit being more valuable than the buildings themselves.
Even in the face of such physical evidence of the humiliation of
Christendom, however, it is hard for churches to entertain alternatives to the Christendom model. The concept of a Christian diaspora, as discussed for example by Karl Rahner,[14] does not seem a
desirable future to churches that were once big and successful.

But if we ask why the quest for alternative forms of the church is
so adamantly resisted, we encounter the real problem confronting
the churches today. It is at the most profound level a problem of theology. How could we have been listening to the Scriptures all these
centuries and still be surprised and chagrined by the humiliation of
Christendom? How could we have honored texts like the Beatitudes
("Blessed are you when men revile you and persecute you and utter
all kinds of evil against you falsely on my account . . ." [Matt. 5:11]),
and yet formed in our collective mind the assumption that Christian
faith would be credible only if it were popular, numerically superior,

and respected universally? How could we have been contemplating the "despised and rejected" figure at the center of this faith for two millennia and come away with the belief that his body, far from being despised and rejected, ought to be universally approved and embraced?

The Pertinence of the Theology of the Cross at the End of Christendom

Just here we find ourselves at the point where the question of this chapter should be addressed as concretely as possible: is there a particular relevance of the theological tradition Luther called the theology of the cross for the present crisis of Christendom and the future of the Christian faith?

The question is moot, for the real crisis of Christendom as it encounters its own demise lies precisely in the poverty and inappropriateness of its theology. One does not blame individuals, or individual congregations, or even entire historical phases of the church for this situation. We have all in some sense been seduced theologically by a history of intellectual and spiritual conditioning that is unbelievably hard to cast off. I have spoken about a very late phase in this conditioning—namely, the almost pathetically naïve phase that emerged in the modern period and has been fashioned by New World optimism and the capitalist-inspired mythology of success. But in the long story of Christian ecclesiastical and theological triumphalism, this has only been a late variation on the theme that was introduced already in the fourth century of the common era with the initial establishment of Christianity under Constantine and Theodosius the Great.

What I mean is that a religion that was ready to become the official cultus of imperial Rome (and historical Christianity was astonishingly ready to do this) and then to adapt itself to every empire in the West that succeeded Rome simply had to have a theology that matched its status. A glorious church could not have an inglorious theology. The very idea of a faith whose central image and symbol

was a crucified Jew now functioning as the official and (after Theodosius) *only* legal religion of the empire that crucified him—such an
idea is absurd and to temporal power unthinkable. I seriously doubt
that any of us has yet come to terms with this absurdity, this incon-
ceivability. Or, to put it otherwise, I do not think that contemporary
Christians, even among those who are serious students and teachers
of the faith, have yet begun to realize how extensively the Christian
faith had to be revamped in order to fulfill the role of religious establishment. We have perhaps begun to realize some of the implications
of it. Some of us, at least, realize that the Jewish basis of this story had
to be submerged and transformed: the humanity of Jesus, a Jew, had
to become a very general, nearly a theoretical humanity, devoid of
particularity—certainly of Jewish particularity—though at the same
time invested subtly, hiddenly, with the particularity of his new
adherents and admirers.

Also, some of us have begun to realize that Jesus' passion and crucifixion, as central as that sequence is in the Gospel accounts, had not
only to be blamed on the Jews[15] but also to be decentralized in favor
of an obviously glorious and triumphant resurrection and reign at
God's right hand. And some of us have begun to realize how the biblical concern for the poor and outcast, for the dispossessed, for the
victims of oppression and abuse and injustice, for children and
women—how all this had to lose its critical bite, its inherent critique
of power, to be reduced at best to a matter of charity toward the
underclasses.

But while perhaps quite a few of us have begun to grasp such
aspects of the great transmutation that occurred in the fourth century
c.e. and beyond, we are still noticeably hesitant to carry such critical
analysis very far; for we too have been conditioned by this history, and
most of us are also rather compromised by our own participation in
the structures of what remains of Christendom. Some of us look
across into the unpromised land of post-Constantinian Christian
diaspora, and we know that some Christians in the future (and some
already now, here and there) will have to make the transition to that
new mode of Christian existence, but we find it impossible or at least
very uncomfortable to put ourselves into that scenario.

Above all, I think, we lack a vision and a hope that are able to give direction to our responses and our planning and to provide a framework of meaning for the seeming losses and reductions that occur to us in this period of transition and temptation. To state that in other terms: we lack a theology that is holistic and bold enough to counter the abiding power of the old theology, namely, the theology that was fashioned gradually by a church that had moved in the space of seven or eight decades from being on the far periphery of power to being a vital part of the power structure, the establishment.

In my various writings I have tried to say that we can find at least the rudiments for such a theological vision and hope in this thin tradition Luther named *theologia crucis*—a tradition that has never really been given a chance to develop itself in a sustained and untrammeled way. In particular, this theology has rarely been allowed to articulate itself ecclesiologically—that is, to become an *ecclesia crucis*.

One suspects that Martin Luther, when in the early phase of his revolt he invented this contrast, *theologia crucis/theologia gloriae,* possessed at least a subconscious and anticipatory awareness of the need to apply the theology of the cross vigorously to the life and mission of the church. For in the line of the pre-Reformers from Wyclif to Hus, Luther found himself sickened by an institution that had not only become very rich and powerful but also, to occupy such a position, forfeited its own deepest insights and its capacity for prophetic vigilance to the point—in the practices of indulgences, for instance—of offering salvation for sale. Certainly the early Luther was not thinking of the theology of the cross merely as "a theology," a way of arranging doctrine; he meant it, clearly, as a vision for the church and its mission in the world. He realized well enough that a theology of the cross that does not translate at once into an ecclesiology of the cross would be a contradiction in terms. In his writings one can see that Luther understood this very well. If in the end his theology did fail to fashion such an alternative ecclesiology, if still today people in Lutheran and other Protestant settings can talk about the theology of the cross while contenting themselves with a church of glory, it is only because the Protestantism that Luther and the others championed itself became so quickly the new establishments of northern Europe and, later, the European satellites.

The question to which all thoughtful Christians and churches need to address themselves today is whether we can find in this alternative theology Luther said was "of the cross" a way of thinking the faith that is not just about doctrine but about being a people of the cross. In some important ways, we have a certain advantage in this respect over the Reformation: namely, it is or at least should be far more evident to us than it was to sixteenth-century Europeans that an imperial Christianity with a triumphalistic theology just does not work in our kind of world. We can be suspicious of that type of Christianity and that kind of theology on historical and empirical grounds, not only theologically and biblically. Since the Reformation, we have had four centuries in which to work out our particularly *Protestant* versions of the ecclesiology of glory, and they have failed as miserably as Catholicism—nay, more so! Our continuing dividedness, our internal denominational strife, our failure to maintain our former prestige vis-à-vis nations and ruling classes and the various controlling institutions of society—all this has made it clear to all but those who will not see that Christian triumphalism in the Protestant mode is a sham—even more obviously so than Catholicism, which at least maintains the external marks of ecclesiastical glory. Particularly in the older, so-called mainline denominations (that is, those formerly most established) the failure of Protestant establishment and of the theology of establishment is palpable. And if the failure of an old system is a condition without which people will not be open to a new, then we are perhaps in a position to explore the theology of the cross as a whole different way of being the church in the world.

Christianity: Participation in God's Suffering for the World

A passage from Dietrich Bonhoeffer suggests what that different way must mean:

Christians range themselves with God in God's suffering; that is what distinguishes them from the heathen. As Jesus asked in Gethsemane, "Could ye not watch with me one hour?" That is the exact opposite of what the religious person expects from God. Man is challenged to participate in the sufferings of God at the hands of a godless world.

The Christian must therefore plunge himself or herself into the life of a godless world, without attempting to gloss over its ungodliness with a veneer of religion or trying to transfigure it. He or she must live a "worldly" life and so participate in the suffering of God. He or she may live a worldly life as one emancipated from all false religions and obligations. To be a Christian does not mean to be religious in a particular way, to cultivate some particular form of asceticism . . . , but to be a human being. It is not some religious act which makes a Christian what he or she is, but participation in the suffering of God in the life of the world.[16]

The theology of glory was fashioned by a religious institution that understood itself to have acquired under God the role of priest to the kingdoms of this world and the glory of them: the official cult of the official culture. As such, Christendom was sometimes capable of achievements that are, by any reasonable standards of evaluation, commendable. Christendom (I have said it before) was not all bad. But its basic, informing image of itself and its worldly mission can hardly be said to have been (in Bonhoeffer's language) that of participant in the suffering of God in the world. At its best, Christendom could be said to think of itself as the comforter, resolver, or even eliminator of suffering—and such a role need not be scorned. But it still presupposes a distance from the world in which God suffers in the suffering of God's creatures. It is better to heal suffering than to inflict it, but healing too can signify distance and usually does. The point that Bonhoeffer is making is that it is just this distance that has to be overcome by any faith that calls itself the body of Christ. The incarnational thrust and presupposition of that nomenclature implies that the place of the church is not above the world but in it. Yes, by all means, *in* it as a movement, not *of* it, but in it, deeply in it, in it in a way that institutions that are really of it are never in it but always trying to transcend, master, and overcome it.

What could it mean for the church today to achieve that kind of intimacy with God's beloved world? Would it make any difference in the way the church is perceived by our contemporaries?

Recently I received a long letter from a professor of religion in a small college in New York State. He wrote to me about my little book *Why Christian?*, which he uses in his classes with undergraduates. He wanted to tell me that his students, who are mostly a generation or two removed from any active involvement in the church, very much identify with the hypothetical, composite student with whom, in this book, I am in dialogue; he says that they find my responses to this student on the whole convincing. However:

> Whereas most students are either convinced or engaged by [the book's chapters] there is one of your discussions that my students find unconvincing: 'Why Church?' (Chapter 6). The subsection discussing other religions is well-received, but the overwhelming majority of students seriously leave the course believing that the church is superfluous, and that one can be a Christian and practice Christianity on his or her own. They tend to believe that the Christian whole (the church, as a sociological and historical phenomenon) is significantly less than the sum total of its parts (i.e., the good Christian men and women who comprise it). This chapter does not get them to rethink their initial assumptions (and biases) quite the way the other chapters succeed.

The professor goes on to say that he tries to supplement my approach by suggesting two points that I have not highlighted in this particular book: (1) that the church is first and foremost an article of faith; (2) that the students' personal experience of church is too greatly shaped by modern Western experience. Still, he admits, this doesn't help much. And he asks, "Can any apology for the church today realistically provide young people with a positive way of thinking about the link between Christian faith and church affiliation? Or, for so many of them, can the former (Christian faith) be salvaged only by jettisoning the latter?"

I know that the concern expressed in this letter is very widespread and that it affects not only the young people but people of all ages and stages in our society. A kind of unreality clings to the churches (with—fortunately—some notable exceptions), and no amount of theological or sociological apologetics can seem to remove it.

It has been my experience that this unreality is removed—or at least countered—only where the aforementioned distance between church and world, faith and life, gospel and context is in some real measure overcome, or, speaking positively, only where the church lives unprotectedly in the midst of the world, where faith is a dialogue with life (not only an internal dialogue of the community of faith itself), where gospel engages and is engaged by context. Or, in Bonhoeffer's language, where the church lives a worldly life, and so participates without too many inhibitions in the suffering of God.

There is, I think, no one way in which this kind of participation may happen. I mentioned the Sojourners of Washington in my book *Why Christian?* I could also have spoken of the Open Door community in Atlanta, Holden Village in Washington State, Taizé, Iona, the East Harlem Protestant Parish, the Church of the Crossroads in Honolulu, and a number of other experiments in removing the once-remove of church from world. I have also often spoken about some of the individual figures who have achieved, for many in our time, the status of symbols of this kind of worldly participation—Simone Weil, Jean Vanier, Mother Theresa, Dorothy Day, Martin Luther King Jr., Bishop Romero. A former student, Alan Tysick, lives directly among the street people in the city of Vancouver, where poverty and drug abuse are rife. But it would be necessary also to think of the intellectual labors of biblical scholars like Phyllis Trible and Walter Brueggemann, preachers both well known and unknown, and congregations where business-as-usual has given place to forms of contemplation and worldly service that assume an understanding of Christian faith and mission quite different from the type called "religious" in the usual sense. There are such things happening, even as the structures of ancient Christendom disintegrate. And one wishes that more of the kinds of young people about whom the American professor wrote in his letter to me could experience such communities, because I suspect the only convincing argument for the church is no argument at all but the experience of its reality.

We are at the beginning of a period in which many things will have to be tried. A few will work; many will not. But the place where the courage to attempt something different—something by way of participation in the worldly suffering of God—begins is thinking critically about the theology that has accompanied Christendom and asking for *another theology*. Not just for a new strategy, or greater commitment to social programs, or more exciting liturgies, or more sincere spirituality—no, for a different theology. And I am comforted by the thought that we do not have to invent such a theology. Unlike what passes for art today, theology does not thrive on novelty! The theology that we need is already there, and indeed it is impressively and profoundly there—from the Old Testament onwards! It is really just a matter of letting go of some of our conditioned beliefs and assumptions and allowing what is there to speak to us as we are, where we are, and when we are.

Part Four

The Way of the Cross

Christ Mocked by Soldiers
by Georges Rouault

chapter 9

On Being Christian Today

Discipleship in a Strange New World

Anyone who has lived on this continent during the past three-quar-
ter-century, as I have, will have passed through changes so vast as to
be a source of continuing astonishment, if not bewilderment. The
world that I encounter today as I leave my house or turn on my television is perhaps as different from the world of my childhood as was
Luther's world from that of Augustine. In a matter of decades we
have passed through alterations that even centuries did not witness
in earlier epochs. Impermanence has become the most permanent of
human assumptions.

This constancy of change has produced in many a kind of psychic
vertigo that reaches out blindly for stability. Religion undoubtedly
offers the most ready recourse in such gropings. The failure of secular*ism,* which we noticed in the previous chapter,[1] as well as the
renewal of supernaturalism in popular Christian and various other
forms, can be traced in part to the sheer transience of a world in
unprecedentedly rapid social transition. A new sense of the transitory
had already begun to manifest itself with the industrial revolution.
"Change and decay in all around I see," wrote the nineteenth-century British clergyman Henry Francis Lyte, and so like countless others since, he prayed that the God who "changest not" should "abide"
with him.

Those who can find in themselves no sympathetic echo of such a prayer have either not lived long enough or are so far out of touch with any alternative to the status quo in the developed world that they possess no criteria of judgment. Religion has always functioned in human life and society as a sphere of reliability, a place to stand, a "rock of ages," a "mighty fortress," and Christian purists deceive themselves if they imagine that their faith permits of no such usage. Like other faiths, Christian belief and belonging regularly entail an element of world-weariness, and a longing for refuge from the shifting and often chaotic daily round. The Bible recognizes, accepts, and even approves this dimension of faith: "Come to me, all you that are weary and are carrying heavy burdens, and I will give you rest," says Matthew's Jesus (11:29); woe betide any Christian movement that in the name of political activism or worldly engagement discards or minimizes this invitation to rest. With few exceptions, the great activists of the Christian movement, including nineteenth- and early-twentieth-century advocates of the Social Gospel, Walter Rauschenbusch, J. S. Woodsworth, and the others, themselves relied upon the securities of faith for the courage and fortitude they needed for their involvement in the world.

There is, however, a fine line between faith and religious escapism. Most of us walk this line every day—and stumble often. Worship, prayer, scholarship—almost anything, including programmed activism—may become a mode of flight from the here and now. Theology has long been labeled an "ivory tower" enterprise, along with every other academic pursuit—and often with justification. It may be reasonably argued that a certain distance from life is requisite to comprehension and responsible behavior. The test of that claim, however, is whether such distance actually functions as the means to better understanding and more accountable involvement in the life of the world. Religion in general, as well as some specific religions, is not necessarily bound to such a test, but Christian faith is so bound.

That, at least, must be said of the Christian faith as it is understood within the parameters of the theological spirit and method we are seeking to interpret in these pages. Given the emphases of the previous chapters in this study, it follows that the fundamental principle that must inform this chapter on *being* Christian is one of profound world commitment. It could be stated as follows: *Discipleship of the crucified Christ is characterized by a faith that drives its adherents into the world with a relentlessness and a daring they could not manage on the basis of human volition alone.* Anselm of Canterbury rightly insisted that genuine faith drives to a quest for understanding *(fides quaerens intellectum).* It could be stated as categorically that genuine faith drives to greater engagement with the life of the world—indeed, that "discipleship" *means,* primarily, just such engagement.

Discipleship is therefore "costly" (Bonhoeffer), for there is that in all of us which resists precisely the high degree of participation in and commitment to creation that following Jesus Christ entails. One of the most poignant of Luther's statements, written early in his career as a reformer, expresses his frustration—exasperation, almost—over the manner of unrelieved public prominence into which he feels himself being propelled: "God is pushing me—he drives me on, rather than leading. I cannot control my own life. I long to be quiet but am driven into the middle of the storm."[2] Similar expressions can be found in the works of Augustine,[3] who desired a life of calm, monastic contemplation and scholarship, and of nearly every notable figure in the history of this faith-tradition, including the prophets of Israel—including also that prophet who frequently sought solitude and who at the last prayed that the cup of destiny should be removed.

It could be said of the theology of the cross, in fact, that its chief *end* is the genesis of a community impelled (pushed!) toward the world despite its own resistance and reluctance. All that has been claimed for this theology in the previous chapters leads to such a conclusion: that it depicts God as one who lays claim to the creation and "will not abandon it prematurely";[4] that it is a theology of worldly engagement and therefore an inherently contextual theology, the incarnational theology par excellence; that it necessarily translates itself into an *ecclesiology* of the cross; etc. There can be no great distinction between theory and practice here, no hiatus between knowing and being/doing. "'Blessed are those who hear the word of God and obey it!'" (Luke 11:28). The measure of our hearing is our obedience. Contemplative or activist, scholar or streetworker, minister or layperson, Christians—according to this tradition—exist under the necessity of *discipleship*.

Discipleship as Outreach: Mission and Ethics

All this evokes the recognition that the goal towards which such *theological* reflection presses is the generation of a missiology and an ethic that adequately express the world-directedness of the theology of the cross. While Christian mission and Christian ethics represent two distinguishable aspects of theological investigation, both assume a single ideational foundation in this tradition; for both stem from the spiritual imperative that the community of the Christ is to be an "apostolic" community—a community sent out into the world. Both assume a single generative source, discipleship, and a single objective, world outreach. Missiology addresses the question of the church's evangelical task in the world—its message; the Christian ethic addresses the question of the manner in which the church tries to live that message in its worldly context, both individually and corporately. A missional church is not only a church with a gospel to proclaim—not only an "evangelical" church; it is also a church that itself tries to understand and conduct itself according to that gospel. This is why the discussion of these two aspects of Christian outreach, mission and ethic, should never be separated. The *ecclesia crucis* assumes that those who would bring good news to the world must submit themselves to the "imperative" that the gospel's "new indicative" announces.[5]

It would be difficult to imagine a less detached theology. "Take up your cross, and follow me" (Mark 8:34)—a command that, given the actual journey of the speaker, is virtually limitless in its demand for involvement. By contrast, it could well be said that the *theologia gloriae* lends itself to both a missiology and an ethic of detachment. I do not of course mean that various forms of what we may consider Christian triumphalism have *lacked* either mission or ethic. To the contrary, the theology of glory can and does produce astonishingly zealous theories and practices of both. Much indeed of the missionary endeavor of Christianity, particularly in the nineteenth century and again in some quarters today, has stemmed from fervent desire on the part of successful, mostly Western churches to carry their messages to the farthest corners of the planet. As for ethics, one is conscious again today, as has been the case often in the Christendom past, that groups in which an unquestioning certitude concerning right and wrong prevails demonstrate a moral eagerness that appears anything but detached. By comparison, ethics emanating from the theology of the cross are bound to seem ambiguous and tentative, since, as we shall see, they presuppose ongoing interaction with the actual life of the world (the context) for which they are intended. But precisely because it is formulated without such interaction with its here and now, must it be said of the ethic as well as the missiology arising from a theology of glory that it is detached. A triumphalistic Christian mission is a mission *to* the world. Beyond superficial matters of language and custom, little account is taken of the fact that the world thus acted upon is—always!—a very specific, unique social context, whose deepest realities are not discernible apart from extensive and informed participation in them on the part of the missionizing body. The history of Christian missions is filled with variations on the theme of the imposition of Eurocentric-Caucasian cultural assumptions upon communities with completely different histories and presuppositions about existence. It is a sad story, despite some noble accomplishments and some laudable consequences; in its wake Christian mission *today* can only achieve legitimacy in the eyes both of the missioners and those being missionized through an agonizing struggle with our missionary past.[6]

Similarly, an ethic that arises out of the theology of glory is typically imposed. It consists of moral precepts derived quite independently of actual human situations. The assumption is that such precepts, especially those gleaned directly or indirectly from reputedly biblical imperatives, are universally and immediately applicable. Thus, without anguish, without doubt and vacillation, the triumphant church already knows what is good and what is evil, and it seeks to implement its moral code without recourse to the specificities of the situation, including the attempts of existing communities to address moral questions on the basis of their own mores and goals.

Our task here, however, is not to assess the shortcomings of triumphalistic Christian missiology and ethics; it is rather to discuss the problems and possibilities of being Christian in the world today, in a way that is consistent with the theological priorities that we have already established. Specifically, what kind of missiology and ethic are suggested by this theological tradition?

We must begin by acknowledging the extreme difficulty of the task. The complexity of the problem is signaled in the title of this chapter by one word: *today*. Our today, as I have suggested in the opening paragraphs above, is so thoroughly steeped in consciousness of the ephemeral, so fast-moving, so diffuse, and withal so unprecedented and new that it is nearly impossible to discern its character and meaning. As the spokespersons of postmodernity keep insisting, the established canons of interpretation seem inadequate. Even the theology of the cross, as it has exemplified itself in the past, falls short of the task. Though those who stand in that tradition will not be greatly surprised by its inadequacy, for this "broken" theology has never thought itself adequate, the shock of the present and impending future is bound to register with any Christian who finds himself or herself confronted by the moral chaos of our historical moment. No Christian community of the past, regardless of its theological predisposition, has had to sort out what it would mean to be a Christian in a world in the grips of such problems as economic and cultural globalism, the unexampled disparity between rich and poor, the technological manipulation of life and death, the complexity of the human relation to the extrahuman, the extreme diversity of human cults and cultures, the terrifying power of clandestine warfare (terrorism), the barely recognized future clash of North and South,[7] etc., etc. Life on earth has never been simple, but today its complexity is both quantitatively and qualitatively daunting. We have never been six billion before, and we have never before lived with so much information about one another.

In his insightful biography of Martin Luther, which is based chiefly on Luther's own correspondence, John M. Todd remarks, concerning the unprecedented need of Reformation theologians to discuss ecclesiology: "In the theology school there had been no regular teaching *De Ecclesia,* on the Church. The Church was all around one, and the need to theorize about it had not arisen. Founded by the followers of Jesus of Nazareth, it was the great 'a priori.'"[8] Something comparable exists for Christian thinking today: in both missions and ethics we find ourselves confronted by existential problems that seem not to have occurred to our immediate predecessors, even when circumstances were such that they *could* have occurred. Although some individuals and critical movements of the late nineteenth and early twentieth centuries had given thought to the problem of Christian missions in a religiously diverse world, the quite monolithic if nominal Christianity of my childhood and adolescence in North America guaranteed that most people, even those on the edges of the churches, would not be inspired to raise any hard questions about the appropriateness of Christian missions at home and abroad. From time to time, missionaries on furlough would address our local congregation, and I do not remember anyone ever asking whether Christianity should be exported to Asian or African peoples or even whether the existing religions of such peoples could be thought in any way legitimate or even preparatory. In Canada, the practice of placing the children of the indigenous ("Indian" and Inuit) peoples into residential schools operated by the churches at the behest of the government, so grave a concern today, was virtually unquestioned. As with ecclesiology prior to the Reformation, Christian missions, understood in quite blatantly expansionist terms, were for us simply "there," given, part of the work of the church to which we all, even children, contributed freely. From World War II onward, this presupposition has been challenged from every side, and no village church is today so remote as to be unaware of it.

In ethics, the changed situation is if anything even more conspicuous, for here a great many of the problems that must be addressed *are,* on account of scientific, technological, and other alleged advances, quite new. Though many in the immediate past, especially we who were young then, protested the tyranny of the moral code inherited from the Victorian era and on its way to becoming middle-class morality, the nature of the good—and more decidedly of the bad—was on the whole firmly entrenched. For some, however, that code was already thrown into disarray by the aftermath of the First World War, and for nearly everyone else it was reduced to relativity in the wake of the Second, at least at the level of personal morality. The greatest challenge to Christian ethics today, however, is not in the albeit complex field of individual morality but in societal and global ethics, where, as I contended earlier, so many problems and possibilities are absolutely without precedent.

Our task now is to ask whether and how, in the face of such innovation, a theology that is of the cross can help to guide the disciple community in fashioning a missiology and an ethic that enables it to *be* in the world today responsibly—employing the current vernacular, to be in the world "as part of the solution, not [as so much Christianity seems to be] the problem."

Faithful Ambassadors of Hope and Love

Clearly, Christianity is a "missionary faith." Not all of humankind's religions are sent out in the way that Christianity is. Though most faiths are proud enough of their basic precepts and the desirability of their approach to want to share their belief in some way, intentional mission is not a necessary concomitant of religion per se. With Christianity as with Islam, the two numerically most powerful world religions today, the compulsion to mission goes well beyond the desire to share belief, and in their most boisterous forms, these two Abrahamic faiths (unlike their Jewish parent religion) tend toward militant expansionism. It is little wonder, therefore, that they frequently clash and that their encounter in today's volatile planetary situation could become earthshaking.

I have no intention of speaking for Islam in this matter—others are doing so.[9] But it is paramount for all serious Christians today to ask whether expansionism of any kind, whether territorial or as a bid for ever-greater numbers of converts, really belongs to the mission of the Christian church. That it has been prominent in the church's past—in Christendom—is indisputable. But does it *belong?* That is, is Christian mission biblically and theologically conceived inherently and necessarily expansionist? Even discounting the possibility that the Great Commission at the end of Matthew's Gospel is a late addition to the text—that is, assuming that the risen Christ actually told his followers to "Go therefore and make disciples of all nations, baptizing them in the name of the Father and of the Son and of the Holy Spirit" (Matt. 28:19), must we believe as Christians that it was the intention of our Lord to inaugurate a community that would strive to convert the entire population of earth ("all nations") to Christianity?

Before we respond to such a question, we had better consider certain realities—some arising from the biblical text, some emerging out of our present global condition.

First, questions arising from the text: If Jesus intended such a massive mission and conversion, why does that intention not inform his recorded teachings? All of the metaphors Jesus uses to depict the community of witness that he is preparing through his teaching and example and will bring to fruition though the later witness of the Paraclete are metaphors of smallness: little things that perform some essential service for bigger things—salt, yeast, a candle, a little town on a hill in a dark night, a pearl, a mustard seed. He speaks of his "little flock," which he sends out "as sheep into the midst of wolves" (Matt. 10:16). He assumes that the missionary vocation of this *koinonia* will involve excruciating isolation, rejection, and suffering—should not the disciple follow the master? There is nothing in the text of the newer Testament that could be construed as imperialistic about this vision—to the contrary! With Constantinian eyes, of course, we may read it as the meager beginnings of something that only *later* became what it was "intended" to be, but surely that kind of interpretation is post-textual, not to say anachronistic.[10]

Nor can this newer Testamental picture of the church be put down to the parabolic-didactic style of Jesus' teaching; for behind it

is the well-established Hebraic theology of divine election, which
Paul again picks up more explicitly (for example, Romans 9–11).
"Election" is by definition and practice a minority concept—that is,
it is precisely something small that exists for the sake of something
big. The most elementary statement of this concept is found in the
so-called Abrahamic covenant: "Through you, all the families of the
earth shall be blessed" (Gen. 12:3). This small people, the Jews (still
today only about fourteen million in number worldwide), sees itself
being chosen for a large responsibility—a representative, priestly,
stewardly responsibility. But it does not fancy *itself* becoming large,
important, powerful—or rather, when it begins to speculate in those
terms, its prophets become nervous and vocal! The great contemporary Jewish writer Elie Wiesel was accurately (if in a modern manner)
articulating this ancient concept of Jewish chosenness when, in an
interview for the *New York Times,* he said: "As a Jew, I do not wish to
make the world more Jewish; only more human."[11]

The so-called Great Commission has frequently been thought
peculiar precisely because, on the surface of it and as it has been her-
alded by a victorious Christendom, it seems so incongruous with
biblical assumptions about the character and mission of the called.
Was this text added later by a church that wanted scriptural warrant
for its expansionist ways? (Certainly the trinitarian formula that is
part of it is regarded by many as a later interpolation.) Or is it to be
interpreted in a manner quite different from the usual Christendom
interpretation? In what follows, I shall opt for the latter possibility.
One may proclaim the gospel universally, hoping to make disciples
among persons of all nations, without assuming either that the proclaimed gospel is going to be heard by all (Jesus even asks at one
point whether it will be heard "hearingly" by *any*! [Luke 8:8]) or that
all who hear will become and remain disciples.

Regardless how this particular text is interpreted, it remains that
the overall biblical picture of the church and its mission does not
support either an imperial ecclesiology or a triumphalistic missiology, and when such are reputedly derived from the Bible, they must
overlook this larger picture and exaggerate the importance of a few
texts or concepts excerpted from the totality. It was not the writer of

the Gospel of Matthew who named the nineteenth verse of his twenty-eighth chapter "The Great Commission." That nomenclature smacks of Christendom, even if the verses it designates belong to the original text.

Second, questions arising from our present global condition: Two empirical realities confront Christians in the West today: (1) that (as I put it in the previous chapter) *we have been Christendom.* That is to say, for a thousand to fifteen hundred years the Christianity that we have known—that we have been—is a certain kind of Christianity. Whether we call it "imperialistic" or "triumphalistic" or "the dominant religion" or simply "Christendom" does not matter so much as the sheer recognition that the faith we profess has been a great force in the world, the religion of the powerful empires of the Western Hemisphere, and of the most successful race where success is measured in terms of economic, technological, military, and pop-cultural innovation and influence. Moreover, the most vociferous Christian groups, at least on this continent, still dream that dream, and those of us who do not dream it and who may indeed want to escape its lasting influence have great difficulty doing so. In short, even when Christians have become critical of the Christendom model of the church, we realize that we "cast shadows not our own"—so that, with respect to the present topic, contemplating an appropriate missiology for today we must recognize that even the most sensitive and politically correct attempts at Christian outreach will be perceived by many both abroad and at home as extensions of our expansionistic habits.

(2) The second empirical reality that confronts us in this connection is the immovable fact of religious plurality, both globally and in formerly Christian territories. For those Christians who embrace an exclusivist view of Christian truth, this does not constitute a problem—at least ideationally and, to a point, tactically. But even they must have begun, after September 11, 2001, to sense that militant religion of *any* variety is today on a collision course with any *other* religion or quasi-religion that sets out to win the world, especially when it is bound up with powerful political entities (as it usually is). In the wake of that act of terrorism, sensitive Christians and sensitive

Muslims have been at pains to explain that such acts and attitudes are adopted only by extremists. But there is a logic of triumphalistic religion that, though it may be taken to extremes only by a militant few, informs the whole body of faith, and the extremists, rather than being mere aberrations, may have to be seen as the few who have absorbed the exclusivistic and uncompromising claims of their religion most unconditionally. Christians, with our history of relations with both Judaism and Islam (to mention only two "competitors"), ought not to need reminding of this. The supersessionistic, anti-Jewish teachings of the Christian centuries prepared wonderfully at the spiritual and attitudinal level for the activity of "the few extremists" who set up the machinery for the elimination of Judaism from Europe. We may say that Christians did not "do it" (the Holocaust), though some who "did it" certainly did claim they were believing Christians; the more important consideration, however, is how hundreds of years of questionable Christian theology and preaching laid the ideological groundwork for those who, whether Christian or neo-pagan, "did it." As always, the question here is not only the deed but the thought that informs and inspires the deed. Unless a self-critical dimension is built into the thinking of a religion, it simply *will*, sooner or later, beget extreme applications of its most salient teachings.[12]

I conclude therefore that Christian expansionism (by whatever name it may be called) is neither biblically sound nor contextually responsible. Without even mentioning the many other barriers[13] to the kind of exorbitant growth mentality[14] that can be found among both conservative and liberal Christian groupings in Northern climes, especially the United States (and I shall not even attempt to speak of the hemispheric South in this connection), these two observations should give pause to any Christians whose missiology falls along triumphalistic lines.

Mission as "Living the Story"

We are presented once again with the question of alternatives to triumphalistic Christian missions. Here we must admit straightaway that any search for alternatives faces extraordinary challenges. For even among the churches or ecumenical bodies that abhor all missionary aggressiveness of past and present there remains such a deep psychic commitment to expansionistic missiological assumptions that it is extremely difficult to overcome their influence sufficiently to achieve openness to another approach. Anyone who has attempted in a seminary or congregational setting to question overt Christian evangelism will have experienced that difficulty. (One of the first questions will likely be, "What about the Great Commission?" And the second will be like unto it: "Didn't Jesus say that *he* was the only way to the Father?")

In keeping with the overall object of this study, therefore, I will insist that the only way in which it will be possible to combat these cloying assumptions of our Christendom past is by embracing another theology! It is not necessary for us to *invent* such a theology.

What would adherence to the theology of the cross mean for a theology of Christian *mission?* There are any number of ways of addressing that question, but I shall do so by utilizing the schema that I proposed in the initial chapter: that is, let us apply to the subject of Christian mission the three theological virtues of Paul as understood within the terms of the *theologia crucis,* in other words, that it is a theology of *faith* (not sight); of *hope* (not finality); and of *love* (not power).

First, a theology of faith, not sight, contains an inherent, critically vital modesty factor. Christians do not *know*—they trust; they do not *possess* truth[15]—they bear witness to the living therefore unpossessible Truth; they do not proclaim *themselves* or *the church* but the one toward whom their faith is oriented (2 Cor. 4:5), whom they experience as being utterly transcendent of their faith as such.

When it is truly foundational, such a theology has no room for the assumption of ultimacy, ownership, or inerrancy. That at least must be said. A theology that bases itself on faith alone *(sola fide)* cannot in its worldly witness legitimately behave as though it were infallible. The revelatory Truth we glimpse is simultaneously a concealed Truth. If we sometimes think we see, it is only "through a glass, darkly" (1 Cor. 13:12, KJV). In its dialogue with those who do not belong to the household of this faith, including, surely, those of *other* faiths, the disciple community may not present itself as though it had seen what no one else could possibly see. It could only prove a contradiction of itself as a community of *faith* were it to act, in relation to these others, as if it had already passed from faith to sight, from trust to face-to-face encounter, from church to kingdom. At the very least in terms of its own self-knowledge, such a community would have to eschew any hint of superiority or condescension in relation to "the others." And that is already a large step toward a sense of mission that is *different*—exceptionally so.

Is it possible to go further? Is it permitted, under the aegis of this theology, to make any positive assumptions about the others? Certainly it is! If I am conscious of the fact that my own stance is one of faith, not sight, I must at least be open to the possibility that the other—a human being like myself—has something to bring to our meeting. At the very least, I should not be able to treat the other as a mere receptacle for *my* message! And if this other also claims to be a person of faith, even though it is not my faith, surely that is already a common attitudinal and epistemological denominator of our discourse. Persons of *faith* may engage in real dialogue, even if the content-dimension of their faiths differs. It is only where one partner fancies herself or himself beyond faith, already a seer, that dialogue between those of differing religious positions cannot occur. In the modesty of faith, therefore, I would try to be ready to hear the message of the other. By the same token, moreover, I would not be allowed to assume in advance that *what* I heard from the other by way of substance or content would as a matter of course differ from or contradict my own theological perceptions. Indeed, the noetic presupposition being faith and the ontic presupposition being the presence in all life of the divine *Logos,* I should be obliged to think that the other *might have positive or corrective insight to bring to me.*

We are speaking here of the modesty that belongs to *faith*. It is not a matter of *personal* humility of bearing, a gift that some do and others do not have. If I find myself being opened to the other, it is not because I am a particularly humble, genial, or extroverted person; it is only because my faith is trust in *Another*—neither in self, nor in system. This Other has begun to teach me to apply the trust I have in him to my way of being with others of my own kind—especially those who themselves name *faith,* some faith, as their point of departure.

Second, a theology that confesses hope, not finality or consummation, will certainly have a mission in the midst of a despairing world, but it will be a mission that recognizes an expansiveness of divine grace that far exceeds its own grasp and representation of this mission. For in the first place it will be hope in *God,* not in its own always-limited appropriation of God's redemptive work. Christian mission is a particular, ongoing attempt faithfully to comprehend and participate in the *missio Dei.* "*God* is at work in the world to make and to keep human life human" (Paul Lehmann).[16] Christians are those who have glimpsed in faith something of the reality and depth of this divine labor and who strive to involve themselves in it. But they know that it is not *their* work, and they know that its end *(telos, eschatos)* eludes them and in its advent *may utterly surprise them.* Therefore they do not, may not, present themselves as a community for which all is finished—a body uniquely knowledgeable of the divine economy, in possession of secret truth concerning God's closure of history, etc. (they are not Gnostics!).

In other words, the bearing or stance appropriate to the church is not that of a community that has arrived but of one that is under way *(communio viatorum)*—that is, a community of hope. And that is precisely how the earliest church regarded itself.

How does this kind of self-knowledge on the part of the disciple community affect its mission, and especially how does it take account of the two contextual challenges mentioned earlier? For my answer, I shall turn to an external source—one, however, in which I was personally involved. In the fall of 2000, five international scholars were invited to take part with two local Presbyterian ministers in an extensive missiological study sponsored by Columbia Theological Seminary in Atlanta and chaired by Walter Brueggemann, the well-known biblical theologian. The eight-member Campbell Seminar met for several hours daily over a two-month period to address a single question: "What is the mission of the church in the twenty-first century?"[17] Over the course of that time various papers were presented, and in the end a common statement was adopted unanimously, the thesis of which declares that "*The mission of the Christian Movement in the twenty-first century is to confess hope in action.*"

That Christian voices representative of virtually all the major regions of the planet would find it necessary to express Christian mission in these particular terms is in itself already highly significant. For one thing, the presupposition of singling out hope as the primary emphasis of the mission is that the human situation to be addressed manifests a certain dearth of hope—indeed, that "despair" (literally the negation *[de]* of hope *[spes]*), whether the overt despair of the poor or the covert despair of the rich peoples of Earth, is the most prominent component of the human condition globally today.[18] The Christian Movement (not institution) bears witness to the hope of the gospel—and not only, not even primarily, in words, but "in action." The consensus statement of the seminar in fact recognizes that the church's *verbal* witness needs to be concentrated chiefly upon itself (for most congregations are ill-prepared to "confess hope") and that in the world at large what is required is the translation of our hope into "action": "In the church, tell the story; in the world, live the story."[19] In view of the triumphalism of the Christian past, "evangelism" normally presupposes *invitation* explicitly or implicitly offered, which in turn presupposes Christian compassion and solidarity with the world in its struggle for justice, peace, and a sustainable ecosphere.

For our present purposes, it is especially important to notice how this vision of Christian mission understands the relation of Christianity to other faiths. The following paragraph sets the tone:

> As the church sheds some of the institutional garments with which its status as religious establishment clothed it, and as Christian communities recover something of the movement-quality *(communio viatorum)* of the New Testament *koinonia*, Christians everywhere are beginning to recognize the *companionable presence* of many others who, even if they do not move

with us in obvious ways, are nevertheless in close proximity and seem to be journeying in the same direction. In a world in which daily life is determined by indifference to ultimate questions and in which the future is being shaped by economic and other forces that do not concern themselves with humanity's "chief end," the presence of genuine faith in many different forms constitutes a source of courage and a confirmation of hope. In our own always inadequate attempts to live as those "sent" by a just and compassionate God, we are becoming more and more grateful for the solidarity of others who, in their own ways, manifest an apostolic vocation. In particular, we cherish the increasing mutuality and support of our parental faith, Judaism, from whose faithful spokespersons we Christians still have much to learn about the world-directedness of God's mission and the prophetic calling of God's people.[20]

In my opinion, the statement of the Campbell Scholars represents a faithful application of the theology of the cross to Christian missiological thought, both as to its identification of the appropriate emphasis of the mission today and in terms of its accompanying approach to religious pluralism.

Third, we said that the theology of the cross is a theology of love, not power. This, were it truly understood and enacted, would render every other commentary on Christian missions unnecessary. Without expecting perfection, without forgetting that at the end of the day we are all "unprofitable servants," without overlooking the various distortions into which love itself falls (sentimentalism, self-love, the blurring of distinction between *agape* and *eros,* etc.), *how might it have altered the history of Christian missions over two thousand years had its watchword been "suffering love" and a consistent vigilance against the quest for power that even lovers can display?* What if every Christian mission—let us say the mission to the indigenous peoples of the Americas—had been undertaken in the spirit of divine love, as it is described, for example, in 1 Cor. 13:4-6?

Love is patient; love is kind; love is not envious or boastful or arrogant or rude, it does not insist on its own way; it is not irritable or resentful; it does not rejoice in wrongdoing, but rejoices in the truth. It bears all things, believes all things, hopes all things, endures all things.

I realize that such a proposal is bound to seem naïve. Everyone knows that love regularly betrays whatever patience, kindness, modesty, and magnanimity belong to it. In practice, whether we are speaking of marriage and family, or friendship, or religion, love is compromised at every turn. Why should we not assume that that would always be the case also with Christian faith? Since to be Christian is (in Luther's familiar phrase) to be simultaneously justified and sinner *(simul justus et peccator),* could we not assume that in its worldly outreach the church would manifest this same duplicity?

Certainly! However, the point is not that Christianity has sinned in its failure to love those whom it sought to evangelize but that its evangelization was so rarely motivated by love in the first place. Or—recognizing the importance of exceptions (for there have been exceptions)—even when the evangelical impulse has been inspired by love of *God,* or of *the gospel,* or even of *humanity* or "people," it too seldom carried with it the kind of concern for the very concrete, flesh-and-blood human beings who were the object of its witness. Had it done so with any kind of consistency, we should not have the kind of disregard for and displacement of non-Caucasian cultures that dogs the history of Christian missions. For love, surely, is incommensurate with such unconcern for the other, even when it is a purely human passion. And the love that is the pattern and inspiration of the Christian mission is a "spontaneous and unmotivated" (Anders Nygren)[21] love, *agape,* that is wholly turned toward the other in disregard of self—to the point of suffering and death, the death of the cross.

No doubt it will be said (it would not be new!) that such a criterion of authentic Christian mission is impossibly utopian, idealistic, and even discouraging from the outset. What must be recognized, however, is that just this love is the canon by which all of our actions as Christians, including mission and evangelism as well as all social outreach and neighborliness, are measured. We may have to confess our failure to attain to it in any and all situations, but that does not excuse us from holding to it as the aim. And when we consider the actual history of Christian missions, can we with anything like objectivity claim that this *has been our steadfast aim,* despite our failure?

Our mandate here, however, is not to judge the past so much as to let the past instruct us for the future. The quest for numbers, for influence, for this or that form of civilization, etc.—in short the quest for power—has not only entailed a flagrant contradiction of this most foundational teaching of Jesus Christ, it has brought untold pain and violence to the human journey. And today that quest, as the basis of Christian mission, can only be pursued with ever greater manifestations of violence. Mission under the aegis of power, however christianly that power may be conceived or reputed to be, is today an evangelical cul de sac. The late Henri Nouwen stated the matter with complete clarity:

> The temptation to consider power an apt instrument for the proclamation of the gospel is the greatest temptation of all. We rationalize and justify the use of power as something good. With this line of thinking crusades took place, inquisitions were organized, Native Americans were enslaved, positions of great influence were desired, episcopal palaces, splendid cathedrals, and opulent seminaries were built.[22]

Why could it not happen, without naïve idealism, that love—God's love, the love that we, being first loved, are learning to show—should be understood by serious ecumenical churches as the first and only unqualified ground for their mission? Only such a sending out could warrant our being linked with the Word *God* sent.

Ethics: Following Christ into the Contemporary Moral Wilderness

The ethic that follows from the theology of the cross is an ethic of discipleship. That is to say, its presupposition is the relationship of faith with the one who bids us, "take up your cross and follow *me.*" This is not merely a poetic or pious way of speaking; it is the heart of Protestant ethical insight. Protestant ethical teaching is not based on natural (or moral) law but on faith in the triune God. Natural law should certainly not be despised or ignored. Its limitations must nevertheless be recognized: it is either so general as to be a cliché ("Good should be done, evil avoided") or else so explicit as to be culture-specific and time-bound. In any case, the ethic appropriate to the tradition with which we are concerned here is not first one of nature but of grace, not of law but of gospel, not of the letter but of the Spirit.

What about *biblical* law? It is to be taken with great seriousness. But it is not to be reduced (yes, reduced) to absolutes. The only absolute to which Christians ought to pay heed is the voice of the Good Shepherd. This pneumatic sense of obedience must of course always test itself in relation to what is given in the tradition. Just as there must be a "test of the spirits" where questions of truth are concerned (1 John 4), so must there be a test of the spirits where questions of the good are concerned; this must mean first of all basic scriptural compatibility. But that is quite different from regarding the laws of the Bible (the Ten Commandments, the Beatitudes, etc.) as absolutes. Such legalism or biblicism should be seen as a defeat of the ethics of discipleship and, specifically, of the church's recognition of the presence and authority of the Holy Spirit. Neither an untested spiritualism nor a literalistic moralism can be accepted here, but only a spiritual listening that is guided by Scripture, tradition, and the ongoing dialogue of the present community of discipleship. The law, in the sense of biblical laws and codes of conduct, should be thought (what the prophetic tradition does think it) "a lamp unto my feet" (Ps. 119:105, KJV), not a set of regulations immediately and thoughtlessly applicable to every situation.

With such an understanding, the disciple community readies itself to enter into the unknownness of present and future—into the wilderness, the moral confusion of its time, the perennial newness of its context. This is an ethic of the cross first of all in the sense that it is discipleship of the crucified one who goes before but also (and therefore) in the sense of its demand for an original exposure to the present and impending future, with its darkness in both the sense of its unknownness and its potential for temptation and evil. The ethics of glory abhor this darkness and only enter it with lights ablaze—namely, the lights of a priori ethical precepts and goals. The ethics of the cross presuppose vulnerability and the risk of engagement. They know neither the questions nor the answers *in advance*. To be sure, the disciple community can call upon its past—the centuries of exposure to human misery and grandeur: after two thousand years, the church is not without experience and moral wisdom. But what it has learned most from its long experience, when it remembers aright, is that its *responses* to the questions of the here and now will be wise and perhaps even redemptive responses only to the extent that the questions themselves have been entered into in all their present novelty and unknownness. The people of the cross does not come to each new situation in the journey of humankind already armed with ready-made answers; rather, it positions itself in such a way as to discover the appropriate "word from the Lord." On the one hand such positioning means divesting itself of foregone moral conclusions that only insulate the church from exposure to real moral questions; on the other hand it means trusting that the divine Spirit, by whom it is led into its contextual wilderness, will also illumine its understanding and provide direction for its response.

The first requirement of the ethic of the cross, then, is that the disciple community must allow itself to be led as deeply as possible into the sphere of *the question*. The question—that is, any matter deserving serious moral deliberation, decision, and action—is never a merely general one, for example, "The Human Relation to Nature" or "Human Sexuality." It is always specific, for the historical conditions under which it is asked are never incidental to its reality. It is precisely the complex contextual specificity of the question that makes it a real and not merely a theoretical question.

To exemplify: (1) any discussion of the human relation to extra-human nature today occurs under historical conditions in which—for the first time in history—human technological prowess, combined with modernity's ambition to control nature and to eliminate chance, has led to the prospect of manifold catastrophe. Homo sapiens is no longer a pathetically vulnerable species at the mercy of overwhelming natural forces and therefore for its own survival required to exercise a certain "audacity" (Thomas Hobbes) in relation to other species and processes; it is on the contrary both quantitatively and qualitatively so masterful in the scheme of things that unless its ancient urge to sovereignty is restrained it may destroy the very resources of the planet on which its own life and future, as well as that of other species, depend.[23]

Under such contextual circumstances, any unqualified reiteration of the biblical injunction to "multiply" and to "subdue" and "have dominion over" the earth must be considered not only redundant but irresponsible; indeed most informed Christians, including most of those predisposed to ethical biblicism, have recognized this and have reconsidered their biblical exegesis and doctrinal conventions accordingly. One could not of course claim in all honesty that Christianity as a whole has rethought its anthropology in the light of the ecological crisis, but a great many Christians of all ecclesiastical groupings and doctrinal persuasions have at least recognized the potential dangers of expressing biblical injunctions in this area without interpreting them in the light of present-day threats to the stability of planetary existence.[24]

And that is instructive, for it represents at least a beginning where exposure to the question is concerned. Wherever the Yahwist's injunction to exercise dominion is interpreted in such a way as to distinguish such dominion from the usual anthropocentric interpretation of that concept, there is an incipient attempt to consider the problem of the relation between humankind and otherkind, not as a theoretical question to which biblical and doctrinal teachings are to be applied without further ado but as a very concrete and highly complex present-day ethical problem that must be entered into in the full consciousness of the contemporary manifestations and permutations of the problem itself. Moreover, these latter are not merely addenda to the ancient question of humanity in its dealings with the rest of creation; rather, they qualify the whole tenor and character of the question, so that conventional responses to it, many of them *reputedly* Bible-based, are effectively ruled out. The more the disciple community allows the specificity of the problem to inform its thought and action, the more excruciating its reflection and decision-making will become. But unless it permits itself to experience this pain (for it *is* pain), it will be incapable of either the spirituality of asking earnestly for divine guidance or the wisdom of responsible human thought and behavior.

(2) A second exemplification of the principle of participatory ethical reflection and action relates to the more personal aspect of the subject. Unfortunately, the (relative) ethical maturity that is being shown by Christians of many persuasions in the area of environmental ethics has not been demonstrated very widely where a number of other pressing moral questions are concerned. Among these latter, none is more conspicuous than in the vast and thorny field of sexual ethics, and within that field the most troublesome issue for most Christians in North America today is that of homosexuality. Here, with notable exceptions, the very first step that I have insisted belongs to the ethic of the cross has simply not been taken: that is, *the question* has not been entered into. Instead, ready-made answers have been paraded ad nauseam—answers that are no answers at all but only preexistent prejudices masquerading as biblical or traditional Christian belief and counsel.

Living with "the question" of same-sex sexuality means, in the first place, recognizing that homosexuality with all its attendant issues is simply a fact of life in our civilization. Contrary to the accusations of the most reactionary elements within the denominations, the question of homosexual orientation and lifestyle was not initiated by liberal or radical groups within the churches themselves. From the 1960s onward, our society at large was thrust into a far-reaching reexamination of all sexual mores and customs, including this one. While this rethinking may have been inspired by the rebellions of the so-called youth culture, it was by no means a merely generational concern, and its outcome included the revamping of the criminal and other codes of law that had been operative for generations. For instance, in Canada it became a punishable offense for organizations to refuse employment to anyone on the grounds of sexual orientation.

This meant that the churches were faced by the need to reconsider their own theological and ethical teachings, which in many cases had formed the moral substructure of the very laws that were now being radically questioned and changed. How, for example, could a Canadian church refuse to consider a self-acknowledged gay or lesbian person for the ministry of Word and Sacraments in the light of the new laws governing employment?

Predictably enough, the ecclesiastical responses to this situation fell into two camps, whose positions quickly polarized: a conservative camp that rejected gay ordination and was at least ambiguous about the acceptance of homosexuality under any circumstances, and a liberal camp that ranged from reluctant recognition of the legitimacy of gay ordination to the celebration of sexual diversity.

It will become obvious that my own sympathies are with the latter group. What will not be so obvious, without further explanation, is that, with important exceptions, I am not satisfied about the way in which *either* of these camps arrived at their conclusions. Indeed, most of the conclusions were *foregone conclusions;* that is, they do not represent what I called earlier "original exposure" to the question. Rather, they express previously held biases for which in the polarized situation various reasons are then discovered.

An ethic arising from the theology of the cross, where this particular moral issue is concerned, must recognize that Christians are confronted here with a genuine problem, one that cannot be resolved by a simple and immediate yes or no, one that cannot be answered merely by consulting the Bible or the classical literature of the tradition.[25] As with the natural sciences, there have been discoveries and insights of the social and medical sciences with respect to human sexual behavior that render many scriptural assumptions and traditional doctrine if not obsolete, at least badly in need of supplementation and interpretation. For example, it is now generally held by scientists, social scientists, and ethicists that homosexual orientation is a "non-chosen" preference,[26] whereas much if not most conventional religious and other "wisdom" has assumed it to be volitional if not deliberately perverse.[27] Again, much if not most traditional morality

where sexual behavior generally is concerned was shaped, if not
determined, by the positive necessity of procreation in sparse and
threatened human populations and in agrarian societies where members of both sexes were under a more or less felt obligation to marry
and produce children.[28] Again, sexuality in the past—especially
though not exclusively in white, Protestant, anglosaxon societies—
has been a highly privatized dimension of life; where acknowledgment of its reality (and variety) was not actively suppressed, it was
generally and deeply *repressed.* Homosexual behavior is by no means
a new phenomenon, but in the past it has been "the love that dared
not speak its name," whereas, in consequence of the sexual revolution of the mid-twentieth century, it is today—along with every
other form of sexual expression—openly present and spoken of.

All such realities of the present greatly complicate the Christian
community's consideration of homosexuality, including the ordination of those who acknowledge it as their sexual orientation; but
without bringing them to the fore of its discussion, the question is
simply not faced and the answers are often destructive of the individuals concerned. If, for example, an ordination committee is still
laboring under the assumption that a gay candidate for ministry is
deliberately perverse ("a pervert"), it is in no position to make a
morally or spiritually responsible decision about that candidate. It is
so thoroughly (and perhaps perversely) stuck in another epoch and
culture that its comprehension even of *the question,* let alone any
viable response thereto, is severely constricted and potentially evil.

But such sociological/psychological ignorance is not the only or
the most troublesome lack in such circumstances. There are even
more important humanitarian and *theological* gaps to be filled.
Why, to begin with, have the churches so readily—unthinkingly—
conceded to the society at large that sex is our defining characteristic as human beings? Neither of our founding traditions—neither
Athens nor Jerusalem—cared to define the human being primarily on the basis of sex or sexual activity or sexual preference. To
the contrary, both traditions sat lightly to that whole area of life[29]
and chose such *spiritual* capacities as "rationality" (Athens) and

"faith/trust/responsiveness/speech" (Jerusalem) as our defining marks. That sexuality (sex-appeal, sexual activity, sexual orientation, etc.) has become so paramount in our assessment of ourselves and others in this society is, from the perspective of our founding civilizations, a sign of our degeneracy. When the church enters no profound critique of this but on the contrary reflects society's preoccupation with sex to the extent of allowing sexual orientation to become the key "issue" in matters of ordination and, in many denominations, the most prominent and divisive subject of all ecclesiastical discourse (the tail that wags the dog), it is a very depressing thought.

Thus, to confront and appropriate at some depth "the question" inherent in this particular moral issue leads into considerations that are far broader and more painful than what a congregation or denomination may have bargained for. From purely sexual-theological inquiries such as "Is homosexuality compatible with Christian faith?" (to which Ken Sehested, a Baptist theologian, counters, "Is *heterosexuality* compatible with Christian faith?"[30]), the honest inquirer is led to confront vexing questions about human nature (What is the place of sexuality in our total life and "with-being"?), the relation of church and society (Why should the church allow its host culture to set the tone for its moral preoccupations?), soteriology (Are we saved *from* sexuality[31]), etc., etc.

It has not been my purpose here to explore in its fullness the complex area of homosexuality in general or the specific question of the ordination of persons who openly acknowledge their homosexual orientation; obviously any such discussion would require lengthy and nuanced treatment beyond the scope of the present subject. My intention has only been to illustrate, by reference to this knotty topic, that the ethic of the cross entails a profound and painful exposure to depths greater than those that first appear. That is the way of the cross, which is just as excruciating in matters of the intellect and the will as it is where actual physical involvement and suffering are involved. The answers to which as persons and communities of faith we might be led by the divine Spirit will gain the only authenticity they need by having passed through the crucible of the *Anfechtungen* (agonies of soul) that accompanied their emergence. For the most part, they will not be brilliant or even persuasive answers, because the only truly authentic answer to the great questions of human existence is the presence of one who gives us the grace and the courage *to live without definitive answers.* That presence cannot be controlled or commanded by any church, ministry, or sacerdotal rites, but it is nonetheless reflected wherever disciples of the Christ have gone far enough with him into their darkness to become witnesses to the light that shines there and only there. Such a witness may be heard in the following sentences:

> I, like many of you, am only a disciple of the poor man from Nazareth. He has made me content with mystery. He has made me less afraid of chaos. He has told me that control is not my task. He, like the cosmos itself, is about two things: *diversity and communion.*[32]

chapter 10

God's Reign, Creation's Future

The Human Background of Doctrine

What we call "doctrine"—*doctrina,* teaching—is at base nothing more than the attempt of the community of faith to answer, from the perspective of the tradition in which it stands, the great, recurrent, yet always newly explicit questions of the human spirit. One of the most persistent of those questions—one that takes on countless forms but is finally always the same—when stated in its most rudimentary form is simply: *To what end?*

The ordinary English word *end* contains two meanings that, though they may be used separately, are never wholly separable: the *end* as termination begets the deeper, existential connotation of the word *end* as goal or purpose. Even when the thing that is ending is relatively unimportant in the grand scheme of things (say, an ad hoc committee or a small-business enterprise), the prospect of its ending causes those involved to ask what end (purpose, *telos*) it has served; indeed this question will have been present, quietly if not openly, throughout the duration of the entity under discussion. That things end—that *everything* ends—necessarily evokes in the minds and hearts of all concerned the question of their meaning and goal. Can the end in any way justify the effort that must be expended in its attempted achievement? Can such an end *be* achieved, to begin with, given the many limitations that must be taken into account, including those of time?

These questions apply in some degree to all individual and corporate human activities, but their intensity increases in proportion to the existential claims their subjects make upon us. To exemplify: As I write (it is November 11, Remembrance Day), a memorial service for the millions of fallen in two great wars and numerous lesser conflicts is being broadcast from my nation's capital, Ottawa. Again we are told, as we are told each year, of the ultimate sacrifices made by our dead compatriots, most of them very young people; again we are assured that their life offerings were nonetheless worthwhile because they died to ensure "a lasting peace." But as we contemplate the real possibility that in a matter of days now the world may be engulfed in yet another war, adding to the literally hundreds of wars that have occurred on the planet since the end of World War II, we ask ourselves, many of us, whether the pursuit of that end has in any way justified the incalculable cost that it has in fact entailed. The "War to End All Wars" (the motto of the promoters of the 1914–1918 "Great War") has not yet been fought, and given the pride and prejudice of nations and peoples, it seems unlikely ever to occur. Yet what lesser end than an end to such persistent violence could justify the snuffing out of even one young life, let alone millions?

End and *end, telos* and *terminus,* confront us at every turn of our historical sojourn, most intensely—for many, obsessively—when we consider, as we do even when we are not intentionally considering it, the reality that our own lives will end. Every report of a "terminal" illness, every death, every funeral hurls at our always-unprepared spirits the question, Why? To what end? But again let me be concrete.

A few days ago I received a telephone call from a young man known to me for several years—a splendid, compassionate, gifted person, a Lutheran pastor for whom the word *pastor* seemed to me to have been invented. He had been diagnosed with multiple melanoma a few months earlier, and now he had come home from the hospital to die in the midst of his dear ones. His friend told me that he would probably die that very day. The dying man's voice was barely audible, but he spoke to me clearly and wonderfully: he spoke of his gratitude for life, for faith, for others. How could I respond? He had come to terms with his ending. But I had not, nor, I imagine, had his wife and children and closest friends—though he, with his characteristic sensitivity, had put us all at ease through his own grace-filled acceptance of his approaching death.

These two immediately past experiences—the one public, the other private and personal—prompt me straightaway to flag two warnings to myself as I set out once again to address this most awesome question—the question to which our tradition attaches the almost clinical term, *eschatology.*

The first warning is this: *No doctrine, no matter how sophisticated, wise, or beautifully articulated, can ever really answer the human question that is posed by the fact that people die—and die, not as "people," but as very, very specific persons, fathers and mothers, grandparents and dear children, unrepeatable individuals with faces duplicated nowhere on earth or in all of history.*[1] That I say not out of a merely humanistic compassion for the lot of creatures (though what Christian should ever despise such humanism?) but out of the Judeo-Christian tradition in which I live and think. For that tradition is nowhere more critical, explicitly (Job) and implicitly (Jesus[2]), than in its polemic against those who provide "satisfactory" answers to the mystery of life, especially its beginnings and its endings but also the sufferings in between. It is a travesty of doctrine when it takes on such colossal pretense. One must do everything in one's power to avoid it, for the temptation to finality is always present.

And the second warning of which I remind myself is the converse of the first: *No doctrine, no matter how tentative or modest and unpretentious it may wish to be, should ever underestimate the combined capacities of the divine Spirit and the human spirit to face and meaningfully to absorb (not just "accept") death—one's own death in particular.* And again I say this, not merely on the grounds of a humanistic appreciation for the "grandeur" of which our species is often capable, but as a Christian who tries to take the grace of God and the "addressability" (Brunner) of the human being *by* such grace both seriously and concretely.

These two caveats, in their fine and complex interweaving, I should like to keep foremost in mind as I attempt once again to explain what I think Christian *doctrina* has to say to the likes of us, creatures who, in the midst of life, are ever conscious of life's inevitable ending. The dialectic suggested by these two warnings is of course more poignantly at work where the *personal* dimension of eschatological thought is concerned, and so I shall begin there.[3] But they have equally important parts to play in any Christian consideration of the more cosmic question of endings—the end of history, of planetary existence, of creation: the end of what we call the world.

As in the previous chapters of this short work, I do not aim to address all aspects of this boundless topic but only to show, so far as possible, what it means when the subject of Christian eschatology is understood within the framework of the *theologia crucis*—that is, when it is seen to be an *eschatologia crucis*.

"A Time To Die . . ."

It belongs to the theology of the cross, we said, that it permits and demands—demands and permits—an exceptional realism. Unlike its opposite, religious triumphalism or *theologia gloriae,* this tradition does not cater to that in human nature which is ready on the slightest pretext to overlook whatever negates in favor of a victorious positive, regardless how shallow the latter may be. In fact the power of the theology of glory lies precisely in its appeal to our human preference for the comforting lie, the other side of our abhorrence of uncomfortable truth. Luther said of the theology of glory that it "calls evil good and good evil"—it confuses, it lies. But the lies of Christian and other forms of religious and quasi-religious triumphalism would have no power to persuade were they not met in us by an inveterate need to be delivered from reality. That need is no sham: reality rarely encourages us to court it open-eyed. There is of course a state of degradation where reality cannot be avoided. Two-thirds of the human population of Earth lives in some semblance of that state. But with a little physical comfort to aid and abet it, the temptation of a rosy worldview that looks past the data of despair can be very effective. It is no wonder, then, that religious, political, and other forms of ideological triumphalism are strongest in relatively affluent societies. The North American success of the funeral industry in covering up the reality of personal death could hardly be duplicated in AIDS-ridden Africa!

The theology of the cross "calls the thing what it actually is." It calls death death, neither sleep, nor transition ("passing"), nor appearance. This theology is centered, after all, in one "crucified, dead, and buried." It rejects the docetism of the Christ's only "seeming" dead—only seeming, to begin with, mortal. The incarnation of the *Logos* means that the incarnate one has both a beginning and an ending, Bethlehem and Golgotha, Christmas and Good Friday. His life moves inevitably toward its ending—and so soon! His suffering, which as we have seen the historic creeds as well as the Gospels accentuate, is not only the suffering inflicted upon him by others but also, simply, the suffering of being human, finite, "being-toward-death" (Heidegger). It is the suffering of a life that is truly and representatively *human* because it is conscious (in Jesus' case exceptionally conscious, surely) of the ending toward which it moves: he was moved by "the grace of God" to "taste death for everyone" (Heb. 2:9).

This realism of the foundational event and symbol of Christian faith, where it is faithfully observed, prevents Christians both from euphemizing death and from resolving it by resorting to the dualistic anthropology presupposed by the concept of the immortality of the soul. Because of the early admixture of Jewish with Greek and Hellenistic influences, historical Christianity has been unable to this day to free itself from the allurements of immortality—and they *are* allurements, for not only does the idea of the soul's immortality seem to explain the *absence* of personhood in the dead human body; it also facilitates our natural longing for the continuance, without a radical break, of our essential self. Yet the price that is paid for this resolution of the dilemma of death is its drastic reduction of the body to the *in*essential, indeed the accidental, the burdensome (the "body tomb" of the Platonists). Nor is this only a repulsion of the flesh and all that pertains to it (including sexuality and, in extreme cases, even reproduction[4]); it is at bottom an option for a redemption theology that supercedes and in effect dismisses creation. Paul, though not without Hellenistic proclivities himself, is still so thoroughly imbued with a Hebraic sense of the goodness of creation and the unity of flesh and spirit in humankind that he is ready to resort to the apparent foolishness of a "resurrected body" rather than betraying this creational-anthropological presupposition (1 Corinthians 15). His argument does not seem to me very persuasive, but how could it be? We should be glad that it is not persuasive, for (see the first warning, above) a satisfactory resolution of the reality of death is a betrayal of the dead.

There is only one resolution of the reality of death that can be entertained by a theology of faith (not sight), hope (not finality), and love (not power), and it is no resolution in the ordinary usage of the term. It is, however, a resolution in its own way: namely, it resolves the *anxiety* (what Paul calls "the sting") of death (1 Cor. 15:55-56), and that is what most requires resolution so far as the living of life is concerned. As for death itself—our death, my death, death as a universal phenomenon—its resolution is only God's possibility. That is what *resurrection* (as distinct from immortality) *means*: Faith affirms that God, who gave life, can give life again—and wills to do so. As God creates *ex nihilo* so God may re-create *ex nihilo*. This is a God who "gives life to the dead and calls into existence the things that do not exist" (Rom. 4:17). Death—death as the fate of all the living, death as "the last enemy" (1 Cor. 15:26)—being God's creature and in some strange way God's servant, can only be negated by God; from our side, its negation is *not yet*: it must be undergone. But the fear of death, preoccupation with death, debilitating anxiety in the face of death, in short the sting of death—this, by grace, and *already,* is profoundly countered in this tradition.

It is countered by *faith,* that is, by that trust in God wrested from us by the divine Spirit who struggles with our spirits, causing us despite our own doubt and fearfulness to say, "Abba, Father" (Rom. 8:15)—that is, to consent. How shall we think of this in the face, not of generalizations and theories about death, but of actual death—particularly our own death and the deaths of those most indispensable to our lives? I do not believe that any one doctrinal answer can be given to this question. I do not know of any method by which, in advance of the actual prospect of imminent death, people may equip themselves to face the inevitable end, though I am sure that facing *life* with trust in God prepares us for facing the end of life. Life itself presents most of us with enough challenges and as it were "little endings" that it is itself a preparation for death, if we are sufficiently attentive to its ceaseless passingness. I believe that Jesus' words to those who will be called upon to suffer for their faith are appropriate here too: "Do not worry beforehand about what you are to say; but say whatever is given you at that time, for it is not you who speak, but the Holy Spirit" (Mark 13:11). That is, at the moment when one's personal demise must be confronted concretely, the necessary courage and the appropriate language will be "given." While I have not myself come to that point, I have witnessed in others who have done so the emergence, on the brink of extinction, of a brightness and clarity of trust in God that I have observed under no other circumstances. Cynicism may put this down to the last bid of the human will to preserve itself, but is it not too mysterious and too moving a phenomenon to permit its reduction to such a paltry explanation? What I heard in the weak and faltering telephonic voice of my friend, dying at a distance, was not a last futile bid for self-preservation but the trust of one whose *mis*trust had been wonderfully diminished, whose spiritual and rational facilities had been cleansed of the usual ambiguity, whose yes had triumphed over the perpetual no of our human duplicity. It was still faith, not sight, but it was a faith that was ready to see, expecting to see. The smudged, opaque glass through which faith sees, so far as it sees (1 Cor. 13:12), had begun to be cleared a little.

And this is why I have had to remind myself, at the outset, not to be so concentrated on the necessity for realism in the face of death as to forget the second caveat, namely, the obligation of the weavers of doctrine to bear in mind the capacity of the Holy Spirit to evoke from human spirits, being hard pressed by their ending, something greater than a mere acceptance of both death and life: something like affirmation, something like gratitude.

The theology of the cross is a theology—we have said, following von Loewenich and others—first of all of faith. But as such it is also and immediately a theology of hope. As von Loewenich writes, "Luther's concept of faith has a strong eschatological character."

> If faith is in the first instance a not-seeing, then it finds its goal (*telos*) in seeing; but this is part of the light of glory. Faith is geared to this *telos,* and thus, in opposition to sight, it is oriented eschatologically. The antithesis is stressed for the sake of the synthesis. For that reason *faith and hope are almost identical for Luther.* . . . For also faith is in the first instance directed to the future. . . . But it is distinctive of hope that it stands in contrast to the reality surrounding us. Hope (*spes*) and physical reality (*res*) are two members of a disjunctive relationship. . . .
>
> Hence in this hope, this bare hope, the first thing to be emphasized is not the positive, but the negative element: hope is not material reality. This reality which surrounds us, and hope, are in conflict with each other.[5]

Faith is not sight, and hope is not arrival at the condition hoped for. Both Pauline virtues beg for a completeness they themselves lack. But their incompleteness is not without its logic: the logic of the cross wants to keep us focused on the cross, which is not only Jesus' cross but the cross of the suffering creation that Jesus represents before God and in our behalf. We are not allowed to abandon that reality in favor of some otherworldly consummation, some paradisiacal ecstasy, and certainly not by regarding this or that present personal or political estate as though it were nicely compatible with that shalom for which Christian hope yearns. There is an ongoing dissatisfaction with "what is" in Christian hope. This applies as much to Christians in the developed as in the developing world, and in the former it should produce a far greater dissatisfaction than it does. For, as Pannenberg affirms, Christian hope "is sharply opposed to the emphatic worldliness of our secular culture"[6]—I would like to

add, however, our secular *and our religious* culture.[7] Too much religion (most of it Christian) on this continent is far too content with
itself and its consumerist context.[8]

Christian hope heightens our awareness of "what is wrong with
the world" (Segundo), including our religious institutions, but it also
gives us the courage to live in the world, to accept ("with serenity")
what cannot be changed in that world and in our own lives and "to
change what can be changed." Such hope provides for faith the necessary trust in life's ultimate *fulfillment* to render possible an exceptional openness to that which presently detracts from the
"abundance" of life promised by the Christ (John 10:10). Without
hope in something like a consummation of the promise of our own
lives, it is natural for us to repress awareness of the many ways in
which they lack fulfillment—in which we are living abysmally unful-
filled lives. It is not necessary, surely, to be able to spell out in detail
either *what* concretely such fulfillment could mean or *how* it could
be brought about. When we try to give specific content to the what
and the how of the vision of consummation that our hope yearns for
and struggles toward, we too often end either with mythic or pietistic language that is dated and incomprehensible[9] or else with ideals
that do not comfort but place further burdens upon ourselves and
others. As Pannenberg rightly notes, "In social life as well as in individual life it is necessary to accept the limitations of our human situation and not to indulge in exaggerated expectations and demands
on our friends and others."[10] Faith longs to be replaced by sight, and
hope by fulfillment, but both faith and hope, in their existential
inseparability, point to a future that is "not yet." And when we try to
force that future, turning the world, or the church, or our own life
with those around us into a visible foretaste, we replace gospel with
law—and law understood not as a "lamp unto my feet" but as an
unreachable ideal and merciless taskmaster.

We are constrained by the anticipation—and more so by the
actual experience—of our own dying to find satisfaction in this
inherently unsatisfactory thing, faith; this trust that fervently longs
to encounter "face to face" the one trusted and that, when it is

brought at last to the impossibility of trusting our own human strength, longs even more ardently for unhindered communion with its Source. What seems to occur sometimes, however, is that in extremis—at that very point where "all earthly helpers fail, and comforts cease"—this unsatisfactory faith, with its hope still unsatisfied, finds that it is *enough*. Not only is it the only possibility available to us then, but it suffices. Job has not yet received answers to his question (he never does; only more questions) when he gives voice to this sufficiency—and even prematurely (proleptically?) translates what he has only heard out of the whirlwind into the metaphor of sight:

> I had heard of thee by the hearing of the ear,
>   But now my eyes see thee. (42:5-6, KJV)

And Paul, the newer Testamental exemplar par excellence of this thin tradition, is content to believe that if we have already "united with [Christ] in a death like his, we will certainly be united with him in a resurrection like his" (Rom. 6:5). And he concludes, "whether we live or whether we die, we are the Lord's" (Rom. 14:8).

With only a few exceptions, and those tangential, biblical literature maintains an astonishing disinterest in the so-called afterlife. It is content to leave heaven to God, and hell too. It affirms judgment because it affirms justice, but it sustains a marvelous modesty about the specifics of the ultimate judgment, because it is persuaded of the abiding discontinuity ("gulf," Luke 16:26) between the ways of God and the ways of humankind. It is clear that God *wills* life, abundant life *(salus)* for all, and it is equally clear that no one under the loving dominion of this God will simply have salvation imposed upon him or her.

Beyond these foundational assumptions, I think, we can only go at the risk of exchanging the eschatology of the cross for an eschatology of glory. If this is construed as a reversion to an existentialist theology "purged . . . of its apocalyptic features" (Braaten),[11] so be it. I shall offer some other reasons for wariness about apocalyptic religion in the next section. Apocalypticism always wants signs and wonders—and of course it will always find them. But the theology of the cross sticks to "the sign of Jonah" (Matt.12:39)—that is, to the faith that sees what is hidden underneath death—*that* death: new life. Though he goes on to register quite other claims, Wolfhart Pannenberg affirms this same sufficiency of faith when, in the essay already quoted, he notes that: "Protagonists of a programme of demythologizing the biblical message had a point in reducing the content of Christian hope to faith in God and in considering all further explication in terms of life beyond death superfluous." He continues:

> Communion with the eternal is indeed the crucial thing. "If only I have you, I do not care for anything in heaven or on earth." This is what Luther found in Psalm 73:25, and the person whose life is so exclusively focused on God may also continue with the same psalm: "My flesh and my heart may fail, but God is my strength and my portion forever." (Ps. 73:26)[12]

The End of the World

Christian eschatology concerns itself not only with the destiny of persons but also with the "fate of the earth" (J. Schell), its species, its processes, its visible and invisible dimensions. Where it is an eschatology of the cross, many of the same presuppositions and conclusions as those pertaining to the personal dimension must be reiterated or, mutatis mutandis, applied. Above all, the termination of the macrocosm, like that of the microcosm, raises the teleological question—the question of purpose. Today, when the end of the world is not only a religious sentiment—the preoccupation of "crazies," as it was in my childhood—but a subject of scientific interest and almost daily reference on account of the many threats to planetary existence, the question of the purpose of life in all its forms is very close to the surface of social consciousness—and perhaps the most repressed of all questions.

It belongs to Christian faith, as to many other religions, to affirm that the world *is* purposed: its existence is neither random nor capricious. It is intended, and it is in essence good, indeed "very good"

(Genesis 1). Beyond this rudimentary affirmation, however, and even with the affirmation of the world's essential goodness, Christianity is deeply divided. For some (in the North American context for an extraordinary number, in fact) this world's purpose is understood to be transcendent of its own future; in fact, its purpose for many advocates of this approach (e.g., the best-selling Hal Lindsey) can only be attained through the ending of the world as such. It would be too drastic, perhaps, to say that for this point of view the purpose of the world as such is to destruct; yet so far beyond the created sphere is the *telos* that moves it that it must be questioned whether those following this line of thought would even wish to affirm the goodness of the creation. For at least the more extreme expressions of this position, in fact, a Gnostic or Manichean tendency to denigrate and deplore the created order (matter being vastly inferior to spirit) is implicit. And this extreme, as with all extremes, represents a tendency so close to the heart of the most self-consciously spiritualistic forms of the faith that one can find, in many places where one would rather not find it, a certain readiness to be done with the world. For such a mentality, the material world, even if it is not the work of an inferior deity like the *Demiurgos* of the Gnostics, is experienced as a sphere of unending sorrow, a vale of tears, a quagmire of temptation, a place of unrelenting struggle between good and evil, etc.; while this world must be endured, salvation entails the effective distancing of the self from its tumults and finally the soul's release from bondage to its necessities.

If what I have claimed for the *theologia crucis* in the foregoing chapters has any validity at all, then one must conclude that such an attitude to the end of the world (in both senses) cannot find any place within this tradition. I have affirmed that the cross of Jesus Christ represents the absolute claim upon the world of the God who created and sustains it, that the message of the cross is that this world is the beloved of God and must not be abandoned, and that the church is that community of faith freed sufficiently from preoccupation with self and institutional survival to seek the welfare of the human city *(civitas terrena)*, to resist that which destroys it, and to

steward the good within it. Such a faith is a clear denial of every continuing propensity within historical Christianity to follow the coun-
sels of all types of spirituality, Christian and non-Christian, for
which creation can only attain its end by passing away. That much
can be said with certainty.

But how, under the aegis of this thin tradition, should we respond
to the question of worldly purpose? If we refuse to make common
cause with those who locate the world's end *(telos)* in and *beyond* its
ending *(terminus),* how can we describe and embrace a purpose that
is both worthy of human faith and credible in the face of the termination of planetary existence that is now a matter of scientific analysis, however distant the end may be, however it may through
changed human attitudes or technological cleverness be postponed?
We have made it clear enough that, if the theology of the cross rejects
world abandonment, it also rejects—or at least seriously questions—
the liberal theology of historical progress that assumes a gradual perfecting of the world. Thus we seem to have opted for a worldview
that looks for a worldly purpose that is neither wholly extrinsic to the
world itself nor wholly intrinsic. We cannot accept a teleology that
locates the *telos* of the world entirely beyond its actual history; nor
can we accept a teleology that finds all the purpose it needs within
the conditions of nature and history, within the *saeculo.* Either this
leaves us at a standstill, or else a third alternative will have to be
found.

We had better recognize from the start that such an alternative is
bound to appear complex, perhaps even contradictory, in comparison with the two positions we have ruled out. For both of those positions are essentially simple (I would say simplistic): that is the secret
of their popular appeal. The first position is simple in the sense that
it resolves the problem of purpose in a world that does not give sufficient evidence of the same by positing a transcendent purpose that
purports not to need any worldly confirmation. The second position
is equally simple, though undoubtedly harder to follow through on
ethically; it resolves the problem of purpose for the world by positing
a consummation toward which the processes of nature and history

are progressively moving. Both positions ask for a single article of belief with respect to the eschatological question: (1) purpose is found in the God who transcends the created order; (2) purpose is built into the created order itself.

In relation to this singularity of faith, what has to be put forward as the *eschatologia crucis* will seem complicated, especially in a religious context such as ours, shaped as it is by the ongoing tussle of these two opposing but simplistic alternatives. For what the theology of the cross calls for is an eschatology that affirms both the transcendent purposing of the world, *yet without bypassing the world,* and the belief that purpose inheres in the structure of the world, *yet without assuming necessity.* The latter clause in each phrase already bespeaks the complexity in question. But this complexity is required if we are to avoid the pitfalls of the two other positions.

We must avoid the pitfall of liberal progressivism, because the world simply cannot bear the burden of providing clear-cut evidence of its own purposefulness. Therefore with the conservative doctrinal tradition we are constrained to locate the agency of worldly purpose strictly in God the creator. But we must avoid as well the transcendentalism that finds the world as such incapable of receiving, approximating, or mirroring that transcendent purpose, for that is effectively to abandon the world to vanity. Thus with the liberal doctrinal tradition we are constrained to affirm that God's purpose for the world must be immanently and not only transcendently understood. For Christians the necessity for seeing purpose *in* and not only *above* or *beyond* the world lies supremely in the incarnation and cross of the Christ. A christological perspective on the subject does not allow us to confine our witness to divine purpose to the transcendent: If God is not only the transcendent sovereign of the world's unfolding but one who in the Christ has actually entered the historical process, history itself must be seen to be purposeful. This christological concentration does not mean that Christians are oblivious of other signs of purpose in nature and history: christocentrism, unlike christomonism, does not translate into a total disinterest in "general revelation" (Brunner), but it does mean that the Christian's entrée into a grateful awareness of worldly purpose is this event—an event that at once recognizes the *difficulty* of finding the world purposeful and provides the insight and courage necessary to affirm such purpose despite all the evidence to the contrary. Belief in the purposefulness of the world is thus for Christians not first a matter of empirical observation (though Luther too knew how to find purpose and wonder in a single grain of wheat), but a matter of faith and hope. If God in Christ has become incarnate (immersed in matter), then matter certainly cannot be conceived as inherently inferior, unreal, or evil. The theology of redemption does not bypass creation but affirms and accentuates its essential goodness. The finite, by grace, has a capacity for the infinite (*finitum capax infiniti*).

With this extraordinarily world-affirming faith as our spiritual point of departure, Christians not only expect to find intimations of purpose in the world at large but *are themselves drawn into the purposing labor of God*. The Christian ethic, as we have already seen, has its genesis and stimulus precisely in this participatory involvement in the *providentia Dei*. While the notion that divine purpose utterly transcends the world itself is thus rejected by this theological tradition, the second (liberal progressive) position is also found unsatisfactory. In saying that through the revelation of the Christ we find transcendent purpose mirrored immanently, *yet without assuming necessity,* we are rejecting the modern liberal belief in progress, that is, the gradual unfolding of ever-greater purposefulness. Nothing at all guarantees such an evolution of the Good. Nothing at all can be assumed about the future as improvement over the past. Superficial improvements such as those in the sphere of applied science, for example, do not automatically translate into cultural, spiritual, or human betterment. To the contrary, it has been said by many in our time that we are a society of improved means to deteriorated ends. The twentieth century, though remarkable in many ways, was after all not the improvement over the nineteenth that its early promoters assured us it would be; nor will the twenty-first century be, necessarily, better than the twentieth—it could be worse, much worse!

What are we left with? We are left, I think, with a deeply meaningful perspective on our world and a highly challenging vocation within it. The world is not *fated* to either evil or unambiguous good, destruction or fulfillment—neither the destruction of the apocalyptic dispensationalists nor the inevitable fulfillment of modernity. Good and evil, wheat and tares, light and darkness, struggle together. Each day brings its new possibilities and its new impossibilities: doors open; other doors close. We believe, as disciples of the crucified one, that the essential goodness of the world, its nature and its history, cannot be thwarted, for God is committed to it in long-suffering love. The God of the exodus and the cross has goodwill toward, and good intentions for, the world. The song of the Christmas angels echoes the ancient faith of the patriarchs: "Glory to God in the highest heaven, and on earth peace among those whom he favors" (Luke 2:14). Yet we are not and cannot be complacent or passive in relation to this assurance; for the measure with which we are grasped by that divine blessing is the measure with which we ourselves are made active participants in its promise.

Apocalyptic and Prophetic Themes in Christian Eschatology

It is just here, I think, that we should consider the difference between an apocalyptic and a prophetic approach to Christian eschatology. "The word 'apocalypse' *(apokalupsis)* means a 'revelation' or 'unveiling,' so that an apocalyptic book claims to reveal things which are normally hidden and to unveil the future."[13] As the well-known American Lutheran theologian Carl E. Braaten notes in the recent collection from which I have drawn several times in this chapter, apocalyptic literature characteristically perceives the world in terms of "spiritual warfare": a "cosmic struggle [is] being fought out on the planet earth."[14] Good and evil, the divine and the demonic, truth and lies, Christ and Antichrist battle for the soul of the creature and the possession of the creation. This colossal struggle is hidden from ordinary sight, but to faith the truth of the situation is revealed.

Braaten (with some of the other contributors to the volume in question) is persuaded that this "apocalyptic perspective" is needed today: "The apocalyptic message is given to communities whose social and cultural worlds are collapsing. The time is ripe and the need is great to recover the apocalyptic imagination in order to strengthen our backbone and stiffen our Christian resistance in face of the rapid moral decline and cultural decay that our society is undergoing."[15] Braaten feels that modern secularity and "one-dimensionality," expressed in the demythologizing programs of modern systematic and biblical theologies from Ritschl to Bultmann, has robbed Protestant Christianity of its apocalyptic clarity, purging the New Testament of its "apocalyptic features," doing away with the "dualistic features of biblical cosmology," and leaving mainline Protestantism with "a wishy-washy attitude on the difference between right and wrong, good and evil, truth and lies, facts and fiction."[16]

One may agree that once-mainline Protestantism is woefully lacking in both theological wisdom and ethical vigor, but is the remedy for this the strong medicine of "apocalyptic imagination" that Braaten recommends? Certainly the cross of Christ, seen from the perspective of the resurrection faith of the church, reveals depths of good and evil, the divine and the demonic, that are theologically clarifying and ethically inspiring, but does not the apocalyptic mindset tend to ignore the distinction between faith and sight, hope and finality, love and power? Does it not lay claim to more revelation than can be glimpsed in an event that conceals while it reveals? Are the faithful already liberated from the realms not only of doubt and ambiguity but also of mystery? Do they no longer see "through a glass, darkly"? "Faith," declared the writer of Hebrews in a sentence so frequently called upon by Martin Luther as to be thought almost his motto, "is the assurance of things hoped for, the conviction of things not seen" (11:1). In a society that has made a certain statement about itself in the fact that apocalyptic works like those of Hal Lindsey become fabulous best-sellers, one has to wonder whether the apocalyptic imagination is not prone to seeing a great deal more than faith, so understood, warrants.

One does not of course imply that there is any comparison between Lindsey and Braaten. Yet as even the restrained and scholarly work of the latter shows, it is difficult for the apocalyptic approach to refrain from identifying "cosmic struggle" too transparently in terms of particular biases of the observer or author. Thus, while Braaten makes passing reference to phenomena such as racism, environmental "poisoning," nuclearism, homelessness, and other contemporary concerns, he seems particularly disturbed by "the culture wars that are fast eroding the fundamentals of religion, morality, and law," and quotes approvingly the proposal of Peter Kreeft that an "ecumenical jihad" be declared upon the same. With many other Americans, he seems to find the most telling evidence of our growing capitulation to the Antichrist in matters sexual:

> When abortion and homosexual behavior, things that clearly contradict the commandments of God and two thousand years of Christian teaching, are accepted as merely matters of personal choice and lifestyle preference, we find ourselves up to our noses in the sludge of social decay and decadence. It boggles the mind. Politicians, the majority of them, tolerate laws of lenience in the name of enlightenment; educators *en masse* endorse them; the media celebrate them. Meanwhile the churches are divided; theologians, many of the best of them, have long since slid down the slippery slopes of relativism and pluralism.[17]

One can readily grant that North American society is morally confused, but if we are looking for evil on the grand scale—"principalities and powers"—would it not be more appropriate to expatiate on social evils by which the whole well-being of the planet is threatened?—the obscene disparity between the few rich and the many poor, the depletion of vital resources and entire species, rampant consumerism in the developed world, etc., etc. And why does Braaten pay so little attention to the problematic political, military, and cultural imperialism of his own nation? Having rather necessarily alluded to the Apocalypse of John, with its background of imperial Rome as the current disguise of "the Beast," he does, it is true, use the term *the American Empire,* which many of his compatriots are reluctant to do. But if it is really cosmic struggle that we are seeking to illuminate, most of the world beyond the United States of America (including those of us in friendly nations who are nevertheless increasingly conscious of the price we must pay for this friendship) would be prepared to elaborate more than Braaten does on the similarities of Rome and America—and indeed of any people, however admirable in other respects, who assume the mantle of Empire.

The language of apocalypse can be very heady stuff, but it can also be extremely questionable and dangerous. When its resort to biblical and medieval imagery (the Devil, Antichrist, cosmic struggle, the Beast and the Dragon, etc.) is not just anachronistic and apologetically irresponsible, it too easily encourages a mood of paranoia and irrationality that is never far from the surface of human social consciousness. Christians in America today, and among America's friends, who resort to the language of "cosmic warfare" and ecumenical "jihad" and a "backbone" stiffened against moral decay and so forth must ask themselves, no matter what their cause, to what extent their witness contributes to the warmongering, enemy-imaging, and self-righteous moral vigilance of a society that needs to locate its problems outside itself in order to be able to maintain its value system and its lofty image of itself intact.

Luther was right to have qualms about the book of Revelation.[18] Even if (as another author in the stimulating volume *The Last Things* suggests[19]) the mature Luther grew less negative in his attitude toward this biblical writing, he remained sufficiently skeptical of apocalypticism and of its contemporary enthusiasts (the spiritualizers and *Schwärmer*) to warrant the supposition that he suspected this approach, too, of too much "glory." The apocalyptic imagination may, under certain circumstances, help the disciple community to discern more clearly "the signs of the times." But if its tendency toward self-righteousness and fanaticism is to be avoided, then even in those special circumstances the apocalyptic impulse needs to be held in check by a sober, apollonian reasonableness that refuses to give in to dionysian frenzy. Dietrich Bonhoeffer, whose name and example are evoked by some in this connection, did not easily or recklessly identify Nazism with absolute evil; the Barmen Declaration, while sharply distinguishing between obedience to the *one* Lord and other reputed "Leaders," reads like a well-considered and nuanced confession of faith and not a revolutionary call to arms against "principalities and powers" that can be correlated unequivocally with evil earthly powers and distinguished with equal alacrity from the reputed good of the earth.

Ernst Käsemann's well-known aphorism that "Apocalyptic was the mother of all Christian theology" may be historically accurate, but it does not mean that this "mother" was a single mother, who parented the church all by herself. If John is tempted by apocalypticism (that is, if the writer of the Fourth Gospel is in fact also the author of the Apocalypse), Paul certainly is not, despite his use of some language that can be co-opted for the purpose. And even if Christians are able to find minimal warranty in Scripture for apocalyptic conceptualization, they ought to be at least equally conscious of the Bible's explicit and implicit *critique* of apocalyptic and its obvious preference for disciplined and measured thought. Above all, the close attention that both Bible and the most prophetic Christian traditions pay to sensitivity to context should help Christians in the affluent societies of the North today to realize that apocalypticism too easily condones a worldview that locates the good too readily in our way of life and looks for the enemy "out there" in the world's Saddam Husseins and Osama bin Ladens—to mention only the most publicized of our current search for enemy images *(Feindbilder)*.

For these reasons I find myself in complete agreement with another of the authors of the important little volume of contemporary reflections on "last things"—Old Testament scholar Paul Hanson—when he affirms that the eschatology appropriate to our context must accentuate the *prophetic* and not the apocalyptic dimension. The prophetic office, as Abraham Heschel insisted, is steeped in a heightened consciousness of the divine pathos—that is, of God's compassion for and solidarity with human creaturehood: God is for us, not forever poised to "zap" us in our wickedness. Even God's judgment and wrath are functions of God's mercy. "Prophetic politics" therefore are the politics of historical responsibility: it is the intention of the prophet, even in his or her most cutting pronouncements, to render those who hear more committed to the flourishing in history of the divine purpose. This is encapsulated, says Hanson, in the Lord's Prayer: "Thy kingdom come, thy will be done, on earth as it is in heaven."

The prophetic approach, Hanson insists, is the normative biblical approach to "last things." It is not implied that the apocalyptic is ruled out entirely. As the two "monumental apocalyptic writings in the Bible, Daniel and the Book of Revelation," demonstrate, there are "conditions" under which apocalyptic eschatological thought is appropriate. These are times when the faithful "found themselves in situations of such extreme persecution that the prophetic model of translating the justice and mercy associated with God's reign into the institutions and structures of society was categorically unviable." Hanson identifies the stand of the Confessing Church under Hitler (he mentions specifically Bonhoeffer and Hans Lilje) as occurring under such conditions. But when the apocalyptic is pursued under less drastic contextual circumstances, it all too regularly stems "not from commitment to God's universal reign of justice and compassion [but] from the lust for human power and the perversion of religion into an instrument of crude self-centered fantasizing."[20]

"What can be stated with a certainty," concludes Hanson, "is this: Given the circumstances within which the church exists in most parts of the Western world today, the biblical model that should guide its interaction with society and world is the prophetic model."[21]

In sum: We do not know how or when this world might end. It is not for faith to speculate about the day or the hour (Matt. 24:36) but only to trust the one whose creature Time is. What we do know is that the God revealed in the continuity of the Testaments and supremely in the crucified one is committed to the creation and to its full realization of the divine intention for it (John 10:10). We ourselves are being granted a sufficient glimpse of God's purposing work and a sufficient freedom from anxiety to participate in that work. Each day, each year, decade, and century, we are given opportunities to exercise critical judgment and active responsibility for the implementation of will of God "on earth as it is in heaven." We are not promised that our work will automatically contribute to the coming reign of God—unlike the nineteenth-century liberals, we can never again indulge in the assumption that that kingdom is just around the corner. But "proximate goals" (Reinhold Niebuhr) are achievable, and if they appear nothing but "gradual measures, minor improvements, piecemeal changes, or just a little bit of progress,"[22] that is unfortunate. They will appear so only to the grand apocalyptic visionaries who cannot be satisfied with anything short of a total transformation—which is to say, the termination of the world as we (and mortals generally) have known it. The faith of the cross does not wish to court or to hasten that ending; it only wishes to pass through it, *en Christo,* to the new being that is already possible within the structures of the old.

Notes

Preface

1. *Thinking the Faith* (1991); *Professing the Faith* (1993); *Confessing the Faith* (1996); Minneapolis: Fortress Press.

Introduction

1. The article was first published by the Washington Post Writers Group and appeared in *The National Post* [Toronto], vol. 5, no. 37 (Dec. 9, 2002) A14.

2. *The Crucified God: The Cross of Christ as the Foundation and Criticism of Christian Theology,* trans. R. A. Wilson and John Bowden (Philadelphia: Fortress Press, 1974), 3.

3. Ibid., 69.

4. John Keats, "Ode to a Nightingale," stanza 6.

1. What *Is* the Theology of the Cross?

1. *Lighten Our Darkness: Toward an Indigenous Theology of the Cross* (Philadelphia: Westminster, 1976). See the revised edition published by Academic Renewal Press (Lima, Ohio, 2001), edited and with a foreword by David Monge.

2. "In English-speaking circles especially [theology of the cross] represents a confessional narrowness or even a gross misinterpretation, and these opinions have had unfortunate effects in ecumenical conversations" ("The Pauline Theology of the Cross," *Interpretation* 14, no. 2 [April 1970] 151).

3. Luther did not employ the term *theologia crucis* frequently, but, as Gerhard Ebeling writes, "the expression serves as an indication of the object of his constant concern, the fundamental orientation of his theological

thought" (*Luther: An Introduction to His Thought,* trans. R. A. Wilson [London: Collins, 1970], 227).

4. It is perhaps surprising to claim that anglosaxon Protestants are "unfamiliar" with the Lutheran side of the Reformation. After living for many decades in both worlds, however—both the anglo-Protestant and the Germanic-Protestant worlds—I have had to conclude that there are significant differences between the two that, with few exceptions, neither profoundly comprehend. English-speaking Protestants tend to lump together all of the Reformers, assuming that Luther differs from the others only in being the pioneering spirit of the sixteenth-century movement away from Rome. But there are factors in Luther's reform—both doctrinal and broadly cultural—that distinguish it from both the French/Swiss and the English Reformation experience. One could say, perhaps metaphorically, that it is the difference between Bach and Handel. A sense of mystery, paradox, and the ongoing struggle between opposites informs Germanic cultural and religious consciousness that is not true of the other western European Protestant groupings. As I have sometimes tried to put it "in a word," neither a French nor an English musician could have composed Brahms's "German Requiem."

It is this profound spiritual/cultural distinction, more than specific ideas or doctrines, that prevents most English-speaking Christians from comprehending in depth the thought of Martin Luther. This is nowhere more manifestly so than in connection with Luther's theology of the cross.

5. The critical theology of Dietrich Bonhoeffer, perhaps the greatest exponent of the theology of the cross in the modern church, was from start (*The Cost of Discipleship*) to finish (the final passages of *Letters and Papers from Prison*) a protest against the substitution of mere doctrine, or personalistic piety, for the more radical and indeed *political* living out of this tradition on the part of a complacent Christendom.

6. *The Crucified God: The Cross of Christ as the Foundation and Criticism of Christian Theology,* trans. R. A. Wilson and John Bowden (Philadelphia: Fortress Press, 1974), 3 (italics added).

7. While the term *Christendom* is often used loosely to refer to the whole body of Christian believers, I shall use it in the more specific historical and etymologically accurate sense to mean the cultic and political predominance of the Christian religion in Western civilization from the fourth century C.E. to the modern epoch. I distinguish sharply between Christendom and Christianity or the Christian faith. See chapter 8 of this study and also

my small work titled *The End of Christendom and the Future of Christianity* (Eugene, Or.: Wipf and Stock, 2002).

8. *Luther's Theology of the Cross: Martin Luther's Theological Breakthrough* (Oxford: Blackwell, 1985).

9. Grand Rapids: Eerdmans, 2001. The learned Scottish theologian T. F. Torrance called Lewis's study "the most remarkable and moving book I have ever read" (from the book jacket).

10. But see Bernhard Lohse (*Martin Luther's Theology: Its Historical and Systematic Development*, trans. Roy A. Harrisville [Minneapolis: Fortress Press, 1999], 36ff.), who traces the "prehistory of [the] formation" of this theology by Luther, demonstrating its "unequivocally antischolastic sense."

11. See Timothy F. Lull, ed., *Martin Luther's Basic Theological Writings* (Minneapolis: Fortress Press, 1989), 30ff.

12. Lohse, *Martin Luther's Theology*, 217.

13. Wendell Berry, *Life is a Miracle: An Essay against Modern Superstition* (Washington, D.C.: Counterpoint, 2000), 60.

14. See Lohse, *Martin Luther's Theology*, 37.

15. Interestingly, Paul Tillich traces this transmutation to Phillip Melanchthon, who "intellectualized faith. The element of trust, or *fiducia*, was shortchanged in favor of *assensus*, of assent or belief in correct doctrine. This led to the blight of Protestant Orthodoxy which lives on in fundamentalist biblicism. Nothing has done more to alienate modern men and women from religion" (George Lindbeck, "An Assessment Reassessed: Paul Tillich on the Reformation," *Journal of Religion* 63, no. 4 [Oct. 1983] 381). See also Tillich, *Systematic Theology*, 3 vols. (Chicago: University of Chicago Press, 1951–63), 2:178.

16. In Latin: *Theologus gloriae dicit malum bonum et bonum malum. Theologus crucis dicit id res est.* In German: *Der Theologe der Gottes unverborgene Herrlichkeit sucht, nennt das übel gut und Gutes übel; der Theologe des Kreuzes nennt die Dinge beim rechten Namen.*

17. *Agape and Eros*, trans. Philip S. Watson (Philadelphia: Westminster, 1953).

18. Martin Luther, Christmas sermon in *Readings in Christian Thought*, ed. H. T. Kerr (Nashville: Abingdon, 1966), 157.

19. See Wilhelm Pauck, "Luther's Faith," in *From Luther to Tillich: The Reformers and Their Heirs*, ed. Marion Pauck (San Francisco: Harper & Row, 1984), 8.

20. In the third century C.E., the Sabellians (or Monarchians), wishing to stress the unity principle in the godhead, were accused of the heresy of believing that God the Father actually suffered in the suffering of the Son. Henceforth, mainstream doctrine avoided any hint of such a belief.

21. See Moltmann, *The Crucified God*, 65.

22. Jon Sobrino, *Christology at the Crossroads: A Latin American Approach,* trans. John Drury (Maryknoll, N.Y.: Orbis, 1978), 182.

23. For instance, Dorothee Soelle in her book *Political Theology* (Philadelphia: Fortress Press, 1971) writes: "By ideology I understand a system of propositional truths independent of the situation, a superstructure no longer relevant to praxis, to the situation, to the real questions of life" (231). Similarly, Gustavo Gutiérrez (*A Theology of Liberation: History, Politics, and Salvation,* trans. Sister Caridad Inda and John Eagleson [Maryknoll, N.Y.: Orbis, 1973], 234–35) writes: "The term *ideology* has a long and varied history and has been understood in very different ways. But we can basically agree that ideology does not offer adequate and scientific knowledge of reality; rather, it masks it. Ideology does not rise above the empirical, irrational level. Therefore it spontaneously fulfills a function of preservation of the established order. Therefore, also, ideology tends to dogmatize all that has not succeeded in separating itself from it or has fallen under its influence. Political action, science and faith do not escape this danger."

Reinhold Niebuhr was also very conscious of the dangers of ideology in theological work: "All human knowledge is tainted with an 'ideological taint.' It pretends to be more true than it is. It is finite knowledge, gained from a particular perspective; but it pretends to be final and ultimate. Exactly analogous to the cruder pride of power, the pride of intellect is derived on the one hand from an attempt to obscure the known conditioned character of human knowledge and the taint of self-interest in human truth" (*The Nature and Destiny of Man: A Christian Interpretation* [Gifford Lectures of 1939; New York: Scribner's, 1949], 194–95).

24. José Míguez Bonino, *Doing Theology in a Revolutionary Situation* (Philadelphia: Fortress Press, 1975), xxvi.

25. Quoted in *MacLeans* 110, no. 3 (January 20, 1997) 15.

26. "He was an adept and thorough thinker. In all his judgements he was motivated, not by a flight away from thought, but by the discipline of the kind of thought that was appropriate to theology. Consequently, the question which concerns him . . . is not that of an antithesis between philosophy and theology in general, but that of an antithesis between good and bad the-

ology, between true theology and pseudo-theology" (John M. Todd, *Luther: An Introduction to His Thought* [London: Collins, 1970], 79).

27. E. Theodore Bachmann, "Introduction," *Word and Sacrament I, Luther's Works,* 55 vols. (Philadelphia: Fortress Press, and St. Louis: Concordia, 1955–86), 35:116.

28. Quoted by Martin E. Marty, *The Christian Century* (Nov. 30, 1983) 119.

29. *Waiting for God,* trans. Emma Craufurd (New York: Harper & Row, 1973), 69.

30. Pauck, "Luther's Faith," in *From Luther to Tillich,* 6–7.

31. *God Hidden and Revealed* (Philadelphia: Muhlenburg, 1953), 57.

32. *The Christian Century* (June 6-13, 2001) 32.

33. Kazuo Kitamori, *Theology of the Pain of God* (Richmond: John Knox, 1965), 46.

34 Paul Tillich, *The Shaking of the Foundations* (New York: Scribner's, 1953), 148. The sermon is titled, "He Who Is the Christ."

2. Theology of the Cross as Contextual Theology

1. See chapter 10 for the elaboration of this point.

2. Luther understood this intuitively, and therefore he would not separate cross and resurrection. The resurrection is not the undoing of the failure of the cross; it is the unveiling of its "success"—that is, of its intentionality, and of the *interiority* of the victory it already achieves. That victory can only be grasped in its fullness if it is premised on the reality of the divine freedom: it might not have happened that way at all! God is not obliged to embrace the fallen creation. Jesus Christ *could have said no to the cross,* that is, to human and worldly solidarity. (That, for instance, is the presupposition of the reference to "legions of angels" that might appear in defense of the arrested Nazarene—well, and of the entire narrative.) The drinking of the "cup of destiny," which is both divine reaffirmation of the decision to love and human affirmation of creaturehood, is already the victory that faith apprehends and celebrates. Not the vindication of God's glory (which does not need vindicating), but the realization of God's compassion: that is the victory. And not the deification and immortalization of the human (which could only be capitulation to religious hubris) but the joyful acceptance of our creaturehood: that is the victory.

3. Wiesel writes that the great gift God gave to humankind was not the gift of beginning—only God can begin—but God gave to human beings

what is perhaps an even greater gift, the capacity to "begin again" (*Messengers of God,* trans. Marion Wiesel [New York: Pocket Books, 1977], 42).

4. See my *When You Pray: Thinking Your Way into God's World* (Eugene, Or.: Wipf and Stock, 2003).

5. Dorothee Soelle, *The Silent Cry: Mysticism and Resistance,* trans. Barbara and Martin Rumscheidt (Minneapolis: Fortress Press, 2001), 179.

6. See in this connection Sallie McFague's *Life Abundant: Rethinking Theology and Economy for a Planet in Peril* (Minneapolis: Fortress Press, 2001). Note especially her "Manifesto to North American Middle-Class Christians," 205–10.

7. See David Suzuki and Holly Dressel, *From Naked Ape to Superspecies: A Personal Perspective on Humanity and the Global Eco-Crisis* (Toronto: Stoddart, 1999), 42.

8. "The Christian ideal has not been tried and found wanting. It has been found difficult; and left untried" (*What's Wrong with the World?* [London: Cassel, 1910], 22).

3. Engaging the World

1. One of the neglected books of our era, Helmut Gollwitzer's *Unwilling Journey: A Diary from Russia* (trans. E. M. Delacour [London: SCM, 1953]), takes its original German title directly from this Johannine verse: *und fuehren, wohin du nicht willst.* It is the great theologian's diary of his life in a Russian prison camp during and after World War II. I can think of no better extended illustration of the thesis of this chapter.

2. This point has often been missed by those who (rightly!) accentuate the suffering that belongs to the Christian life. Dietrich Bonhoeffer, who is sometimes held up as an exemplary martyr, was adamant on the point: suffering is *not* the object of discipleship; only *obedience* ("Follow me!") can be that object. This theme, which the young theologian developed in his *Nachfolge* (*The Cost of Discipleship,* trans. R. H. Fuller [London: SCM, 1959]) is the leitmotiv of all his subsequent writings, in which "obedience" is more and more explicitly defined in terms of worldliness—that is, profound involvement in one's worldly context. Suffering is not sought, but is the inevitable consequence of such involvement.

3. "The Christian is not a *homo religiosus,* but a man [*sic*], pure and simple, just as Jesus was man, compared with John the Baptist anyhow. I don't mean the shallow this-worldliness of the enlightened, of the busy, the comfortable or the lascivious. It's something much more profound than that,

something in which the knowledge of death and resurrection is ever present. I believe Luther lived a this-worldly life in this sense" (*Letters and Papers from Prison,* trans. R. H. Fuller [London: SCM, 1953], 168).

4. See for example Paul Tillich, "Introduction," in *Systematic Theology,* 3 vols. (Chicago: University of Chicago Press, 1951–63), 1:6–8.

5. As an example of Christian apologetics, see my *Why Christian? For Those on the Edge of Faith* (Minneapolis: Fortress Press, 1998).

6. The famous statement is found, in fact, in the first paragraph of book one: "*Tu fecisti nos ad te, Domine, et inquietum est cor nostrum donec requiescat in te.*"

7. On a personal note, and to illustrate the point under discussion, I may say that the very first course that I took in theology was titled not "Systematic Theology" or "Philosophy of Religion" but "Christian Apologetics." It was taught by the most dignified Anglican bishop I have ever known, a great scholar, and it was designed to take on all the questioners of religious faith current in the first part of the twentieth century—Durkheim, Freud, Nietzsche, Marx, and others—because it belongs to the apologetic tradition to face, squarely, the foe and the denier. But since there is a foe and denier in all of us, it is addressed as much to the believer as to the unbeliever.

8. "Nature and Grace," in *Natural Theology,* trans. Peter Fraenkel (London: Geoffrey Bles/Centenary Press, 1946).

9. Ibid., 65ff.

10. See my *Remembered Voices: Reclaiming the Legacy of "Neo-Orthodoxy"* (Louisville: Westminster John Knox, 1998).

11. Hitler certainly oversimplified both Nietzsche and Wagner. Yet he could legitimately *make use of* both, because both registered serious complaints about the Christian faith. In Nietzsche's case, the complaints are explicit; in Wagner's they are ambiguous enough that, for example, his last great opera, *Parsifal,* can still be attended by devout Christians who imagine that this tale of the Holy Grail is a kind of Christian passion play. That it is no such thing is perhaps best appreciated by discerning Jews, who refuse to identify genuine Christianity with the kind of anti-Semitism cloaked by the opera and made very explicit in Wagner's writings.

12. See my essay "Barmen: Lesson in Theology," *Toronto Journal of Theology* 1, no. 2 (fall 1985).

13. It would be difficult, in fact, to find a more *contextually sensitive* statement than Barth's response to the same Emil Brunner at the time of the suppression of the Hungarian revolution by the USSR. Brunner, like others

at the time, complained that Barth did not denounce Marxist oppression with the same kerygmatic ardor as he denounced Nazism. Barth replied: "You do not seem to understand. At the moment I am not rousing the Church to oppose Communism and to witness against it, in the same way as I did between 1933 and 1945 in the case of National Socialism. . . . The Church never thinks, speaks, or acts 'on principle.' Rather it judges spiritually and by individual cases. For that reason it rejects every attempt to systematize political history and its own part in that history. Therefore, it preserves the freedom to judge each new event afresh. If yesterday it travelled along one path, it is not bound to keep to the same path today. If yesterday it spoke from its position of responsibility, then today it should be silent if in this position it considers silence to be the better course. The unity and continuity of theology will be best preserved if the Church does not let itself be discouraged from being up-to-date theologically" (*Against the Stream: Shorter Post-War Writings* [London: SCM, 1954], 113ff.).

14. *Luther's Theology of the Cross,* trans. Herbert J. Bouman (Belfast: Christian Journals, 1976), 52–58.

15. For the teaching of Paul on the subject, see Charles B. Cousar, *A Theology of the Cross: The Death of Jesus in the Pauline Letters* (Minneapolis: Fortress Press, 1990).

16. See Paul Tillich's seminal essay on this distinction, "The Two Types of Philosophy of Religion," in *Theology of Culture,* ed. Robert C. Kimball (New York: Oxford University Press, 1959), 10ff.

17. *Jesus: The Crucified People* (New York: Crossroads/Meyer-Stone, 1989).

18. Moltmann, *The Crucified God: The Cross of Christ as the Foundation and Criticism of Christian Theology,* trans. R. A. Wilson and John Bowden (Philadelphia: Fortress Press, 1974), 4.

19. *The Crucifixion of Jesus: History, Myth, Faith* (Minneapolis: Fortress Press, 1995), 217.

4. The Crucified God

1. I capitalize the word *Theology* when it refers explicitly to the doctrine of God; lowercase *theology* signifies the discipline of systematic (dogmatic, constructive, etc.) theology.

2. Kenneth Clark, *Civilization* (London: British Broadcasting Corporation and John Murray, 1969), 77–78.

3. In an extended conversation with me in 1989, Kitamori stressed repeatedly his conviction that North American Christians on the whole

were incapable of appreciating the biblical concept of God's *suffering* love *(agape)* because our culture had so sentimentalized love, removing from it the pain that is always involved in profound relationships of love. His theology of the pain of God may be best exemplified in the novels of his compatriot Shusaku Endo, who was influenced by Kitamori. See especially Endo's *Silence,* trans. William Johnston (Tokyo: Sophia University Press, 1969). See also my essay, "Theological Reflections on Shusaku Endo's *Silence,*" *Interpretation* 33, no. 3 (1979) 254–67.

4. "For the sake of clarity, this sentence ['God is love'] is to be read with the emphasis on the word God, whereas we have fallen into the habit of emphasizing the word love. *God* is love; that is to say not a human attitude, a conviction or a deed, but God Himself is love. Only he who knows God knows what love is" (Dietrich Bonhoeffer, *Ethics,* trans. Neville Horton Smith [London: SCM, 1955], 173).

5 Cited by James Carroll in his *Constantine's Sword: The Church and the Jews* (Boston: Houghton Mifflin, 2001), 15 (italics added).

6. "Innocent III was unquestionably a man of personal humility and piety, but no Pope ever had higher conceptions of the papal office and under him the papacy reached its highest actual power" (Williston Walker, *A History of the Christian Church* [rev. ed.; New York: Scribner's, 1959], 259).

7. Whether a new Christendom is being born among the churches of the Southern Hemisphere (Africa, Asia, Latin America) is a question that we shall have to tackle later; my argument here refers to the historical Christendom of the West (including parts of the Near East).

8. I say "fortunately" because Paul's point would be lost if the problem to which he alludes were narrowly defined. *Whatever* his (or our) particular "thorn," what it betokens is a lack of self-sufficiency, the knowledge of which makes the human being open to undeserved and unearnable grace.

9. Robert McAfee Brown, ed., *The Essential Reinhold Niebuhr: Selected Essays and Addresses* (New Haven: Yale University Press, 1986), 22.

10. This refers to the mutuality or interdependence of the being and acting of the three *personae* of the Trinity. Each person—Father, Son, and Spirit—reflects the others. The dogma is based on John 10:28-38 and was important in the thought of the Cappadocian fathers, Augustine, Hilary, and many others.

11. As many have pointed out, the only term in both the Apostles' and the Nicene Creeds descriptive of the *life* of Jesus as distinct from his birth, death, and resurrection is the term *suffered.*

12. *Atonement in Literature and Life* (Boston: Houghton and Mifflin, 1906), 232.

13. On the question of Christian supersessionism see the excellent study of R. Kendall Soulen, *The God of Israel and Christian Theology* (Minneapolis: Fortress Press, 1996).

14. As Moltmann points out, Luther gleaned this phrase from "the theology of the mysticism of the cross in the late Middle Ages" (*The Crucified God: The Cross of Christ as the Foundation and Criticism of Christian Theology,* trans. R. A. Wilson and John Bowden [Philadelphia: Fortress Press, 1974], 47). A reference in Luther himself is found in Martin Luther, *Luthers Werke: Kritische Gesamtausgabe (Schriften),* 65 vols. (Weimar: H. Böhlau, 1883–1993), 1:614, 17.

15. *Letters and Papers from Prison: The Enlarged Edition,* trans. Reginald Fuller, Frank Clarke, et al. (London: SCM, 1953), 361.

16. See Barth's discussion of "The Perfections [Attributes] of God" in "The Doctrine of God," *Church Dogmatics,* 4 vols. (New York: Scribner's, 1955–57) 2:322ff.

17. *The Shaking of the Foundations* (New York: Scribner's, 1953), 148.

18. For an interesting discussion of Luther's relation to Anselm, see Bernhard Lohse, *Martin Luther's Theology: Its Historical and Systematic Development,* trans. Roy A. Harrisville (Minneapolis: Fortress Press, 1999), 223ff. Lohse argues (contra Aulen) that Luther's atonement theology cannot be identified with any one of the three dominant types of theory, yet he is inclined to distinguish Luther from the Anselmic emphasis on "satisfaction." And he notes that "the importance of the victory motif should not be ignored"—which is at least a guarded and partial acceptance of Aulen's famous hypothesis in *Christus Victor* (trans. A. G. Herbert [London: S.P.C.K., 1953]).

My own view on the subject is that, when Luther's theological perspective is understood as an (unsystematic) elaboration of the *theologia crucis,* it could not possibly give rise to the species of divine transcendence and impassivity that Anselm's soteriology assumes. While, therefore, it is entirely possible and historically explicable to find in Luther's writings reminiscences of all three major theories of atonement, the soteriology by which Luther is grasped throughout fits *none* of the extant theories in any neat manner but is uniquely his own; and this is nowhere more in evidence than in his readiness to see *God* ("The Father Almighty" of the creeds) under the sign of the cross.

19. Jürgen Moltmann, "The Crucified God," *Theology Today* (1974) 18.

5. The Grandeur and Misery of the Human Being

1. In one of her novels, the Canadian writer Margaret Laurence comments on the crucifixion window in the church of her childhood. Jesus appeared to her as "a slightly effeminate traveling salesman, expiring with absolutely no inconvenience on what might in other circumstances have been a cross" (*The Diviners* [New Canadian Library 3; Toronto: McClelland and Stewart, 1971], 41).

2. Langdon Gilkey, *Through the Tempest: Theological Voyages in a Pluralistic Culture* (Minneapolis: Fortress Press, 1991), 7–8.

3. See chapter 10.

4. See Mary Jo Leddy, *Radical Gratitude* (Maryknoll, N.Y.: Orbis, 2002).

5. Elie Wiesel, *The Town beyond the Wall,* trans. Stephen Becker (New York: Holt, Rinehart and Winston, 1964).

6. Albert Camus, *The Myth of Sisyphus: And Other Essays,* trans. Justin O'Brien (New York: Vintage, 1955). The famous title essay begins with the line, "There is but one truly serious philosophical problem, and that is suicide" (p. 3).

7. Cited in David Suzuki and Holly Dressel, *From Naked Ape to Superspecies: A Personal Perspective on Humanity and the Global Eco-Crisis* (Toronto: Stoddart, 1999).

8. See Margaret Visser, *Beyond Fate* (CBC Massey Lectures Series; Toronto: House of Anansi, 2002).

9. Blaise Pascal, *Pensées,* VI, no. 347.

10. See Douglas John Hall and Rosemary Radford Ruether, *God and the Nations* (Hein/Fry Lecture Series; Minneapolis: Fortress Press, 1995), 13ff.

11. Martin Luther, *Church Postil Sermons,* trans. John Nicholas Lenker (Minneapolis: Lutherans in All Lands, 1905), 1:10–11.

12. Hendrikus Berkhof, *Christian Faith: An Introduction to the Study of the Faith,* trans. Sierd Woudstra (Grand Rapids: Eerdmans, 1979), 193.

13. The NRSV translation "obligation" is certainly too mild!

14. Nor can this "human" act be attributed to "the Jews." The unspeakable history of Christian accusation against the Jews as "Christ-killers" cannot be settled in a footnote, but I wish in this connection to draw attention to the phrase in this sentence that speaks of human beings "who are entirely and accurately representative of human behavior" in their rejection of God "whenever God comes close enough" (Berkhof). It is true that the people depicted by the Gospels as being instrumental in securing Jesus' condemnation before the Roman authorities are Jews. But the leap from that datum to the racist charge against all Jews as slayers of the Christ is not

only psychologically damning (damning, namely, of the Christians who made it!), it is both historically absurd and theologically reprehensible.

Historically: *All* the persons described in the Gospels are Jews (unless otherwise specifically identified), including the disciples, Joseph and Mary, the women and children, the authors of the accounts, and of course Jesus himself. Those Jews actively engaged in seeking Jesus' apprehension are only *some* of this great collectivity, and most are singled out by name. Moreover, those who actually *determine* the judgment and *effect* the crucifixion are *not* Jews but Gentiles.

Theologically: Even more importantly, it belongs to the profound scriptural understanding of (priestly) representation that those human beings who brought about Jesus' death, whether actively or passively, whether as Jews or as Romans or whatever, *were acting representatively in behalf of (fallen) humanity.* They were (in the words of my text) "entirely and accurately representative of human behavior whenever and wherever the spontaneous and unmotivated loved of God comes close enough to US to judge OUR unloveliness and sham."

The apparent incapacity of the shapers of early (and later!) Christian dogma (including some of the great names of the patristic period) to grasp (or perhaps deliberately to ignore) this *representational* nuance of the tradition of Jerusalem should be seen as the greatest intellectual and spiritual tragedy in the history of Christian theology. (See in this connection Gerard S. Sloyan, *The Crucifixion of Jesus: History, Myth, Faith* [Minneapolis: Fortress Press, 1995], esp. chap. 3, 72–97.)

15. See Paul Tillich, *The Protestant Era,* trans. James Luther Adams (Chicago: University of Chicago Press, 1938), 196: "This idea is strange to the man of today and even to Protestant people in the churches; indeed, as I have over and over again had the opportunity to learn, it is so strange to the modern man that there is scarcely any way of making it intelligible to him."

16. In *The Evangelical Dictionary of Theology* we find the following definition of *justification:* " a forensic term, denoting a judicial act of administering the law—in this case by declaring a verdict of acquittal, and so excluding all possibility of condemnation. Justification thus settles the legal status of the person justified" (Walter A. Elwell, ed. [Grand Rapids: Baker, 1984], 593). Over against such an interpretation, John Macquarrie writes: "The principal danger is that justification gets separated from actual growth in righteousness or in the Christian virtues, the process traditionally known

by another archaic term, 'sanctification.' Justification gets thought of as something external, a so-called 'forensic' justification, a kind of acquittal or 'declaring just' that takes no account of the actual condition of the person so acquitted" (*Principles of Christian Theology* [London: SCM, 1966], 305).

17. Joseph Sittler, "Hammer, the Incarnation, and Architecture," *The Christian Century* (March 27, 1957) 394–95.

18. Paul Tillich, *The Shaking of the Foundations* (London: SCM, 1945), 153ff.

19. See Wilhelm and Marion Pauck, *Paul Tillich: Life and Thought* (New York: Harper & Row, 1976).

20. Martin Luther, *Luthers Werke: Kritische Gesamtausgabe (Schriften)*, 65 vols. (Weimar: H. Böhlau, 1883–1993), 7:336.

6. Jesus Christ—and Him Crucified

1. See "Related Sections in the Trilogy" at the end of this book.

2. "When *Thou* is spoken, the speaker has no *thing;* he has indeed nothing. But he takes his stand in relation" (Martin Buber, *I and Thou*, trans. Ronald Gregory Smith [Edinburgh: T. & T. Clark, 1937], 4).

3. Tillich's actual formulation of this principle is articulated in an essay interestingly titled, "The End of the Protestant Era?" It bears careful study, for one has the distinct impression that very few self-defined Protestants either understand or (especially) conduct themselves according to this principle—which is quite possibly why Tillich wondered, in this early essay, whether the Protestant era had in fact come to an end. He defined the principle thus:

> The central principle of Protestantism is the doctrine of justification by grace alone, which means that no individual and no human group can claim a divine dignity for its moral achievements, for its sacramental power, for its sanctity, or for its doctrine. If, consciously or unconsciously, they make such a claim, Protestantism requires that they be challenged by the prophetic protest, which gives God alone absoluteness and sanctity and denies every claim of human pride. This protest against itself on the basis of an experience of God's majesty constitutes the Protestant principle. This principle holds for Lutheranism as well as for Calvinism and even for modern Protestant denominationalism. It is the principle which makes the accidental name 'Protestant' an essential and symbolic name. It implies

that there cannot be a sacred system, ecclesiastical or political; that there cannot be a sacred hierarchy with absolute authority; and that there cannot be a truth in human minds which is divine truth in itself. Consequently, the prophetic spirit must always criticize, attack, and condemn sacred authorities, doctrines and morals. And every genuine Protestant is called upon to bear personal responsibility for this.

(*The Protestant Era*, trans. James Luther Adams [Chicago: University of Chicago Press, 1948], 226.)

4. Karl Barth, *Evangelical Theology: An Introduction*, trans. Grover Foley (New York: Holt, Rinehart and Winston, 1963), 7.

5. Karl Barth, "The Task of the Minister," in *The Word of God and the Word of Man*, trans. Douglas Horton (New York: Harper and Brothers, 1956), 213.

6. Barth, *Evangelical Theology*.

7. Walther von Loewenich, *Luther's Theology of the Cross* (Belfast: Christian Journals, 1976), 151.

8. It is not incidental to Luther's option for a theology of the cross that he distrusted abstraction and the search for absolutes and preferred to think the faith concretely and with a view to what Whitehead called "the livingness of things." John Todd writes of the young Luther: "The thing which really stands out is that he disliked the abstract statement, and preferred to see life as a flux, rather than as a status. From Augustine's *De Vera Religione* he dug out a reference to prime matter, which enabled him to propound a dynamic theory of the nature of things. We live moment by moment, in a continuum, in God's presence" (John M. Todd, *Luther: A Life* [New York: Crossroad, 1982], 55).

9. Douglas John Hall, *Lighten Our Darkness* (Philadelphia: Westminster, 1976), 133ff. (rev. ed.; Lima, Ohio: Academic Renewal, 2001), 130.

10. See my discussion of H. Richard Niebuhr in *Remembered Voices: Reclaiming the Legacy of "Neo-Orthodoxy"* (Louisville: Westminster John Knox, 1998), 93–106.

11. Brian Gerrish, "What Do We Mean by Faith in Jesus Christ?" *The Christian Century* (Oct. 6, 1999) 936.

12. If I use the concepts of "livingness" and *fluxus* often in this discussion, it is in part because this is a consciousness that I think I share with Luther, and part and parcel of the theology of the cross. As John Todd has observed, "The young lecturer's words show that from these early days Luther began to prefer the dynamic and personal, even biographical,

approach to theology, rather than an intellectual structure, and 'summas' based essentially on a philosophical outlook, reaching back to Aristotle for their assumptions. He quickly began to feel that a philosophical approach was even a betrayal of the message of the New Testament. Aristotle earned in these margins the title 'rancid philosopher' and was often designated 'pagan' with some special force, and a betrayer too of the Augustinian tradition of Luther's own Order. *Life, far from being a settled planned matter, was a fluxus, a flow of events, and in those events, man met his God"* (*Luther: A Life,* 54, italics added).

13. See Tillich's discussion of the three "Types of Anxiety" in *The Courage to Be* (London: Nisbet, 1952), chap. 2, 30–59.

14. See Berry's penetrating essay "What Are People For?" in *What Are People For?* (San Francisco: North Point, 1990), 123ff.

15. For a lengthier discussion of this, see my essay "Despair as Pervasive Ailment," in Walter Brueggemann, ed., *Hope for the World: Mission in a Global Context* (Louisville: Westminster John Knox, 2001), 83–93.

16. Søren Kierkegaard, *The Sickness unto Death,* trans. Walter Lowrie (Princeton, N.J.: Princeton University Press, 1951), 28ff.

17. "Suffered" is the only word in the Apostles' and the Nicene Creeds describing Jesus' *life.*

7. The Church and the Cross

1. For a fascinating contemporary commentary on the much-neglected book of Lamentations, see Kathleen M. O'Connor, *Lamentations and the Tears of the World* (Maryknoll, N.Y.: Orbis, 2002). An early sentence in the book sets the tone: "For readers who begin from a place of suffering, Lamentations is a book of comfort" (p. 3).

2. See my essay on Bonhoeffer in *Remembered Voices: Reclaiming the Legacy of "Neo-Orthodoxy"* (Louisville: Westminster John Knox, 1998), 63–74.

3. The possible documentation for this observation is of course too extensive to cite; however, I would like to direct the reader to three works which illustrate, in three quite different ways, the point being made: (1) a book by Mary M. Solberg, who was inspired to explore Luther's *theologia crucis* by her work in El Salvador during that country's brutal civil war (*Compelling Knowledge: A Feminist Proposal for an Epistemology of the Cross* [Albany: SUNY Press, 1997]); (2) the multiauthor volume edited by Walter Wink, *Homosexuality and the Christian Faith: Questions of Conscience for Churches* (Minneapolis: Fortress Press, 1999), which sensitively documents the plight of gay and lesbian persons and the recovery of "biblical fidelity"

(Ken Sehested); (3) Walter Brueggemann, ed., *Hope for the World: Mission in a Global Context* (Papers from the Campbell Seminar; Louisville: Westminster John Knox, 2001), especially the essays of H. Russel Botman (South Africa), Damayanthi M. A. Niles (Sri Lanka and United States), Ofelia Ortega (Cuba), and Janos Pasztor (Hungary).

4. "Ode to a Nightingale," stanza 6.

5. T. S. Eliot, *The Complete Poems and Plays* (New York: Harcourt, Brace, 1930), 196.

6. Jürgen Moltmann, *The Crucified God: The Cross of Christ as the Foundation and Criticism of Christian Theology,* trans. R. A. Wilson and John Bowden (Philadelphia: Fortress Press, 1974), 1.

7. See Gustav Aulen, *Christus Victor: An Historical Study of the Three Main Types of the Idea of Atonement* (London: S.P.C.K., 1953).

8. Moltmann, *The Crucified God,* 1.

9. *Systematic Theology,* 3 vols. (Chicago: University of Chicago Press, 1951–63) 2:29ff.

10. Ernest Becker, *The Denial of Death* (New York: Free Press, 1973).

11. Gustav Aulen's *Christus Victor: An Historical Study of the Three Main Types of the Idea of Atonement* (trans. A. G. Hebert [London: SPCK, 1953]) is as relevant today as when it was written half a century ago; for the atonement theory that it challenges, that of Anselm, is as dominant today as it was then.

12. Martin Luther, *The Table Talk of Martin Luther,* ed. Thomas S. Kepler (New York: World, 1952), 320f.

13. Walther von Loewenich, *Luther's Theology of the Cross* (Belfast: Christian Journals, 1976), 127.

14. See D. Premen Niles, ed., *Between the Flood and the Rainbow: Interpreting the Concilliar Process of Mutual Commitment (Covenant) to Justice, Peace, and the Integrity of Creation* (Geneva: World Council of Churches Publications, 1992).

15. See my *God and Human Suffering: An Exercise in the Theology of the Cross* (Minneapolis: Augsburg, 1986).

16. See Larry Rasmussen's "An Ethic of the Cross," in idem, *Dietrich Bonhoeffer: His Significance for North Americans* (Minneapolis: Fortress Press, 1990), 144ff.

8. The Theology of the Cross and the Crisis of Christendom

1. It has become fashionable in religious—and even some secular—circles today to claim that secularism has ended. For example in a recent (and

deliciously ironic) editorial for the *New York Times,* the well-known commentator Peter Steinfels writes: "That the world has indeed become postsecular is now virtually beyond debate, though whether this is good or bad is definitely not. Religion is booming on several continents, sometimes literally with rockets and artillery shells. Resurgent forms of ancient faiths have filled in voids created by the collapse of effective state institutions or secular ideologies, whether socialist or nationalist" ("Swapping 'Religion' for 'Postsecularism,'" *The New York Times* [August 3, 2002]). One may agree that as an "ism" the secular mentality no longer enjoys the popularity that garnered a whole spate of enthusiastic books *from Christian authors* in the 1960s. Secular*ism* failed as an ideology, a substitute for religion. But that does not mean that the secular *mentality* has disappeared from the face of the earth. For at base what was called "secularism" (the nomenclature was assigned in the middle of the nineteenth century) was not at first an "ism" at all but simply the growing recognition of countless persons that human beings could from now on no longer count on solutions to human and planetary dilemmas offered from some transcendent vantage point in the manner of the Deus ex machina. The species, they felt, would have now to work out its possibilities for survival and life-enhancement within the confines of the *saeculo.* That assumption, I would say, still informs most of the thought, planning, and activity that is undertaken—at least in the West. As such, of course, Christians could not embrace the full implications of such a preconception; for it effectively ruled out transcendence. Yet they *could and did* embrace the sense of human *responsibility* that such a point of view assumes because in their own faith tradition they knew that God has assigned the human species a stewardly role in creation and that very much of what was called "religion," including the Christian religion, tended to deprive Homo sapiens of this role or excuse humankind for its failure to act responsibly.

In this sense, Harvey Cox and others who wrote enthusiastically about secularity in the 1960s were entirely correct, in my opinion, in finding in the Judeo-Christian tradition the historical ideational *source* of the secular position. The God of the Scriptures is not a God who does everything for you: rather, God calls us as creatures to a life of extraordinary responsibility, and "salvation" implies reclaiming that responsibility. In that sense at least, Christians ought to be grateful that the secular mentality has not disappeared along with secular*ism.* But how could it disappear in any case—apart from a total metamorphosis of the human creature? For at base it is nothing more than an extension of the oldest self-understanding of human beings—

including Aristotle's classical definition, "Man is a rational animal." What else could human "rationality" mean than the assumption that *thinking* is for the purpose of *acting* thoughtfully? And that is the fundamental premise of the secular mind-set. Christians do not attack that premise; they only attack its exaggeration—namely, the belief that human thinking and acting will be inevitably redemptive.

2. *The Presence of the Kingdom,* trans. Olive Wyon (London: SCM, 1951), 37.

3. See Karen Armstrong, *The Battle for God* (New York: Knopf, 2000).

4. See Philip Jenkins, "The Next Christianity," *The Atlantic Monthly* (Oct. 2002) 53–75, and his book *The New Christendom: The Coming of Global Christianity* (Oxford: Oxford University Press, 2002).

5. Jenkins's analysis makes a great deal of this fact, but I question whether his work is in this respect as revelatory as he thinks. It represents in this and in several other respects a very United States–oriented perspective—in other words, one that is exceptionally concentrated on American perceptions and sensibilities. Most of us who have worked professionally in the churches, especially those who have ecumenical experience, have long known that Africa, Asia, and Latin America increasingly dominate Christian growth statistics, and at least some of us have tried to comprehend the deeper meaning of this fact.

6. Jenkins, "The Next Christianity," 57–58.

7. "By any reasonable assessment of numbers, the most significant transformation of Christianity in the world today is not the liberal Reformation that is so much desired in the North. It is the Counter-Reformation coming from the global South. And it's very likely that in a decade or two neither component of global Christianity will recognize its counterpart as fully or authentically Christian" (ibid., 68). "At present, the most immediately apparent difference between the older and newer churches is that Southern Christians are far more conservative in terms of both beliefs and moral teaching" (Jenkins, *The New Christendom,* 7).

8. Jenkins in an interview with Katie Bacon, "Christianity's New Center," *The Atlantic Monthly* (September 12, 2002) 34.

9. Jenkins, *The New Christendom,* 202.

10. I say that Jenkins "almost" overlooks the questions that present-day Christians have to raise about the language of Christendom because, while he does recognize the militant and exclusivistic behavior of Christian powers during the Middle Ages ("widespread intolerance . . . crusades, heresy

hunts, religious pogroms" [*The New Christendom,* 12]), he does not ask *theological questions* about the whole notion of a Christianity in search of √ power through proximity to power. Is the dominion of the Christian religion a biblically and theologically justifiable model of the movement begun by Jesus Christ? To raise that kind of question is to ask simultaneously whether *any* application of such a term as *Christendom* still has legitimacy.

11. A strange and unfortunate lacuna in Jenkins's analysis, it seems to me, is his failure to recognize that in the South there are many Christians who do *not* represent the kind of conservativism that colors many of the more militant forms of Christianity in the three continents named. Like many scholars whose point of departure is chiefly statistical, he is dismissive of minorities that, while not powerful in the usual, quantitative sense of the term, are spiritually and intellectually powerful because they represent long and tried traditions of Christian scholarship, a lively awareness of Christian ecumenicity, historical connectedness with confessional traditions like Calvinism, Lutheranism, Thomism, etc. Who at this point can discern the ways in which such minorities may grasp and shape more popular movements that are in great need precisely of such intellectual and spiritual leadership?

Beyond that, it may be questioned whether even the popular Christian movements in these contexts qualify for the status of the next Christendom. When I asked my friend and former doctoral student Ishmael Noko, General Secretary of the World Lutheran Federation, whether he thought Christendom were being reborn in his native Africa, he was visibly puzzled by my question. Christendom, in his (highly educated) view, entails power—political power, economic power, the power of global decision-making. And few African churches or movements qualify. Even where nations (like Zambia) have seemed to embrace Christianity in an official way, large questions are to be raised about its reality and its nature. Most African Christians are not only poor, as Jenkins repeatedly tells us, they are powerless. Many of them are women, of whom one could almost say "doubly powerless." In short, majority does not add up to power any more than minority connotes utter powerlessness. Numbers can be very deceiving—as readers of the Bible ought to know.

12. Indeed, it would have to include classical Protestant, Catholic, and Orthodox traditions as a whole, for none of them can be absorbed into categories like "conservative," "fundamentalist," "biblicist," or "evangelical" in the way that these categories are used in North America and elsewhere today.

13. See Mark A. Olson, *Moving beyond Church Growth: An Alternative Vision for Congregations* (Minneapolis: Fortress Press, 2002).

14. See Karl Rahner, *Mission and Service: Essays on Pastoral Theology,* vol. 1, trans. Cecily Hastings (London: Sheed and Ward, 1963), 3ff.

15. See Gerard S. Sloyan, *The Crucifixion of Jesus: History, Myth, Faith* (Minneapolis: Fortress Press, 1995).

16. Quoted from John A. T. Robinson, *Honest to God,* fortieth anniversary edition (Louisville: Westminster John Knox, 2002), 82.

9. On Being Christian Today

1. See pp. 246–48, n. 1.

2. Martin Luther, in a letter of 1519 to Staupitz, in John M. Todd, *Luther: A Life* (New York: Crossroad, 1982), 148.

3. See Peter Brown, *Augustine of Hippo: A Biography* (Berkeley: University of California Press, 2000), 199–200.

4. Dietrich Bonhoeffer, *Letters and Papers from Prison,* ed. Eberhard Bethge (3rd ed., enl. and rev.; London: SCM, 1967), 336–37.

5. John Coleman Bennett, who exemplified this connection in his scholarship and life more consistently than any Christian theologian/ethicist I have ever known, always commented with great approval on the practice of my own denomination, the United Church of Canada, of incorporating these two dimensions of Christian outreach in one ecclesiastical department. In those days (the 1950s) that department was designated "Evangelism and Social Service." He felt that this did greater justice to both mission and ethics than when the two "prongs" of Christian outreach were separated. (See his *The Radical Imperative: From Theology to Social Ethics* [Philadelphia: Westminster, 1975].)

6. See Barbara Kingsolver, *The Poisonwood Bible* (New York: Harper Collins, 1998).

7. See again Philip Jenkins, *The New Christendom: The Coming of Global Christianity* (Oxford: Oxford University Press, 2002).

8. Ibid., 154.

9. See Karen Armstrong, *Islam: A Short History* (rev. ed.; New York: Modern Library, 2002).

10. Besides my trilogy, I have discussed the church in these terms in several works: *The Reality of the Gospel and the Unreality of the Churches* (Philadelphia: Westminster, 1975); *Has the Church a Future?* (Philadelphia: Westminster, 1980); *The Future of the Church* (Toronto: United Church

Publishing House, 1985); *The End of Christendom and the Future of Christianity* (Harrisburg, Pa.: Trinity Press International, 1995; reprint: Eugene, Or.: Wipf and Stock, 2002).

11. I cannot vouch for the exact wording of Wiesel's statement, since I do not have the article at hand, but this was certainly the gist of what he said.

12. Consult Rosemary Radford Ruether, *Faith and Fratricide: The Theological Roots of Anti-Semitism* (New York: Seabury, 1974); Ulrich Simon, *A Theology of Auschwitz: The Christian Faith and the Problem of Evil* (Atlanta: John Knox, 1978); James Carrol, *Constantine's Sword: The Church and the Jews* (Boston: Houghton Mifflin, 2001); R. Kendall Soulen, *The God of Israel and Christian Theology* (Minneapolis: Fortress Press, 1996).

13. For example, ecumenical disarray and inter-Christian competitiveness: How shall Christians who cannot even manifest a working unanimity in established Western and Northern contexts mount missions that are anything but divisive both at home and abroad?

14. See Mark A. Olson, *Moving beyond Church Growth: An Alternative Vision for Congregations* (Minneapolis: Fortress Press, 2002).

15. "No one, not even a believer or a church, can boast of possessing truth, just as no one can boast of possessing love" (Paul Tillich, *On the Boundary: An Autobiographical Sketch* [New York: Scribner's, 1966], 51).

16. Paul Lehmann, *Ethics in a Christian Context* (New York: Harper and Row, 1963).

17. See my write-up of this fascinating experiment in *The Ecumenist* 38, no. 2 (spring 2001) 1–4.

18. See my essay, "Despair as Pervasive Ailment," in Walter Brueggemann, ed., *Hope for the World: Mission in a Global Context* (Louisville: Westminster John Knox, 2001), 83–93.

19. Walter Brueggemann, ed., *Hope for the World: Mission in a Global Context* (Louisville: Westminster John Knox, 2001), 19.

20. Brueggemann, *Hope for the World*, 18.

21. *Agape and Eros*, trans. Philip S. Watson (London: S.P.C.K., 1957), 91ff., passim.

22. Henri Nouwen, *In the Name of Jesus* (New York: Crossroad, 1989), 58.

23. Such restraint includes limiting our own reproductive capacities. As Rosemary Ruether stated in a 1995 lecture at the Vancouver School of Theology titled, "Ecofeminism and Healing Ourselves, Healing the Earth": "To

allow endless human fertility to populate the earth is no more compassionate than to allow so many plants to jostle one another in a garden that none has space to grow. . . . We need to limit our numbers as well, while at the same time creating conditions for those who live to grow optimally. . . . But we need also to seek the most compassionate ways to limit numbers, starting with limiting the affluence of those groups who consume the most and empowering all women throughout the world to be the decision makers on their own reproduction, rather than cutting down the lives of the born through disease and violence, as is presently the case" (unpublished text, 14).

24. An exemplary recent work in this connection is Sallie McFague's *Life Abundant: Rethinking Theology and Economy for a Planet in Peril* (Minneapolis: Fortress Press, 2000).

25. The reader is strongly advised to study the question of biblical interpretation with respect to this question as treated by the Finnish biblical scholar Martti Nissinen (*Homoeroticism in the Biblical World: A Historical Perspective,* trans. Kirsi Stjena [Minneapolis: Fortress Press, 1998]). Nissinen writes:

> It is important to remember that "sexuality," with its derivatives "homosexuality" and "heterosexuality," is a modern abstraction with no equivalent in the Bible or other ancient sources. This means that the distinguishing of sexual orientations, with the accompanying rationales and justifications, also is a modern phenomenon with a quite different basis and motivation for argumentation from the way ancient sources deal with same-sex eroticism. . . . Paul's arguments are based on certain Hellenistic Jewish moral codes that are culture-specific and that had their own trajectory of tradition. If these moral codes are regarded as binding in our time, the authority of the Bible might become confused with the authority of the Hellenistic Jewish synagogue.
>
> Paul cannot be held responsible for things he does not appear to know about—such as sexual orientation, which is not a voluntary perversion but an aspect of gender identity that manifests itself in different ways, including love. (124–25)

26. See, for example, David G. Myers, "Accepting What Cannot be Changed," 68, and Lewis B. Smedes, "Exploring the Morality of Homosexuality," 79, in Walter Wink, ed., *Homosexuality and Christian Faith: Questions of Conscience for the Churches* (Minneapolis: Fortress Press, 1999).

27. For example, Paul, in one of the "three" biblical references "which unequivocally condemn homosexual behavior" (the other four are ambiguous), Rom. 1:26-27, seems to assume that the persons of whom he is speaking "were heterosexuals who were acting contrary to nature, 'leaving,' 'giving up,' or 'exchanging' their regular sexual orientation for that which was foreign to them. Paul knew nothing of the modern psychosexual understanding of homosexuals as persons whose orientation is fixed early in life or perhaps even genetically" (Walter Wink, "Homosexuality in the Bible," in Wink, *Homosexuality and Christian Faith*, 34–36).

28. "For most of human history, the sexual life of humans, like that of other animals, was immediately related to the reproduction of offspring. The nearly exponential growth of the population in the twentieth century has made both possible and necessary the exploration of human sexuality as a reality of its own" (Maria Harris and Gabriel Moran, "Homosexuality: A Word Not Written," in Wink, *Homosexuality and Christian Faith*, 75).

29. Despite the preoccupation of Christian and other moralists with sexual matters, the Bible spends relatively little time on the ethics of sex; in fact, Walter Wink states frankly that "the Bible has no sexual ethic. Instead, it exhibits a variety of sexual mores, some of which changed over the thousand-year span of biblical history. Mores are unreflective customs accepted by a given community. Many of the practices that the Bible prohibits, we allow, and many that it allows, we prohibit. The Bible knows only a love ethic, which is constantly being brought to bear on whatever serious mores are dominant in any given country, or culture, or period" (Wink, "Homosexuality in the Bible," in idem, *Homosexuality and Christian Faith*, 44).

30. Ken Sehested, "Biblical Fidelity and Sexual Orientation," in Wink, *Homosexuality and Christian Faith*, 60.

31. If, as some conservative Christian groups have insisted, homosexuality can be "cured" by Christian conversion and true belief, should it be thought that all sexual libido that is not inspired by procreation is sinful and in need of subjection to the ministrations of grace?

32. Richard Rohr, OFM, "Where the Gospel Leads Us," in Wink, *Homosexuality and Christian Faith*, 88.

10. God's Reign, Creation's Future

1. "It is an amazing thought that for every person who has ever lived . . . there has never in the past been anyone genetically identical to that person and never will be in the future unless the person is cloned" (Margaret Somerville, *The Ethical Canary* [Toronto: Penguin, 2000], 63).

2. E.g., John 9:2.

3. In doing so, I am reversing the order in which I have usually treated the subject, especially in *Confessing the Faith* and *Why Christian?*

4. E.g. "the perfect" among the Cathari of the twelfth century forswore reproduction.

5. Von Loewenich, *Luther's Theology of the Cross* (Belfast: Christian Journals, 1976), 89–90 (italics added).

6. Wolfhart Pannenberg, "The Task of Christian Eschatology," in Carl E. Braaten and Robert W. Jenson, eds., *The Last Things: Biblical and Theological Perspectives on Eschatology* (Grand Rapids: Eerdmans, 2002), 1.

7. It may be a consequence of his western European matrix, but I find Pannenberg's analysis in this work both too quickly critical of secularity and too unaware of the problems of a society like that of the United States that is still excessively religious. The situation is even more complicated than this suggests, because most of the so-called secular hopes of North American society have been and are inspired by our regnant religions, which are chiefly called Christian.

8. For an imaginative contemporary documentation of this statement, see Mary Jo Leddy, *Radical Gratitude* (Maryknoll, N.Y.: Orbis, 2002).

9. Beyond that, there is always a very real danger that specifying the content of eschatological fulfillment will involve some highly questionable ethical and theological assertions. I find such in a recent statement of Robert W. Jenson, where—albeit en passant—he affirms that in the last judgment, "the robber baron will be condemned for his exploitation of the helpless, and reparation made. The brutal parent will be rebuked and the harm done the children repaired" ("The Great Transformation," in Braaten and Jenson, *The Last Things,* 39). How can a posthistorical reparation undo the historical pain of lives ruined by capitalist exploitation or parental abuse? And are we asking the still-exploited and still-abused of the world to take comfort in such a resolution?

10. Pannenberg, "The Task of Christian Eschatology," in Braaten and Jenson, *The Last Things,* 2.

11. Braaten, "The Recovery of Apocalyptic Imagination," in Braaten and Jenson, *The Last Things,* 19.

12. Pannenberg, "The Task of Christian Eschatology," in Braaten and Jenson, *The Last Things,* 3.

13. *The Oxford Dictionary of the Christian Church,* ed. F. L. Cross (3rd ed.; Oxford: Oxford University Press, 1997), 69.

14. Braaten, "The Recovery of Apocalyptic Imagination," in Braaten and Jenson, *The Last Things,* 14ff.

15. Ibid., 16.

16. Ibid., 16–19.

17. Ibid., 28.

18. See Bernhard Lohse, *Martin Luther's Theology: Its Historical and Systematic Development,* trans. Roy A. Harrisville (Minneapolis: Fortress Press, 1999), 333: "However much he [Luther] may have pointed to the imminent inbreaking of the end time, there is no lack of evidence that Luther reckoned on a longer historical development."

19. Philip D. W. Krey, "Luther and the Apocalypse: Between Christ and History," in Braaten and Jenson, *The Last Things,* 135ff. Of course, Krey's interpretation of Luther's attitude toward this biblical writing *is* an interpretation.

20. Paul D. Hanson, "Prophetic and Apocalyptic Politics," in Braaten and Jenson, *The Last Things,* 64. Hal Lindsey's *Late Great Planet Earth* (Grand Rapids: Zondervan, 1970) is specifically cited.

21. Hanson, "Prophetic and Apocalyptic Politics," in Braaten and Jenson, *The Last Things,* 64.

22. Braaten insists Jesus never "talked" that way! ("The Recovery of Apocalyptic Imagination," in Braaten and Jenson, *The Last Things,* 21).

Related Sections in the Trilogy

The Cross in Our Context	The Trilogy
1. What *Is* the Theology of the Cross?	*Thinking the Faith,* Preface, Introduction (pp. 11–66)

2. Theology of the Cross as Contextual Theology	*Thinking the Faith,* Part I: The Disciple Community (pp. 69–244)
	    1. The Meaning of Contextuality in Christian Thought
	    2. Discerning *Our* Context
	    3. Components of Our Context

3. Engaging the World	*Thinking the Faith,* Part II: The Discipline (pp. 247–449)
	    4. Elements of the Discipline
	    5. Theological Method
	    6. Knowing in Christian Faith and Theology

4. The Crucified God	*Professing the Faith,* Part I: Theology: The Christian Doctrine of God (pp. 43–183)
	    1. *"Credo in Deum"*
	    2. Questioning the Father Almighty
	    3. A Suffering God?

Index